THE

SUBSTANCE

OF

SPACETIME

Also by Andrew M. Ryan
The Labbitt Halsey Protocol, a novel

THE

SUBSTANCE

OF

SPACETIME

INFINITY, NOTHINGNESS, AND THE NATURE OF MATTER

2ND EDITION

ANDREW M. RYAN

Published By

GADFLY

Leesburg, Virginia

Published by:

Gadfly, LLC
P.O. Box 147
Leesburg, Virginia 20178
Publisher@GadflyLLC.com
GadflyLLC.com

First Edition as *The Law of Physics*, published 2008
© 2008 Andrew M. Ryan
ISBN: 978-0-9802088-1-8

Second Edition, *The Substance of Spacetime: Infinity, Nothingness, and the Nature of Matter*, published 2016
978-0-9802088-4-9 Trade Paper
978-0-9802088-5-6 eBook
978-0-9802088-6-3 Kindle

Cover background image star field courtesy NASA's Hubble Space Telescope.

Printed in the United States of America
10 9 8 7 6 5 4 3

Library of Congress Control Number: 2016931024

To Jill

Table of Contents

Figures & Tables

THE

SUBSTANCE

OF

SPACETIME

Introduction

What *is*? It is the most basic question of ontology, and has occupied philosophers and scientists ever since man first began plumbing the depths of reality. In its purest form, the question concerns the nature of *sub-stance*—literally, that which is presumed to "stand under" all that exists. This is the stuff that makes something *real*, to which, in some way, an object's properties adhere. It is the existence beneath the thing, the *thing-in-itself*, stripped of its particulars and accidental characteristics.

Through the ages, any number of substances have been proposed. There are mental substances, physical substances, divine substances, mathematical substances, composite substances, and ideal substances, among others. They are frequently described as perfect, atomic, uniform, indivisible, or undifferentiated. Some thinkers have denied the whole notion of substance. We cannot directly experience this hypothetical stuff they argue, but only the superficial properties that objects show to our senses. What then justifies the claim that there is something beneath what we experience?

Though a great deal of effort has been expended on this question, it is far from obvious that we have made any headway whatsoever. Ask a physicist what the fundamental substance is and you will likely get a description of *energy*, either in the guise of multidimensional *strings* or as something that corresponds to the *E* and the *m* in $E=mc^2$. But if you press the issue, ask him what this stuff really is, where it came from, or why it behaves as it does, you will discover there is nothing more to the story; it is nothing but a mysterious quantity that makes the equations work. Ask a contemporary philosopher and he will gladly regale you with the history of substance from Heraclitus to Heidegger. But ask him which theory is correct and you will get a blank stare.

As different as the various concepts of substance are, they have one thing in common. They are all utterly impotent. It is impossible to take any particular notion of substance in hand (Leibniz's monads, for example) and apply it to something that exists. One might hope that if a particular substance had anything of value to say about the beings it comprises, we could extrapolate from its characteristics to figure out how objects actually work. Unfortunately, that simply is not the case.

Without exception, concepts of substance are entirely beholden to the workings of the human mind. How we think and perceive and what we believe we know always inform— even determine—our judgments about the nature of reality. Man thinks, "My mind is logical and mathematical, hence reality must be as well." These restrictions on the nature of substance are certainly understandable; if we cannot think, perceive, or know something (if it is neither *empirical* nor *rational*) it cannot be expected to form the basis of a concept. Yet it is not at all axiomatic that reality outside of our own heads is similarly circumscribed by human frailties. Restricting ourselves to substances that can be perceived by the senses or formulated in rational terms simply because those are the skills we have, is reminiscent of the drunk who searches for his car keys under the lamp post because that is where the light is good. With nothing to go by, it is just as likely that the fundamental substance is irrational and imperceptible *and yet exists just the same.*

None of the substances proposed through the ages has ever been successfully applied to reality in order to explain the nature of physical objects. Invariably, the definition of the substance itself is the end of the project. It is as if the philosopher in question believed an intrepid scientist of the future would pick up the ball and run with it, even without an instruction manual or any tangible examples of how to use it. By contrast, the current volume is exactly that *second* book, the instruction manual. Instead of presenting the philosophical thought that got me to this point, I will instead jump ahead and demonstrate how the substance I have uncovered actually works. I decided to do it this way because the world does not need another painstakingly derived but otherwise useless substance. Yes, many fascinating insights were required in order to get here, and I may write about them someday. But a demonstration is always vastly superior to an argument. For the time being, then, this book can be thought of as volume two of a one-part series.

My aim is to explain all that is, the first principle of ontology. But that means I have nothing with which to get started. I cannot very well assume the existence of any substance if it is substance I hope to explain. It appears then that the only way to begin this discussion is to assume *nothing*, and so that is what I will do.

1

Spacetime

The Void

Easily the most perplexing question one can possibly ask is, "Why is there something rather than nothing?" Existence is not an obviously reasonable state of affairs, whereas nothingness does not seem to require any explanation at all. Confronted with an endless void, utterly empty, barren, and cold, one might say, "Well, of course. What did you expect?" But existence, once given any thought at all, quickly becomes an intellectual abomination. It is no wonder that the gods, before they got around to burdening us with all sorts of ethical dicta, first busied themselves with creation. That there are things is more puzzling than any of the things that are.

If the efforts of current cosmologists are any indication, the assumption of nothing is not as easy as it sounds. Typically, it is conceived as a quantum field devoid of matter, but already fortified by the laws, forces, and fields with which physicists are familiar. By contrast, the nothingness I have in mind is what we can call *true nothingness*, an emptiness so complete that it lacks even the structure and energy of a quantum field. To get our bearings, we can think of this brand of nothing as *contentless*, *void*, or *uniformly empty*. These and similar ideas draw attention to the fact that nothingness completely lacks any positive properties. It is defined entirely by absence; it is the opposite of existence. At first glance, this does not bode well for the universe. Without God or something else inexplicable to break the monotony, nothing appears to follow from nothing; *ex nihilo, nihil fit*. This conclusion has certainly been the favorite of philosophers as well as common sense for as far back as one cares to look. It is also the reason modern cosmologists recoil from true nothingness and feel compelled to supplement the void with ready-made quantum fields. But it may be that there is more to the void than meets the eye.

Though it may not yet imply any *thing*, the void does seem to imply infinity and eternity. Placing an edge or boundary somewhere in the void and declaring an end to it involves the imposition of something, and something is more than nothing. Any such boundary violates our assumption as well as raises the question of what lies beyond it. Consequently, assuming nothing implies an infinite expanse of it. Only the *ad hoc* addition of some object—however nebulous or abstract—into the void can prevent it from being infinite. Likewise, there is no temporal beginning or end to the void either. Even if time is defined as nothing more than the passage of events, and there are no events actually occurring, the void *qua* nothingness imposes no restrictions on any hypothetical events that might happen to occur there. For the special case in which there are no events, time can be conceived as simply a *degree of freedom*, much like the three dimensions of space. It makes no difference that there is nothing there, only that, if there were, it would be unrestricted in the temporal dimension just as it is unrestricted in the three spatial dimensions.

It is critical here to note that infinite space and time are not new assumptions but simply an elucidation of the original assumption of nothing. Infinity follows necessarily from nothingness; it is not something that has been added to it. Nothingness *is* four infinite degrees of freedom. It is that which *does not get in the way*. Any object introduced into the void is absolutely unaffected by it. The object is, while the void is not. A philosopher might object here by claiming that I have introduced the notions of *dimension* and *expanse*. Why not assume instead that nothingness is dimensionless? If I were to do that, however, the void would oppose the existence of objects with which we are already familiar, and in that respect, it would not be nothing. Nothingness, after all, is not only or even primarily *way out there*, inaccessible and impossibly distant. Rather, it is all around us, not getting in the way of everything that exists. Only an infinite and eternal four-dimensional expanse—four infinite degrees of freedom—can completely fail to oppose the existence of all that exists. In essence, our familiar four-dimensional world guarantees that nothingness possesses four infinite degrees of freedom.[1]

Infinity

It appears then, that the assumption of nothing implies an infinite, four-dimensional expanse of space and time (not yet *spacetime*, which is significantly different)—still nothing to be sure, but at least a somewhat more interesting version of it. To take another step toward existence we need to examine this curious notion of *infinity* that is inextricably bound to the assumption of nothing.

The first thing to notice is that infinity is an inherently irrational concept. Though we may understand in a strictly formal sense what the word *infinity* means, it is not possible to conjure up an accurate representation of the idea in our minds. The best we can do is acknowledge that however far we go we can always go farther. But man cannot wrap his head around anything truly boundless. Moreover, the machinery of logical and mathematical reasoning also breaks down when applied to infinity. The crux of this breakdown comes from the fact that the *cardinality* (size) of all infinite sets is the same regardless of how those sets are defined. For example, the set of all integers is the same size as the set of all odd numbers even though, intuitively, it seems like

---

1   To be perfectly rigorous here, this claim could be made even less controversial by stating it as a hypothetical, *viz*, that the following theory is [provisionally] based on an infinite, four-dimensional universe. But should it ever be discovered that this assumption is untrue (as it would be if String Theory were proven correct), the theory described in this book would be invalidated. Or, more simply, this theory is true *only* for an infinite four-dimensional universe.

there should be twice as many of the former as the latter. The even numbers are missing from the set of odd numbers but not missing from the set of integers. Therefore, the set of integers must in some sense be the larger of the two even if we concede that both are infinite. But this raises the question of how one infinite set can be any larger than another. They both go on forever.

Any number of paradoxes can be formulated by applying the above observation to hypothetical situations. David Hilbert's paradox of the *Infinite Hotel* is one example. In it we are to imagine a hotel with an infinite number of rooms and then wrestle with various notions of vacancy and occupancy. Specifically, would an infinite number of guests result in full occupancy? The answer appears to be no. If a new guest arrives we simply move the guest in room one to room two, the guest in room two to room three, and so on, making room for the new guest. Since there is no end to the number of rooms, even an infinite number of guests cannot fill them all. In this and every other paradox of infinity the problem centers on treating infinity simultaneously as a *number* and as the concept of unboundedness. A number is a discrete, definable entity, while *unboundedness* is exactly the opposite. All numbers are unique, their values rigorously determined, whereas all unboundedness *qua* infinity is the same. But because we can define infinite sets in much the same way that we define particular numbers, it appears as though different infinities are equal and unequal at the same time.

These sorts of paradoxes are interesting but they are only relevant outside of pure mathematics if there are in fact genuine infinities in the physical world. Currently, physicists reject infinities as meaningless and none of the accepted laws of nature require them. On the contrary, an infinite answer to an equation describing a physical phenomenon is regarded as evidence of a mistake. Consider that if there were any infinite physical quantities they would, by definition, take over the entire cosmos. Infinite gravity would pull everything in with an infinite force. An infinite force would generate an infinite quantity of energy.

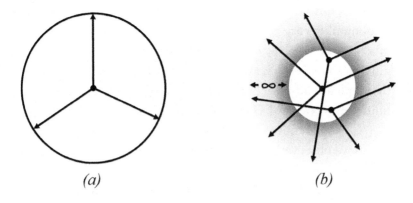

(a)   *(b)*

Figure 1.1:   Infinite and Euclidean Spheres
While only one point (the center) is equidistant from every point on the surface of a finite, Euclidean sphere (a), every point in the interior of an infinite sphere (b) is equidistant from the surface. Hence, every point in an infinite sphere can be thought of as its center.

Infinite energy in turn would impart an infinite expansive or implosive velocity to everything in the universe. Nothing in our experience justifies these crazy conclusions; hence infinity is never relevant or even possible in the real world.

Yet infinite nothingness appears inescapable. And as with the paradoxes discussed above, it is easy to construct a contradiction between the finite character of any discrete region of the void, and its infinite character taken as a whole. Imagine, for example, an infinite spherical region of the void (**Figure 1.1**); being infinite, the void can contain any number of infinite subregions just as we can define any number of infinite sets using only a subset of the integers (odd numbers, for example). Any discrete point selected anywhere inside of this infinite sphere is by definition an infinite distance from the surface. And because all infinite quantities are equal (equally boundless), every point in the sphere is also an equal distance from the surface. However, the only point in a sphere that is equidistant from every point on the surface is the very center of the sphere. Therefore, the line connecting any point inside the sphere to its surface is a radius of that sphere. That is, every point in the sphere, no matter

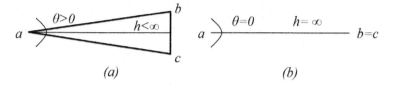

Figure 1.2:   Infinite and Euclidean Triangles
As long as the height of the triangle is finite, the angle at *a* is greater
than zero and the points *b* and *c* have a positive separation. But when the
height becomes infinite, the angle goes to zero and points *b* and *c* become
the same point.

where it is, is the same point, namely, the center. The paradox
is obvious: every point in an infinite sphere is the center of the
sphere, the same point. There is a clear logical contradiction between infinite geometry and Euclidean geometry. Indeed, there
is a contradiction between infinity and every variety of math and
logic, because every infinity must be treated as both a particular
number as well as an equally unbounded quantity. Or again, infinity can be defined in many different (and mutually exclusive)
ways, but always ends up equally infinite just the same.

The above paradox is even clearer if we create a simple
isosceles triangle (**Figure 1.2**) and vary the height. As the height
increases, the angle at *a* decreases, and if the height becomes
infinite, the angle becomes zero. However, if this angle becomes
zero, points *b* and *c* become the same point. This is true regardless of how far apart in absolute terms *b* and *c* really are. That is,
b and *c*, from the standpoint of infinity, are the same point even
though they are not *really* the same point. Under normal finite
conditions, these sorts of paradoxes are no more than interesting intellectual observations having no relationship to reality.
But if we are agreed that the void is genuinely and unavoidably
infinite, we cannot simply leave this problem unaddressed. The
points in an infinite sphere are either all in the center or they
are not. Points *b* and *c* either have a particular separation or they
do not. The void is either infinite or it is not. In none of these
examples can we have it both ways.

From an intuitive perspective, we might try to resolve this matter by pointing out that, with infinite distances at our disposal, it is always possible to "stand back" from an object, however big that object might be, far enough to reduce it to a pin point. Venus, for example, looks to the naked eye like a point, but only because it is so far away. If we launch a space probe to get a closer look, its true size becomes evident. There is no paradox to unravel. But though this might seem to resolve the issue, it ignores the categorical difference between *extremely big* on the one hand and *infinite* on the other. As we increase the height of our triangle, the distance of a from b and c is not merely great enough to make b and c look the same, it is great enough to render them mathematically as the exact same point. The angle at a from an infinite distance is not just very, very small, it is exactly zero. And this is true whether we initially define the base to be an inch or a light year wide. This disparity results in a real, intractable mathematical contradiction. There appears to be a kind of *tension* between the Euclidean and infinite characters of the points b and c. The question now is, do we treat this tension as entirely theoretical, or is it in some sense real?

Eternity

Whether or not the tension between Euclidean geometry and infinite geometry is real as opposed to entirely conceptual, we can, nonetheless, speculate about what would happen if this tension tried to work itself out. In general, any two discretely defined points within an infinite space *tend* toward the same point. That is, however distant from one another two points are when conceived from a finite perspective, they are the same point when conceived from an infinite perspective. That disparity is the essence of the geometric tension between them. Even so, it seems perfectly obvious that this tension, the tendency of points to merge, is merely a figure of speech. The void after all is absolute nothingness. And in any case, points have no physical extent. They are nothing but mathematical abstractions,

infinitesimals. It is meaningless to ascribe to them any characteristics whatsoever, particularly anything as definite as a tendency
to merge with other points. Or is it?

One outstanding question from cosmology concerns
the ultimate fate of our universe. Right now it is expanding and
there is some doubt about whether it will continue to do so or
will instead reverse course one day and begin contracting. I will
address this question in Chapter 4. For now we can treat it as
simply a thought experiment. In particular, what will happen if
the cosmos goes on expanding *forever?* The void provides an infinite degree of spatiotemporal freedom to anything that exists. If
the momentum of expansion exceeds any force of contraction,
there will be, literally, *nothing* out there to get in its way. So
where does it go?

Mathematically, if we divide any quantity, however large,
by infinity we get zero, expressed by the equation,

$$x/\infty = 0.$$

Put simply, if we distribute any finite amount of stuff over
an infinite expanse (**Figure 1.3**) it will eventually cease to exist
altogether; becoming infinitely diffuse is theoretically equivalent
to disappearing. If our cosmos does not reverse course, it has
no other choice but to succumb to this strange equation. But
because it is expanding at a finite rate, it will require an eternity
to undergo this transformation. As I discussed earlier, infinite
time (eternity) is, like infinite space, an infinite degree of freedom. Eternity says, "Take all the time you need," not, "This is
never going to end." This infinite degree of temporal freedom
offers no resistance to any process that occurs within it, but it is
not something over and above that process. Time does not *flow*;
it is not a force that acts on things as if from outside. Physical
phenomena tend to evolve in a specific way, from more to less
orderly (increasing entropy), but that fact reflects only the phenomena themselves, not the temporal degree of freedom that
permits them to occur. If no phenomena are occurring, time,

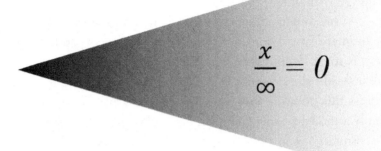

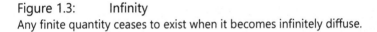

$$\frac{x}{\infty} = 0$$

Figure 1.3:   Infinity
Any finite quantity ceases to exist when it becomes infinitely diffuse.

like space, appears as nothingness—with no beginning and no end. However, as merely a facet of nothingness, we are under no obligation to explain how it has no beginning. It is not as though time, *qua* nothingness, has always been flowing at some finite rate and could not possibly have gotten here (the present moment) had it not started at some particular time.

Once our cosmos has "taken all the time it needs" in order to blink out of existence according to $x/\infty = 0$, we are confronted with the same sort of paradox, the same sort of tension, between Euclidean and infinite geometry that I introduced above. In particular, it now makes sense to solve the equation for x, suggesting that any infinite expanse of nothingness is equivalent to some specific quantity of something, given by:

$$x = 0 \cdot \infty.$$

That is, if we gather up an infinite quantity of nothing we do not have nothing anymore, but instead we have some particular amount of something. Without question, it is much easier to swallow this idea when we imagine something (e.g., our cosmos) ceasing to exist after eternal expansion than it is when we try to imagine something coming into existence after, presumably, an eternal collapse of nothingness itself. Yet, theoretically, there is no difference. All that distinguishes the two cases is the physical mechanism. We already know our cosmos is expanding, so it requires little to imagine it expanding forever. On the other hand, it borders on the absurd that an infinite expanse of infinitesimal points, nothingness itself, might somehow coalesce into our entire universe.

Ex Nihilo – The Eternal Dialectic

The tension (dialectic) between infinite and Euclidean geometries strikes common sense as nothing more than a conceptual subtlety, an entirely abstract phenomenon or mathematical artifact. Logic dictates that the presence of a paradox is evidence of an error in reasoning. It is most definitely not evidence that reality itself is paradoxical. Yet the void is stubbornly infinite while the four dimensions of space and time are equally stubbornly Euclidean (finite). Therefore, notwithstanding its seemingly abstract nature, in the absence of any compelling reason to doubt it, we must at least consider the possibility that this tension is real, that the infinite-finite dialectic has a physical effect.

The entities to which this tension applies are dimensionless, infinitesimal points—the fundamental elements of any geometry. Being infinitesimal, a point has no mass, no size, no extent of any kind. It is, at least from a Euclidean perspective, nonexistent, a mere abstraction. Therefore, whether or not it makes any sense to say so, it would require no effort to move such an entity. Having no mass, no force is required to push a point around. Or again, having zero mass, a *zero force* would suffice to move a point, particularly if we had an eternity over which to apply such a force. And it is exactly a zero force that we have at our disposal, namely, the theoretical tendency of points to merge in order to reconcile the dialectic between infinite and finite geometries.

The tension between points in the void is a formal abstraction, a zero force. However, given that the entities to which this force applies are also formal abstractions and have zero mass, and that an infinite temporal span is available over which to apply this force, it is not only possible but absolutely certain that points will gradually coalesce. Or again, though this tension is apparently nonexistent (nonphysical), so too are the points to which it applies—they both belong to the same ontological category. In essence, eternity transforms nothing into something just as it turns something into nothing. Infinite time and infinite space come together and give rise to *spacetime*, the fundamental substance of reality.

Collapse

To get a sense of what is going on here, consider the infinite spherical sub-region I mentioned earlier. In that case, the geometric tension manifests itself as a tendency of points to coalesce at the Euclidean center of the sphere. This can be understood as a tendency of points to merge or as a weak (infinitesimal) attraction between nearby points. As the density of spacetime in the central region increases, so too does the force of attraction of that region on the surrounding space. Each point is attempting to merge with all the other points within the infinite sphere. The more spacetime points there are in a region, the more powerfully that region attracts the ambient space in its vicinity. Over time, the rate of convergence increases in proportion to the density of spacetime in the central region.

It is not obvious that it makes any sense to talk about how long this process takes. With no events other than the collapse of space itself, time shows itself for what it really is, merely an infinite degree of freedom. There is *nothing* at this point in the story against which we can judge its rate. The phenomenon of spacetime collapse plays itself out according to its own dynamics. It could just as easily be thought of as mind numbingly slow as incomprehensibly fast. All that changes is the relative rate at which, as the attractive force in the center increases, spacetime accumulates. Eventually, therefore, it stands to reason that the convergence occurs at a virtually (perhaps actually) infinite rate, pulling in space fast enough to transform the nothingness of the void into the somethingness of spacetime.

One critical aspect of this phenomenon is that the tension, the dialectic, between infinite and finite geometries is a genuine *tension*. As such, it pulls in both directions, driven by both paradoxical poles. It is not, as the above discussion might at first suggest, committed to transforming Euclidean geometry entirely into its infinite counterpart. It seeks an *equilibrium state* midway between the two, which is why I have introduced the seemingly incongruous term, *dialectic*, to describe the relationship. As a result, the attractive force of the increasingly dense spacetime at the center of a collapsing region will eventually begin stretching the space way out at the infinitely distant surface of that sphere. Over some indefinite period this stretching will become critical. And after building up for eternity, the tension between the collapsing sphere and the rest of the void will finally *rip* the space connecting them. Space itself tears under the stress.

The *ripping* of space along the surface of an infinite sphere is an inherently incomprehensible concept, depending as it does on the also incomprehensible concept of infinity. In some respect, therefore, it should be treated metaphorically. Referring to Figure 4, we can see that the tension on the surface of an infinite sphere is also infinite, resulting in an infinite implosive velocity of the space at that location. To say that this infinitely imploding surface rips away from the rest of the void is simply to say that this phenomenon, as a whole, extricates itself from the rest of the void so as to become a discrete, bounded cosmic entity. *Rip*, then, is defined as: moving away (imploding) at an infinite rate. It is not necessary (though it is, arguably, permissible) to imagine, at the extremity of the infinite collapsing region, a violent physical separation of two entities that were previously connected.

When this rip occurs, the surface of the sphere snaps down toward the core of its region. The velocity with which any

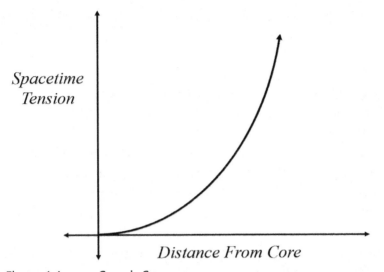

Figure 1.4:   Cosmic Snap
The tension between adjacent spacetime points increases in proportion to the square of the distance from the core. That tension, in turn, is re-sponsible for the distribution of velocities when the surface of the infinite region rips free of the rest of the void.

point in space moves toward the core is directly proportionate to the tension (**Figure 1.4**) it possessed when the surface finally snapped. And that means the velocity of each point is propor-tionate to the square of its distance from the center. The farther a point is from the center the faster it moves toward that center, because that is where the tension was greatest when the surface snapped free. This phenomenon is essential to the subsequent evolution of our cosmos. What we will see in the next chapter is that the Big Bang depended on extremely high but also perfectly uniform pressure. A typical collapsing mass does not reach a uni-form pressure. The pressure in a collapsing protostellar cloud of hydrogen, for example, is greatest in the center. Such an uneven distribution of densities would not have created our universe. Only because the surface of the collapsing region of space was held back by its resistance to stretching could it then snap down toward the center with exactly the right distribution of radial ve-locities to arrive at the core all at the same moment. Moreover,

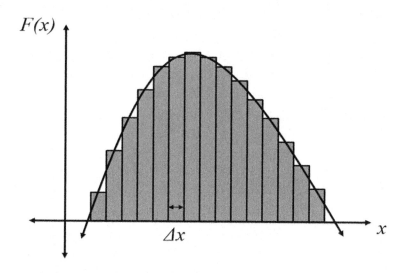

Figure 1.5: Infinitesimals
In integral calculus, the area under a curve is calculated by adding together an infinite number of rectangles. As Δx approaches zero, the rectangles become infinitesimal in size but infinitely numerous. Yet because the region is bounded—by the function and the x-axis—even an infinite number of them results in a finite area.

the extreme high pressure of the Big Bang would also not have been reached had the velocity of the collapsing space not been so dramatically increased by the snapping of the sphere away from the rest of the void. This snap instantly converted an eternity of pent up potential energy into the kinetic energy that ultimately collapsed space into the condensed sphere that exploded into our cosmos.

Something else important occurs when the spherical region tears away from the rest of the void. Our cosmos suddenly becomes a *bounded*, though still infinite, entity. When we calculate the area of a region (**Figure 1.5**) under, for example, a parabola, we use an infinite number of infinitesimal rectangles. But because the region is bounded we get a finite answer. Our universe, therefore, can contain an infinite number of spacetime points and yet still exhibit the finitude associated with a bounded phenomenon. That is how we can end up with a finite quantity of mass and energy in our universe despite the fact that it is composed of an infinite quantity of nothingness. In the equation, $x = 0 \cdot \infty$, the number x is a discrete finite value because the infinity involved is bounded in some way. Presumably, if the entire void collapsed into one location, x would be infinite as well. However, I suspect such a fanciful notion as *entire void* is utterly meaningless, even by comparison to the mind-bending ideas we've been dealing with thus far.

The Cosmological Constant

The region of spacetime that became our cosmos ripped free of the void when the tension between its infinite and Euclidean poles exceeded its maximum threshold at the surface of the sphere. The Euclidean pole pulled out toward the void as the infinite pole pulled in toward the center. As a result, the total quantity of spacetime that constitutes a universe is a *multiversal* constant; all universes have the same mass. Any collapsing region tears away from the void at exactly the same point in its evolution, right as the tension between its infinite and finite poles reaches its maximum threshold.

Furthermore, the tension between the adjacent points in the ensuing universe reflects the total quantity of spacetime in the region at the moment it was separated from the void. As I argued earlier, the force of attraction between adjacent points is a function of their density. This force manifests itself, even to this day, as the *coherence* of spacetime, its inherent resistance to both excessive compression and decompression. The exact value of this coherence is the *cosmological constant* itself, and it underpins every other constant in the universe, from the vacuum pressure to the mass of a neutron. When spacetime is stretched, its infinite pole *pulls* it back toward its equilibrium pressure. If it is compressed, its finite pole *pushes* out against whatever is compressing it. The value of this equilibrium pressure, the cosmological constant, reflects the quantity of spacetime that broke away from the rest of the void. If there were more of it, the equilibrium pressure would be higher, reflecting the greater attractive force exerted by the additional spacetime points. If there were less, it would be lower because the finite pole has no problem with points at greater separations. As we will see, the equilibrium pressure, the coherence, of spacetime dictates the behavior of everything in the universe. It is the fundamental force of nature from which all the others are derived.

Substance (A Brief Overview)

Though its origin may be difficult to comprehend, space-time itself is remarkably simple stuff. Having collapsed out of the infinite void over eternity, it is nothing but compressed space. It became compressed when the edges of the region from which it collapsed snapped free from the rest of the void, catapulting it toward the center at a velocity proportionate to the square of its distance from the center. The snap transformed eons of built-up potential energy into a phenomenal quantity of kinetic energy that crushed space well past its equilibrium pressure, all the way down into an exceedingly and uniformly dense sphere—a kind of Euclidean minimum. We know an equilibrium pressure exists because the collapse of space from the void depended on the internal attraction of space when it was *below* this pressure, whereas the tremendous force of the Big Bang, as well as the current expansion of the cosmos, depends on the internal repulsion of space when *above* this pressure. Indeed, we will find that the pressure of intergalactic space (~2.7 on the Kelvin scale) is very close to, though slightly higher than, the equilibrium pressure of spacetime.

All of the energy in the cosmos is contained in the pressure and velocity of spacetime. In the current epoch, because it is marked by the ongoing decompression of the Big Bang, positive pressure dominates. Though, as I have just shown, negative pressure dominates the long spans of time during which space-time coalesces out of the void. Still, because negative pressure plays a critical role even in our epoch, we must define *energy* as the *absolute value* of the pressure of spacetime[2]. As a result, negative spacetime pressure (in the form of implosive force) yields positive energy. From this we can conclude, based on $E=mc^2$, that mass is also defined by the pressure of spacetime. Mass composed of positive pressure spacetime is *matter*; mass composed of negative pressure spacetime is *antimatter*. The quantity of matter greatly exceeds the quantity of antimatter because our current epoch is dominated by positive pressure spacetime; its finite, Euclidean pole is actively striving to restore equilibrium. One could argue that the interminable span during which spacetime collapses out of the void is characterized by a preponderance of antimatter. However, as I will show, there are no naturally occurring particles of antimatter. Spacetime itself is neither matter nor energy, but is the fundamental substance on which they both depend. What we normally think of as *solid matter* is composed of spacetime that still possesses the enormous compression value associated with the Big Bang. In the following chapter I will explain how this phenomenon is possible.

Traditionally, a gravitational field is represented as spacetime *curvature* on a two-dimensional surface. Clearly this is meant as an analogy. Curvature in three dimensions is geometrically meaningless. But it is generally left to the imagination to decide what the genuine, three-dimensional equivalent might be. Transforming this analogy into a meaningful reality (**Figure 1.6**), we get, not spacetime curvature, but a spacetime *pressure gradient*. The depth of a two-dimensional spacetime curve is analogous to the intensity of its pressure in a real three-dimensional universe. In every case in which curvature seemed to make sense, pressure gradients make far more sense. And in every other case, including within the atomic nucleus, curvature only obscures the truth, while pressure gradients make it perfectly clear.

In summary, every phenomenon in the universe can

---

2   The relationship between pressure and energy is not linear, but hyperbolic, related to the Lorentz Factor. As spacetime approaches extreme pressures (related to either high velocities or strong gravitational fields) the corresponding energy increases without bound.

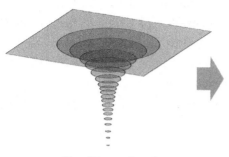 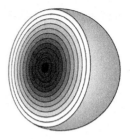

Two Dimensional   *Three Dimensional*
Spacetime Curve   *Spacetime Pressure*
                                  Gradient

Figure 1.6:   Spacetime Curvature
A three-dimensional curve is meaningless, whereas anything but a three-dimensional pressure gradient is meaningless. The traditional analogy of spacetime curvature, therefore, translates into a pressure gradient in a real three-dimensional universe.

be understood as the interactions between regions of different spacetime pressure. Spacetime strives to reach its equilibrium state. In our epoch, that means most phenomena will be dominated by high pressure, expansive or explosive events. Differences in pressure manifest themselves within spacetime gradients, not curves. A three-dimensional curve is meaningless, whereas anything but a three-dimensional pressure gradient is meaningless. This brief overview is enough to get us started and these concepts will become clearer as they are applied to actual phenomena. We now know enough to see how matter arises from compressed spacetime. But first there is one final order of business before we move on.

I started this book by asking the most basic question of ontology. What *is?* We now know enough to give a provisional answer.

Reality is the evolution of the eternal dialectic of infinity and finitude. The tension between these two paradoxical poles of Nothingness manifests itself in Being as the coherence of space and time—the equilibrium pressure of spacetime.

As promised, the fundamental substance of the universe is both irrational and imperceptible and yet exists just the same. The rest of this book is devoted to proving beyond any reasonable doubt that the above statement is the *Law of Physics*—the ontological principle underlying all that *is*.

2

Protons

The Big Bang

When the resistance of spacetime to additional compression finally overcomes the tremendous kinetic energy of its collapse, it is left as a hyper-compressed sphere of perfectly uniform density. This uniformity is critical and is the result of the snap, the tearing of space, along the surface of an infinite bounded region. Every point in space is accelerated toward the center at a rate proportionate to its tension when the sphere snapped free of the void. That tension is equal to the square of the distance of a point from the core. Hence, the entire mass arrives at the core simultaneously, resulting in a sphere of uniform pressure and density. There is no need to assume this sphere is a *singularity*. In fact, a singularity would imply infinite potential energy, and while the Big Bang was certainly impressive, there is no evidence it was infinite. The instant it comes to a halt it immediately begins decompressing at a rate proportionate to the Lorentz Factor associated with its internal pressure.

As cosmologists have already suggested (though for different reasons) the first fraction of a second saw the nascent cosmos expand to many times its initial volume and at many times the speed of light. The first question we might ask is why the universe at its maximum compression does not simply collapse into a singularity under its own gravitational pull as predicted by Relativity Theory. The answer is that spacetime is always repulsive at pressures above its equilibrium value—when its finite pole dominates its infinite pole. There are no exceptions.

Gravity is not simply a measure of the total mass of an object. To form a gravitational field there must be a spacetime pressure gradient. In its initial condition, there is no spacetime field, only the void, surrounding the cosmos. And within the sphere of spacetime itself the pressure is equal everywhere; no gradient means no gravity. In general, spacetime, when above its equilibrium pressure and not organized into complex matter (atoms), is not attracted but repelled by gravitational fields. The Big Bang is explosive, pure and simple. There is no paradox.

In the tiny fraction of a second after the Big Bang, the universe expands at a preposterously high, inflationary velocity, far above the speed of light, proportionate (according to the Lorentz Factor) only to its internal pressure. This is so because the void surrounding the expanding sphere offers no resistance to its expansion. This dramatic increase in volume is accompanied by a correspondingly precipitous drop in pressure but not, as we might expect, uniformly everywhere at the same rate.

The initial velocity of the inflationary expansion is proportionate to the initial pressure. This velocity cannot be slowed because there is no compressed spacetime ("normal space") occupying the void into which the universe is expanding.[1] The void as always does not get in the way. As a result, except for the first instant, the actual expansion rate of the universe exceeds the preferred expansion rate and by an ever increasing amount. The internal pressure of the expanding sphere drops precipitously as the volume increases, but the velocity continues to increase. The velocity increases (the universe accelerates) because of the diminishing but still positive force applied by the decompressing spacetime, and because there is nothing (the void) to slow it down.[2] Had the sphere begun its expansion at a lower pressure,

---

1   The speed of light in a vacuum, c, is its speed through spacetime at its equilibrium pressure. There is no analogous speed limit for objects traveling through the void. Interestingly, Newtonian physics applies precisely, at all velocities, in the void.

2   To eliminate any ambiguity here, the *force* in question is the finite pole of the eternal dialectic between infinity and finitude. As described in Chapter 1, the infinite pole of absolute nothingness tends to pull space together, while the finite pole tends to push it apart. The force of expansion provided by the finite pole is

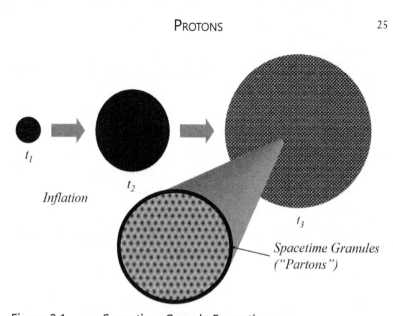

t_1

Inflation

t_2

t_3

Spacetime Granules
("Partons")

Figure 2.1:   Spacetime Granule Formation
During the inflationary period, the pressure drops while the expansive velocity continues to increase. The disparity between the accelerating expansion of the whole cosmos and the slowing expansion of individual points
results in the formation of spacetime granules.

the expansion rate would have been lower by a proportionate
amount. Therefore, the early expansion of the universe results
in an ever increasing disparity between the actual expansion rate
and its preferred or necessary (as dictated by the finite pole)
expansion rate. That disparity leads to the formation of *spacetime
granules* (**Figure 2.1**).

Unlike a standard explosion, the Big Bang is not composed of a large quantity of inert matter being propelled away
from a center of detonation. Every single point in the expanding
sphere contributes equally to the expansion and propels itself
away from neighboring points with equal intensity.[3] At the very
first moment, the repulsion of those spacetime points manifests

currently referred to as *Dark Energy*, and it performs the same function today that
it did during the Big Bang. The infinite pole, then, could be referred to as negative
dark energy.

3   In this context, the word *point* does not refer, as in Chapter 1, to an infinitesimal spacetime point but rather to a very small (sub-nucleonic) discrete region.
Though it is small, it is composed of an infinite number of spacetime points, just like
everything else that exists.

itself in the expansion of the entire cosmos. As the pressure drops, the intensity of repulsion (the acceleration) drops proportionately though the overall velocity continues to increase. That means the expansion of each granule within the sphere is exceeded by the expansion of the universe as a whole. Something has to give. Very soon after the bang, the individual granules within the sphere have plenty of room to expand at a rate proportionate to their decreased pressures. If we look closely at one of these granules, we see that its own internal pressure demands a rate of expansion considerably lower than that of the whole sphere, and indeed it is now expanding at exactly that lower rate. Each one of these granules constitutes a local expansion that is slowing in proportion to its decreasing pressure, even as the whole cosmos is accelerating geometrically. Each granule of spacetime is a pressure gradient, denser in the center and progressively less dense as it approaches the limits of the adjacent granules. At the surfaces of these gradients the spacetime rapidly approaches its equilibrium value because the volume it is expected to fill vastly exceeds the lower rate at which it is now expanding.

Very quickly, the pressure at the surfaces of these granules drops all the way to the spacetime equilibrium pressure (SEP). To reiterate, the cosmological constant is the pressure of spacetime at which its infinite and finite poles are perfectly balanced. When this happens, the granules begin to exert an increasingly powerful resistance to any further expansion; the infinite pole begins to exert itself. However, the momentum of the entire cosmos greatly exceeds this resistance and it keeps right on expanding at the same breakneck pace. This moment, when the increasing volume of the cosmos outstrips the ability of the expanding granules to fill it *without their surfaces falling below the equilibrium pressure of spacetime*, marks a major event in the evolution of the universe.

So long as the granules are pushing out against the expanding cosmos, everything proceeds apace without any significant changes. After all, the goal of spacetime is to reach its equilibrium pressure. But as soon as the geometrically expanding volume of the cosmic sphere reaches the point at which the surfaces of the granules are no longer pushing but are instead being pulled, spacetime quickly changes course. The resistance of spacetime to stretching is analogous to the surface tension of water, except that it increases in intensity with increased stretching. If we imagine the whole universe at this moment, we see a huge expanse of granules with their surfaces under increasing stress from the expanding sphere. Given the dynamics of a spherical expansion, the rate at which any two granules are moving apart is proportionate to the distance between them. Granules on opposite sides of the sphere are moving apart much faster than two adjacent granules. Also, the strength of the attraction along the surfaces of any two granules is related to the intrinsic resistance of spacetime to further stretching—to the force exerted by the infinite pole. Essentially, we have a tug of war between the expanding sphere and the attractive granules. Very quickly, this unstable state of affairs must be resolved.

What happens is that the universe fractures into an inconceivably complex network (**Figure 2.2**) of interlaced *filaments*, the scale of which corresponds to the distance at which the attraction between the granules is just barely exceeded by the pull of the expanding sphere. For the sake of simplicity, I will assume that a typical filament ranges anywhere from a few centimeters or so in diameter to no more than a few kilometers. The ideas to follow are not dependent on the exact dimensions, just so long as they are much larger than the granules and much smaller than stars—roughly halfway between the extremes of magnitude that characterize the cosmos. Because the fracture of the cosmic sphere is perfectly symmetrical, the exact geometry of the filaments is invariably chaotic, balanced on a knife-edge between the competing forces. What this means is that neither the momentum of cosmic expansion nor the surface tension of adjacent granules dominates the phenomenon. And when com-

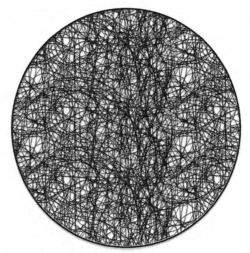

Figure 2.2:　　　Partonic Filaments
A view of the cosmos at the end of the inflationary period. Because this shape is a fractal, this view could be 100 kilometers or 100 million light years across. The large-scale isotropy and small-scale anisotropy of the universe is a consequence of this fracturing process. A computer simulation will no doubt reveal that the actual shape is far more complex than the one pictured here. But it will, like this one, be a highly compressed analog of the observed filamentous architecture of the cosmos.

peting forces are balanced so precisely, the resulting geometry naturally reflects this balance at every location and at every scale—a shape referred to as a *fractal*.

Deceleration

Before we continue our investigation into the formation of protons, we must take note of another consequence of the critical moment following the inflationary period. As mentioned, the rapidly expanding sphere of the cosmos was in a tug of war with the intrinsic attraction, the surface tension, of the granules. That war resolved itself in the formation of filaments of granules. But in so doing the cosmos was dramatically decelerated as it was forced to break the bonds between the granules along the surfaces of all of those filaments. This is important because at its highest rate of expansion, the cosmos would have been flung to the far reaches of the void in very short order had something not arrested its motion. The collective inhibitory effect of pulling apart the granules—borrowing the terminology of particle physics, I will refer to these granules as *partons* from now on—along the surfaces of the filaments slowed the cosmic expansion rate to a more familiar value.

Looking more closely at these filaments, we can see that the total surface area of the cosmos—the total surface area of all the filaments taken together—is proportionate to the force that was needed to separate them. The finer the structure of the network (the smaller they are), the greater the total surface area. That surface area in turn is proportionate to the surface tension that held those partons together. And each parton was bonded to adjacent partons with an equal force. The amount of force required to separate the filaments, therefore, is proportionate to the number of partons actually separated, and that is proportionate to the total surface area of the entire network taken as a whole. Consequently, the amount of momentum sapped from the rapidly expanding cosmos can be precisely calibrated. If the filaments were large (low total surface area, implying fewer broken partonic bonds) the cosmos would have lost relatively little momentum while separating them. Correlatively, if the filaments were small (high total surface area, implying more broken partonic bonds) the cosmos would have been slowed much more. So the question now is: How much was the universe slowed? The answer is subtle but very important.

Scientists are understandably made queasy by phenomena that could have evolved differently but seem to be very precisely calibrated to give us the cosmos as we actually find it. The exact value of the cosmological constant (equilibrium pressure of spacetime), the size of a proton, the extreme weakness of gravity compared to the other forces, etc., seem unreasonably perfect for life as we know it. Such unlikely coincidences are more like winning the lottery than discovering a physical law, and often prompt uncomfortable applications of the anthropic principle. When we find an event such as the deceleration of the

initial inflation of the Big Bang that could have happened along
a continuum of values, we need to offer a reason that it turned
out the way it did that does not involve dumb luck. We need to
explain why the cosmos, expanding at perhaps millions of times
the speed of light, was slowed to a dead stop all at once even
though it could have been slowed far less, allowing it to continue
expanding off into the void and leaving matter too thinly distributed to create any complex and interesting configurations.
Thankfully, in this case there is a good explanation.

When the cosmos fractures into filaments, there are
two important considerations: the momentum of the cosmos as
a whole and the attraction or surface tension binding adjacent
partons to one another. Once the pressure along the surfaces of
the partons has dropped below the equilibrium value of spacetime, each one exerts an equal—and increasing—attraction on
adjacent partons. Across the entire cosmos, the total attractive
force contained in these interpartonic bonds exceeds the total
momentum of the expanding universe. That may sound like a
bold claim, but it follows from an extrapolation of the behavior
of any two adjacent partons. Regardless of how rapidly the universe expands, its speed is driven by the expansive ambitions of
the individual partons, and no two adjacent partons repel one
another with more force than the breaking point of spacetime itself. Indeed, any two adjacent partons are nearly stationary with
respect to one another and are highly attractive at their surfaces.
Spacetime attempts to reach its equilibrium pressure by expanding, but that expansion is checked by its equally strong resistance
to stretching below its equilibrium pressure. It does not behave
like compressed gas being released into space. Its resistance to
expansion below its equilibrium pressure holds it together no
matter how high its initial pressure or how rapid its initial expansion. Therefore, no two adjacent partons taken in isolation from
the whole can repel one another with enough force, regardless
of their initial pressures, to break the bond on their surfaces.
That means that, collectively, the force of attraction between all

the partons exceeds the momentum of the universe.

Though the *total* attractive force is greater than the *total* momentum, that is only because the *collective* effect of the interpartonic bonds is so great. Individually, partons are very tiny and their bonds are—at least by comparison with total cosmic momentum—very weak. What we need to do is look at the conditions just before the universe fractures. At that moment the total momentum of the cosmos is devoted to stretching the interpartonic bonds. If that momentum exceeded the total bond strength (which we have seen that it does not) then the cosmos would break apart in such a way that much momentum would remain and the filaments would continue expanding away from each other at great speeds, possibly becoming too distant from one another to form the universe as we know it. But because the collective bond strength exceeds this momentum, we have an equilibrium condition. And wherever an equilibrium condition exists, the resolution must conform to that equilibrium.

At the moment the cosmos fractures, the interpartonic bonds are stretched near their breaking point. But because their total strength exceeds cosmic momentum, only a specific fraction of them must break in order to restore equilibrium. As we have seen, the total surface area of the resulting network of filaments is proportionate to the force required to create it, and that force is exactly equal to the momentum of the cosmos when the fracture occurs. The number of interpartonic bonds that break will be the absolute minimum necessary to counterbalance the momentum. Or, looking at it from the opposite perspective, the momentum of the universe, because it is less than the total interpartonic force, breaks exactly the number of bonds that correspond with its total energy. Either way we look at it, the momentum of the cosmos is completely sapped when it fractures the partons into filaments, and the size of those filaments is directly related to the momentum so sapped. In brief, the universe comes to a dead stop. The inflationary expansion is over.

It may be difficult to imagine, but we are still within the first few moments[4] after the Big Bang. The partons of which our network of filaments is composed are nothing but unstable spacetime gradients—minuscule bits of Big Bang. Left to themselves they would decay in far less than the blink of an eye. Yet when we consider these events at extremely small time increments, we can resolve the amazing structure that develops. Now we need to look more closely at one of these filaments.

Protogenesis

When the surface tension holding the cosmos together fractures, creating the filaments of partons, those partons recoil at their surfaces back toward the equilibrium pressure of spacetime. I point this out only because it implies that there is no longer any rapid expansion going on within the filaments, just as there is no longer any rapid expansion generally. The filaments are separated from one another and their behavior is determined only by their own internal properties, which are determined entirely by the partons of which they are composed.

Partons are highly unstable, each one a moment of expansion, a spacetime pressure gradient that wants nothing more than to explode outward until it reaches its equilibrium pressure. That being the case, whatever happens next must happen very rapidly in order to preserve the structure implied by these ephemeral entities. If we look closely at the filaments, what we find is a very important asymmetry. Now that the filaments are separated, drifting alone in the void, the partons near the surface are less constrained than the ones in the interior. In other words, the outer partons can expand more freely than the inner partons. It might seem that the filaments would simply evaporate, starting from the surface and moving toward the center. But that is not what happens. Bear in mind, the surfaces of the partons

---

4   Current theory has provided very precise predictions for the duration of this brief inflationary period. Clearly, those predictions will not apply to this new theory, though it is still quite likely that the inflationary period was very brief.

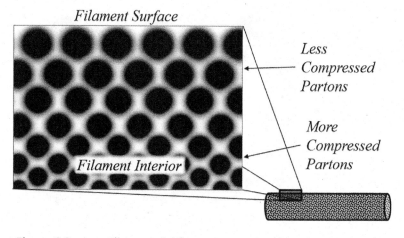

Figure 2.3: Filament Surface
The partons on the surface of the filaments are less constrained and decompress more freely than the partons in the interior.

are mutually attractive so long as they are at or below their equilibrium pressures. Though the partons do expand somewhat, they do not drift apart, and this is where the asymmetry in pressure (between the surface and interior of the filaments) becomes critical. It is also important to note that because the partons are moving through the void (at least near the surfaces of the filaments), their rectilinear velocities can greatly exceed their expansive velocities; they can move around a great deal before they decay. Movement through the void can be superluminal (essentially infinite), whereas the expansion of the partons is proportionate only to their internal pressures.

As the outer partons expand, their pressures drop. As their pressures drop, adjacent partons, those closer to the center, move into the slightly more decompressed partons (**Figure 2.3**). Every parton attempts to expand into whatever surrounding region offers the least resistance, and that means partons closer to the center (more compressed) rush into the relatively low pressure regions occupied by partons closer to the surface (less compressed). This movement of the more compressed partons into the less compressed ones tends to recompress those

Parton
Convection
Cells

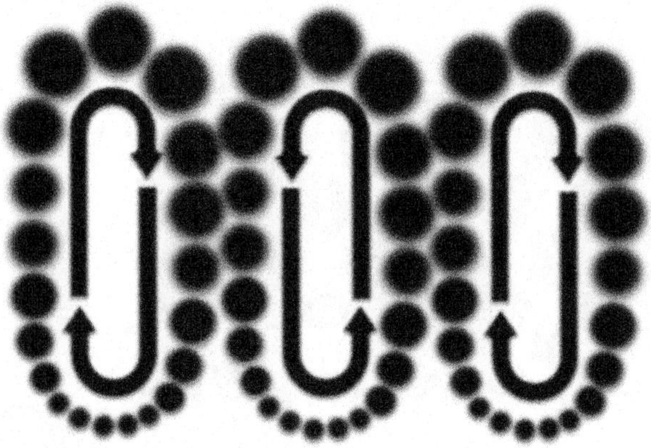

Figure 2.4:   Parton Convection Cells
Because the partons are mutually attractive at their surfaces, instead of flying apart they exhibit convection currents. The filaments boil.

that were attempting to decompress, pushing them back into the filament away from the surface. Overall, this motion results in a vast number of localized convection currents, partons alternately decompressing and recompressing as they migrate into one another on the basis of relative pressure differences (**Figure 2.4**). In a sense, the filaments begin boiling, and it is here that something truly amazing happens.

In order to establish a local equilibrium, all we need is for a precise number of partons to begin circulating together. That number is just however many partons are required in order to create—while in convective circulation—a total average pressure that is equal to the internal pressure of each of the participating partons. It might seem unlikely that the exact number of partons would happen to assemble themselves in just the right way to create a stable circulation, but the contrary is true. They have no choice but to assemble themselves that way. As partons circulate within the filaments, stable configurations will spontaneously dissociate themselves from the rest as soon as they come together because, as a stable particle, they no longer require the overall circulation in order to maintain their own local equilibria. As a result, stable convective parton circulations (I will refer

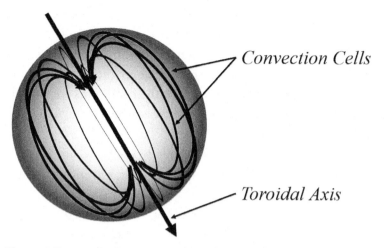

Figure 2.5:   Parton Convection within a Proton
Partons circulate through the proton's major axis, around the surface, and
back through the core. By way of this convective motion they are compressed in the interior and allowed to decompress on the surface. The
constant disparity in pressure drives the proton's circulation. Note: though
only the surface and major axis are shown here, this particle is solid and
partons circulate, in direct contact with one another, throughout the entire
volume of the proton.

to them as *protons* from now on) at the surfaces of the boiling
filaments break free of the circulating mass and drift away into
the void (**Figure 2.5**). Very rapidly, the entire cosmic network
disintegrates into protons in this way. Each proton is exactly the
same size because only a very specific number of partons can
maintain but not exceed an average pressure that exactly balances the internal pressure of all of its constituent partons.

This phenomenon does not rely on a lucky coincidence
of partons magically coming together in the right numbers.
Rather, within the roiling mass of partons, virtual protons are
implied by any association that is, by virtue of its own internal
characteristics, stable. To use an analogy, consider the manner in
which raindrops form in a cloud. Small droplets of water vapor
coalesce on dust or pollen particles and gradually increase in
mass. These protodrops, in turn, collide and combine. At some
point, gravity exceeds their buoyancy and they fall. It is not a

coincidence that the same amount of water comes together in each drop. The quantity of water that constitutes a drop is implied by the entire system. When a drop forms, it falls, but not before. Likewise, a proton forms whenever the local circulation of partons happens to form one. Yet, the conditions are such that the necessary number of partons will easily come together over and over.

Nevertheless, it is reasonable to assume that many, perhaps most, of the partons do not find their way into protons. If several protons form in a region, only a very specific number of partons can be used. Any leftover partons would not be able to move to other regions fast enough to become part of a proton before decompressing to the point at which they are no longer suitable for convective circulation. Moreover, unstable associations—those with too few or too many partons—will rapidly decay.[5] This has several important consequences. As these leftover partons decompress and unstable associations decay, the void is very rapidly filled with spacetime at its equilibrium pressure, setting the stage for "normal physics." It also means that our newly minted protons are blasted away from their places of origin by the leftover decompressing partons. Finally, it means the cosmos enters another period of rapid expansion (though far slower than the Big Bang), as these decaying partons expand to their equilibrium pressure. This expansion is governed by the equation, $E=mc^2$, in which c^2 is the factor by which a parton expands in order to reach its equilibrium pressure (the cosmological constant). Viewed from a cosmic perspective, we now have protons being propelled in all different directions and mixed together in all different concentrations. Such asymmetric distribution is critical for the subsequent evolution of galaxies and stars.

---

5   For reasons that will be explained in later chapters, neither neutrons nor other intrinsically unstable particles persist at this point in cosmic evolution. If a neutron did form, it would not be able to capture a proton in order to sustain itself because there is, as yet, no "normal space" surrounding these phenomena to facilitate the formation of atoms.

Proton Spin

A proton is a nearly spherical convective circulation of partons. As the partons are circulated through the major axis of the proton, they are compressed. They are then allowed to decompress as they circulate through the particle and around its surface. It is the constant disparity between the pressure on the surface and the pressure in the core that drives the circulation and maintains the proton's equilibrium. Each parton is a pressure gradient that observes the inverse square law—very dense in the center and progressively less dense near its surface. At their surfaces, the partons are in direct physical contact; there are no forces-at-a-distance and no particles (i.e., gluons) are exchanged between them. Their relative motions are determined exclusively by their mutual reactions to their differing pressures and to their momenta.

To understand the angular momentum characteristics of the proton, we need to examine any one of an infinite number of possible sets of radially symmetrical cross sections (**Figure 2.6a**). Each cross section intersects two opposing convective cells. We can draw in the angular momentum vectors for each cell (**Figure 2.6b**), and then use simple vector addition to calculate the net value for the entire object. Incredibly, no matter what set of cross sections we select, the net angular momentum for the proton as a whole always has a value of exactly zero (**Figure 2.6c**).

This zero angular momentum value is fascinating because it means the whole object does not, like a gyroscope, resist any effort to push it out of a particular orientation. No matter how vigorous the convection, any applied force will cause the object to move or rotate just as if it were a solid, stationary ball. It also means that a tremendous amount of energy (kinetic) can be stored inside the proton without it having the slightest effect on anything outside of the particle. Correlatively, no matter how energetic the proton is internally, even the slightest exter-

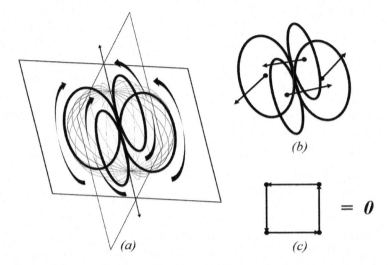

Figure 2.6:   Proton - No Angular Momentum
Various radial cross sections (a) of a proton reveal angular circulations (b) that might seem to contribute to the proton's spin. However, when we add the angular momentum vectors of all possible circulations (c) they sum to zero. Hence, protons have no intrinsic spin.

nal force can have an effect on it. In fact, the proton, because it possesses no net angular momentum, will only move in response to externally applied forces.

During their formation, protons represented an equilibrium condition that exactly balanced the internal pressure of each parton against the average pressure of the entire particle. The proton, by turning itself inside out, concentrates the explosive force of the partons into its core rather than out beyond its surface. One very interesting aspect of this equilibrium is that it was achieved in the void, not in normal space (space infused with spacetime just above its equilibrium pressure). That means the proton is the only configuration of matter that is stable— though just barely—in the void. In normal space, the proton is what we might call *superstable*. By modulating its rate of convection, a proton can very precisely regulate its internal pressure. It does this by drawing spacetime in through its northern pole and expelling it from its southern pole (**Figure 2.7**).

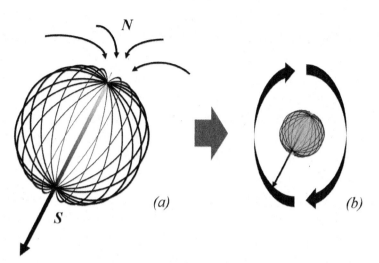

Figure 2.7:   Proton Rotation
Spacetime is drawn in through the north pole and expelled from the south pole (a), resulting in a disequilibrium state—high pressure around the south pole and low pressure around the north pole. As the poles push and pull on the ambient spacetime, the proton rotates (b) in order to put the north pole into a region of higher pressure and the south pole into a region of lower pressure.

If we look closely at the north pole of a proton, we find partons being rapidly pulled down into the proton's interior. Any ambient spacetime that is in contact with the surfaces of these partons will resist decompression below its equilibrium pressure, thereby being pulled down into the interior along with the partons with which it is in contact. Once inside the proton, the ambient spacetime is dramatically compressed, contributing to the pressure of the entire particle in direct proportion to the proton's rate of convection.[6] The faster the proton circulates, the more spacetime is drawn in and the higher the internal pressure becomes. This relationship enables the proton to precisely regulate its pressure by modulating its convection. That is the reason protons are so amazingly stable in normal space.

---

6   In fact, the pressure in a proton's core is proportionate to the Lorentz Factor associated with the proton's convective velocity. Linear increases in convective velocity, as the ambient spacetime approaches c, result in geometric increases in core pressure.

When the spacetime that is drawn into the proton is expelled from the south pole, it is emitted as an extremely focused and intense beam or jet of compressed spacetime. This jet in turn compresses the ambient spacetime around the south pole well above its equilibrium value. At the same time, the spacetime around the north pole is being dramatically decompressed as it is pulled in. Since spacetime resists both decompression below and compression above its equilibrium value, the proton must rotate in such a way that the north pole is moved into a region of higher pressure while the south pole is moved to a region of lower pressure. In essence, the jet of spacetime coming from the south pole pushes against the ambient spacetime, which in turn pushes back against the proton, causing it to spin. Since the proton has no net angular momentum of its own, it does not resist this spinning at all. Proton spin comes entirely from the pushing and pulling of the ambient spacetime in response to the proton's convective circulation.

Termination Shock

With no angular momentum, the proton's rotation is governed almost entirely by the action of the south polar jet— the north pole contributing a small but perhaps important component as well. The jet, in turn, is governed by the proton's convective velocity. If, then, we examine the system after one full rotation, we will find, surrounding the proton, a very dense ring of spacetime at a distance that marks the termination shock of the jet.

Termination shock occurs, in general, when the forced or fast flow of a substance succumbs to the steady or slow flow of that same substance. The most celebrated example of this phenomenon is the termination shock of the solar wind, way out at the inner edge of the solar system. In fact, due to sudden and pronounced changes in the prevalence of cosmic radiation at its current location, it is believed that the Voyager I spacecraft has recently passed through the termination shock. A far less gran-

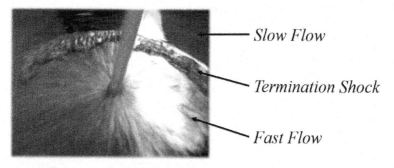

Figure 2.8: Termination Shock
The phenomenon of termination shock prevents a substance from dissipating smoothly all the way out from a high-pressure point of origin. Instead, it stops abruptly at a specific distance from its source.

diose but still instructive example of termination shock can be created in a kitchen sink (**Figure 2.8**).

Termination shock is interesting for many reasons, not least of which is its applicability to the solar wind, but my focus for now is on nothing more than the simple fact that it exists at all. What it means for the proton is that the energetic south polar jet, at a well-defined distance from the particle, will suddenly succumb to the ambient spacetime, driving up the pressure at that radius. The spacetime pressure does not dissipate gradually, either smoothly or turbulently, off into the distance with no specific stopping point.

Derivative Axes

The simplest possibility is that the proton spins in a circle, but it is obvious that such a pattern would merely clear a two-dimensional disk around the particle and lead to a significant disequilibrium between the spacetime in that disk and the spacetime in the surrounding areas (**Figure 2.9a**). Another possibility is that the proton spins such that the simple disk just mentioned itself spins around what we might call a *derivative axis*, thereby sending both the north and south poles of the proton through every point in a spherical volume around the particle. That is certainly an improvement, but even this motion sends the

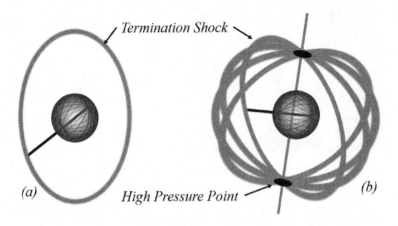

One Rotation   *Multiple Rotations*

Figure 2.9:   Multiple Rotations
After one rotation (*a*), the south polar jet clears a two-dimensional disk, while the termination shock creates a high pressure ring around the proton. After multiple rotations (*b*), the proton rotates on a derivative axis in order to minimize the pressure through which its jet passes, but the jet has no alternative but to pass through the poles of the first derivative axis with each rotation, resulting in two high pressure points.

poles through some points more than others. In particular, the proton's north and south poles—its major axis—pass through the poles of the first derivative axis on every primary rotation but only pass through any given point on the equator once per total derivative cycle. To remedy this, we must introduce a second derivative axis.

This next axis is derived from the first derivative axis by drawing a line through the two points through which the major axis passes most frequently (**Figure 2.9b**). With the second derivative axis, we are definitely getting closer to an equilibrium condition. However, even this axis sends the major axis through certain points more than others. And because the proton has exactly zero angular momentum of its own, there is nothing else acting on it except for the pressure exerted by the spacetime in its immediate environment. Consequently, if the pressure in the spherical volume of space around the proton can be made even

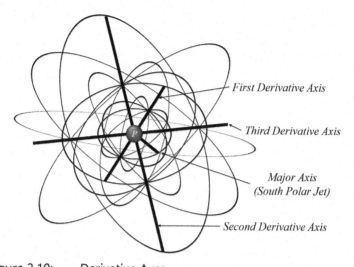

First Derivative Axis

Third Derivative Axis

Major Axis
(South Polar Jet)

Second Derivative Axis

Figure 2.10:   Derivative Axes
Each derivative axis sends the south polar jet through its poles more frequently than its equator. Hence the poles of each derivative axis must,
like the major axis, rotate such as to reduce the pressure variations. In this
diagram, the axes are shown with different radii for clarity. In a real atom,
they are all the same size.

more uniform, however nit-picky this might appear, the proton
must rotate in such a way to make it so, giving rise to the third
derivative axis.

The third derivative axis is derived just like the second
one, by drawing a line through the poles of the one preceding it.
And the fourth, fifth, sixth, and n^{th} derivative axes (**Figure 2.10**)
are the same, each one responsible for fine-tuning the equilibrium pressure of the spherical volume immediately surrounding
the proton. If we look at the proton up close, what we see is
simply the major axis (the south polar jet) moving through an
incredibly complex pattern that seems to magically avoid pass-
ing through any particular point more than any other. Nevertheless, despite this complexity and apparent randomness, there
remains an echo of all of those derivative axes that gave rise to
its ultimate motion. To see this, we must have a closer look at the
nature of these axes.

The first thing to notice is that each axis spins somewhat

more slowly than the one from which it is derived. This is so because the pattern that makes any n^{th} derivative axis necessary only emerges after the $n-1$ axis has rotated long enough to begin creating a disequilibrium in the ambient spacetime. Therefore, the major axis spins the fastest, the first derivative axis somewhat slower than but nearly as fast as the major one, the second derivative axis more slowly than the first and the nth slower than the $n-1$. Moreover, the *difference* in rotational velocity between any two successive axes increases as n increases, because the total number of rotations implied by any particular axis increases exponentially as a function of n.

The next important aspect to notice is that each successive axis is responsible for maintaining a smaller fraction of the total equilibrium than its predecessor. The greatest disequilibrium is created when the highly compressed spacetime is first emitted from the proton's south pole; the simple circular motion of the major axis contributes more, simply by moving any direction at all, than any of the derivative axes. Similarly, the first derivative axis is responsible for mitigating the effects of the major axis' simple circular motion. By the time we get all the way to the nth derivative axis, we are dealing with only the smallest fraction of the disequilibrium. Nevertheless, a somewhat counterintuitive fact emerges from these considerations. The purpose of all of these various interdependent rotations is to alter the path of the major axis in such a way that it passes through every point in the sphere with equal frequency. As a result, the motion of the major axis is defined by the path of the nth derivative axis, while the path of the first derivative axis is defined by the path of the $n-1$ axis, the path of the second derivative axis by the path of the $n-2$ axis, etcetera. Hence, the intensity of any axis is inversely proportional to the fraction of the equilibrium for which it is responsible.

Let us look at this relationship in a slightly different way. According to our discussion, the major axis moves in a simple circle. The first derivative axis in turn rotates the circle of the

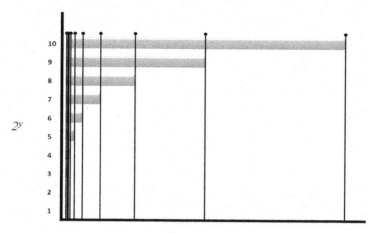

2^y

Wavelength

Figure 2.11:   Emission Spectrum
The exponential relationship between the derivative axes results in a distribution of wavelengths that closely mirrors any one of the observed electromagnetic spectral series of hydrogen.

major axis. The second derivative axis rotates the poles of the
first derivative axis. Finally, the nth axis rotates the poles of the
n-1 axis. This progression of axes is as much an explanatory tool
as a description of reality. In fact, the major axis never actually
spins in a simple circle. The complex pattern implied by all *n*
axes defines the path of the major axis right from the start. The
dynamics of the derivative axes do not imply that any particular
axis ever existed independent of the rest. Rather, this model of
proton spin is designed to rigorously explain the path of the major axis itself. Which is not to imply that these derivative axes do
not really exist. Indeed, if we graph (**Figures 2.11 and 2.12**)
the various axes and their intensities, we get a very interesting
picture. You may recognize it as any one of several series of lines
from hydrogen's electromagnetic emission spectrum.

As mentioned, there is an exponential relationship between the axes. If, for the sake of simplicity, we assume that each
axis must rotate only twice in order to generate the next one,
then the first derivative axis implies two rotations of the proton,
the second derivative axis implies 2 x 2 or 4 rotations, the third,

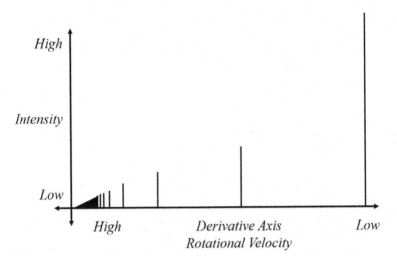

Figure 2.12:   Rotational Axes Graph - Intensity vs Velocity
The intensity of any axis is inversely proportionate to the fraction of the disequilibrium for which it is responsible. Combined with the exponential relationship depicted in Figure 2.11, these dynamics give us not only the wavelengths but also the relative intensities of the lines in hydrogen's electromagnetic emission spectrum.

2 x 2 x 2 or 8, etc., which generates a graph like Figure 2.11 over the first ten derivative axes. Since this is an entirely notional model, figures 2.11 and 2.12 do not exactly replicate any of the series of lines in hydrogen's EM spectrum. However, this is very obviously the type of phenomenon that could generate them.

Energy States

The lines in Figure 2.12 are not meant to represent any particular series. At this point in the discussion, it could be the *Lyman, Balmer, Paschen*, or any of the other series (**Figure 2.13**). They all operate according to the same principle, though each of them represents a distinct energy state of the atom. The first thing to note is that, contrary to the current quantum model, an energy state is defined by an *entire series*, not by only one of its spectral lines. Every hydrogen atom emits the entire series all at once. Atoms do not fluctuate between the various lines within a series. When an atom changes energy states, it immediately be-

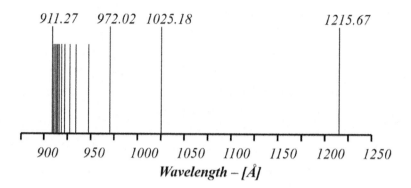

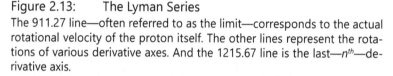

Figure 2.13:   The Lyman Series
The 911.27 line—often referred to as the limit—corresponds to the actual rotational velocity of the proton itself. The other lines represent the rotations of various derivative axes. And the 1215.67 line is the last—n^{th}—derivative axis.

gins emitting all the lines within a different series. Correlatively, no single atom ever emits lines from two different series at the same time.

The purpose of an energy state is to maintain a uniform pressure in the immediate vicinity of the proton. That means the convective velocity of the proton must evacuate spacetime from that region at the same rate that it is reabsorbed. It might appear that this equilibrium could be accomplished by simply varying the convection rate of the proton in exact proportion to the ambient spacetime pressure. That is, as the ambient pressure (temperature) gradually rises or falls, the convection rate slows or increases at the same continuous rate. However, the relationships between all the derivative axes that characterize a convective pattern—an energy state—are related only to the geometric demands of those axes, which are indifferent to the smooth continuous pressure changes around the atom. Most importantly, only certain series of axes are able to evacuate spacetime at the same rate that it is absorbed. As a result, the proton must jump between discrete energy states rather than slowing or accelerating continuously in direct response to the ambient pressure. If we were to speed up a proton only slightly, placing in between two accepted energy states, spacetime would either be evacuated faster than it is absorbed, or vice versa, resulting in a disequilibrium condition. The proton cannot maintain a constant convective velocity unless the pressure of the spacetime in its immediate vicinity is also constant. This idea is far from intuitive and merits some further explanation.

As mentioned, a single energy state of hydrogen is defined by an entire series of derivative axes. The fact that hydrogen only exhibits one well-defined set of such series (e.g., the Lyman, Balmer, and Paschen series) means that for some reason nature excludes any, seemingly plausible, intermediate wavelengths. Why should that be? In other words, why should the hydrogen atom not be allowed to spin at whatever velocity best reflects the ambient pressure at every moment? Why instead should it be required to jump back and forth between a limited set of energy states, none of which is perfectly suited to the local conditions? The answer is literally *complex* (see Chapter 9 for more detail), and would be difficult to glean from even a perfectly clear computer simulation because the rigid relationships between the derivative axes within a series cannot be visualized in any straightforward way. Nevertheless, these relationships exist and are decisive.

If we assume, as above, that each axis must complete two, and only two, rotations to give rise to the next axis, then it follows that each axis (from the major axis all the way to the nth axis) is capable of evacuating neither more nor less than a well-defined fraction of the spacetime in the proton's vicinity. Alternatively, the major axis would be capable of evacuating twice as much spacetime (by itself) if it could complete four rotations instead of two before creating the next axis. The same variations and restrictions apply to all of the derivative axes as well; each one is capable of evacuating no more or less spacetime than is associated with its particular intensity over the course of exactly two rotations. Put as simply as possible, this means that each of the axes in a series restricts and is restricted by all of the others. If the major axis were to speed up only slightly, perhaps in response to a minor change in the ambient spacetime pressure, all of the other axes would also speed up, but (and this is the critical point) in an exponential, non-linear, and ultimately unpredictable way. Such a state (in between two of nature's approved energy states) would not be able to maintain the delicate equilibrium between the ambient spacetime pressure and the rate at which spacetime is evacuated from the atom. Each energy state, therefore, corresponds to a unique internal constant pressure between the proton and its electronic shell, a concept to which we will now turn.

The Electronic Shell

Looking at the entire phenomenon of a hydrogen atom (**Figure 2.14**), we have a proton nucleus pulling spacetime in through its northern pole and expelling it from its southern pole. Its rotational pattern exhibits the complex geometry of one entire series of derivative axes. Because the proton evacuates a spherical region of space in its immediate vicinity, we can conclude that the spacetime pressure between the nucleus and the electronic shell, with the exception of the south polar jet, is lower than the pressure of the ambient spacetime just outside of the atom. The electronic shell in turn is the spherical surface at which the polar jet's outward pressure is balanced by the inward pressure of the ambient spacetime in the atom's vicinity. To visualize this, imagine the proton gathering up the spacetime within the atom, concentrating it into its south polar jet, and then firing it at the electronic shell. The rate at which any series of derivative axes evacuates the atom and concentrates the associated spacetime into a jet determines the pressure inside the electronic shell. If the proton rotates very rapidly, the internal pressure drops. When the proton slows down, the internal pressure rises.

From these considerations, it is clear that an *electron* is not an independent particle of matter, but is rather the *bump*

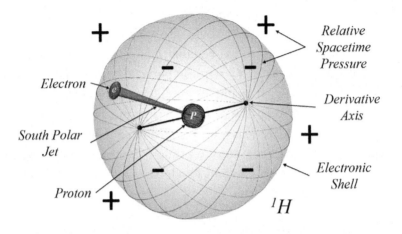

Figure 2.14:   Hydrogen
The hydrogen atom has a primary electron at the end of the south polar jet, which tracks the course of the nth derivative axis. The poles of every other derivative axis can be thought of as derivative electrons (only two shown here). The pressure inside the electronic shell is negative relative to the ambient spacetime. And the electronic shell is the termination shock radius at which the atom achieves cosmological equilibrium.

on the electronic shell at which the proton's south polar jet is balanced by the ambient spacetime—a phenomenon captured by the principle of *termination shock*. This is the reason protons and electrons have an "equal but opposite charge"; they are both part of the same phenomenon. Atomic electrons would not exist without the protons that generate them. Still, if we treat an electron as a discrete particle, we can see that it is a point of high pressure that corresponds to and balances the low pressure inside the atom. The faster the proton spins, the lower the internal pressure and the more intense the electron becomes. This explains the perhaps counterintuitive fact that EM waves from cold hydrogen atoms (atoms in low energy states) are shorter and more intense than waves from atoms in high energy states. At low temperatures, atoms must rotate more rapidly in order for their internal pressures to remain proportionate to the low ambient pressure.

We can refer to the electronic shell as an atom's *cosmological equilibrium*, a concept that dominates everything in the universe from atoms to stars. In general, this equilibrium state reflects the competing requirements that spacetime decompress from the highly compressed condition left over from the Big Bang, while not recompressing the ambient spacetime that has already decompressed and which now constitutes the vacuum pressure of the cosmos. Notice that the electronic shell of an atom would not exist were it not for the ambient spacetime, near its equilibrium pressure, pushing back against the proton's polar jet (creating its termination shock). Nor would the polar jet exist. The electron is nothing more than the point at which these two—polar jet and cosmos—collide.

By way of foreshadowing, *free electrons* and *beta particles* are similar to atomic electrons though obviously they are not generated in the same way. Any positive pressure shock wave (longitudinal wave) propagating through spacetime is phenomenologically similar to the positive pressure point on an atom's electronic shell. In later chapters, we will examine several of the myriad ways in which such longitudinal waves are generated.

Intrinsic and Extrinsic Mass

In the previous chapter, I mentioned briefly that spacetime is not itself either energy or matter but is rather the substrate upon which the latter depend for their existence. *Matter* and *energy* refer to the intensity of spacetime pressure. And because spacetime has an equilibrium pressure, it has the *capacity to do work* (possesses energy) at both positive and negative pressures. At negative pressures, spacetime *pulls* (driven by its infinite pole), while at positive pressures, it *pushes* (driven by its finite pole). Hence, negative pressure gives rise to positive energy and positive mass, and that means energy must be defined as the *absolute value* of spacetime pressure.

We have just seen that the pressure inside the electronic shell of a hydrogen atom is lower than the surrounding space.

We know this because the proton evacuates spacetime from that region, lowering its pressure relative to the local region. If the pressure of that surrounding space is very close to the equilibrium pressure of spacetime, lowering the pressure even further can yield a negative value. Since negative pressure results in positive energy and mass, the mass of an atom is at least partly determined by its rotational velocity or energy state, leading to a very complex situation.

Obviously, the overwhelming majority of a hydrogen atom's mass comes from its extremely high-pressure proton nucleus. This mass would remain even if the particle were returned to the void, effectively ending any discussion of polar jets and electronic shells. Therefore, we can refer to the proton itself (the partons) as the *intrinsic mass* of the hydrogen atom. If this mass were to change, the nucleus would no longer be a proton but something else entirely. On the other hand, the rotational velocity of the proton can and does change rather dramatically in response to external conditions. That rotational velocity determines the intensity of the pressure within the atom and therefore the fraction of the atom's mass that is associated with the energy generated by that pressure. We can refer to this phenomenon as *extrinsic mass* since it fluctuates according to the behavior of the proton, but would disappear completely if the proton were returned to the void.

For the time being, it is enough to file away this distinction between intrinsic and extrinsic mass in the back of your mind. The process of weighing a particle and disentangling these two different contributions to its mass will have to wait. Ultimately, this concept will be instrumental in explaining atomic binding energies, as well as the curious behavior of neutrons. But before we can examine it any further, we must first gain a better understanding of gravity and neutrons. To understand those we must have a look at somewhat larger phenomena—stars.

3

Neutrons

The theory developed in the previous chapter dealt with the genesis of protons out of spacetime during the Big Bang. It explained a great deal, including the basic elements of the EM spectrum of hydrogen, but there is already a fly in the ointment. Anyone familiar with modern cosmology will immediately point out that *neutrons* were not among the particles discussed. Without neutrons, neither helium nor lithium could have formed, though the formation of these elements just after the Big Bang is a fundamental part of the standard model. According to the theory I am developing here, there is no such phenomenon as *Big Bang Nucleosynthesis*, because there were no neutrons available to form complex atoms.

This aspect of the theory is a potential problem because it is well known that there is considerably more helium in the universe (roughly 25% of its total baryonic mass) than can be explained by stellar nucleosynthesis alone. There are not now nor have there ever been enough stars, as they are currently understood, to account for all of this helium. Any new theory of nucleosynthesis must make up this deficit.

Another challenge for this theory is to explain the curious uniformity of neutrons the universe over. The pressure under which protons formed was decisive for determining their complement of partons. As we will see, neutrons also depend on a particular pressure to determine their mass. Yet stars come in all different sizes, which would seem to imply that they have different internal pressures. More mass means more gravity, which means higher pressure. Different pressures should give rise to particles of different mass, because the number of partons necessary to maintain equilibrium is inversely proportionate to the pressure under which they formed. High pressures would create smaller particles with fewer partons, while lower pressures would create larger particles with more partons. Yet there is no evidence that neutrons, regardless of where they came from, vary by the slightest amount. The neutrons that make up my computer keyboard are the same as neutrons in the Andromeda Galaxy. This vexing issue is not even addressed by the standard model, but will be the primary consideration of the theory to follow.

Finally, this new theory must take seriously the colossal energies released by *gamma ray bursts (GRBs)* and *supernova* explosions. The standard model argues that a star's core gradually fills with metals (astrophysics refers to all elements heavier than helium as metals) as it burns progressively heavier elements in a series of fusion reactions. The star runs out of fuel when it either generates a large iron core (iron being the heaviest element that liberates energy during fusion) or, if it is a smaller star, when its gravitational force is exceeded by the nuclear binding energy of whichever element it last created. In either case, the only thing left over to account for the death of a star, supernova or otherwise, is the gravitational energy of a heavy metallic core. Notwithstanding the heroic efforts of mathematical physicists, there is simply no way to explain the energy of a supernova with nothing more to work with than a hot metallic ball. And, as we will see, the standard model completely collapses when confronted with the most energetic phenomena in the universe—gamma ray bursts. What I will show, unbelievable as it might sound, is that *nuclear fusion* has nothing to do with how a star generates its energy. The cosmic abundances of elements as well as their binding energies—the primary clues used to justify the standard model—may well be the greatest red herrings of all time.

Galactic Stars

If the theory of the Big Bang from the previous chapter is correct, then the asymmetric manner in which protons were created and subsequently ejected from the filaments that spawned them is more than sufficient to explain their eventual gravitational aggregation into large clouds and finally protostars. This theory also requires that all first-generation stars be composed entirely of hydrogen, because the equilibrium conditions during the Big Bang can only explain protons, not neutrons. To make things interesting, we will start with a protostar (actually a protogalaxy) of at least 10 million solar masses. In the early universe, dense and rich with matter, gigantic hydrogen clouds such as this would have been commonplace. The standard model states unequivocally that such an enormous mass would quickly collapse under its own weight into a supermassive black hole (indeed into the ones currently occupying the cores of galaxies) without going through a main sequence stage at all. This theory is not correct. Supermassive black holes came from supermassive *galactic stars*. And though these stars are long extinct, there are very good reasons to believe that they existed.

Our first question is, What could possibly prevent such a massive star from completely collapsing? The standard model argues that the gravitational force of such a star would far exceed any outflow of energy from hydrogen fusion. It could not maintain a *hydrostatic equilibrium* and would continue collapsing through both electron and neutron *degeneracy pressures* all the way down to a black hole. Indeed this is more or less what would happen were it not for one major oversight of the standard model: the cosmological equilibrium.

In a hydrogen atom, any outward pressure is met by an equal and opposite inward pressure exerted by the ambient spacetime slightly above its equilibrium pressure (the vacuum pressure). The proton's south polar jet pushes up against the electronic shell, which is nothing more than the radius at which the outward pressure of that jet is balanced by the inward pressure of spacetime. I call this the proton's *cosmological* equilibrium because the ambient pressure of spacetime (what is traditionally thought of as "empty" space), though not exactly constant everywhere in the universe, is usually very near its equilibrium value, at least by comparison to extreme locations such as stellar cores or atomic nuclei. Every expansive phenomenon in the universe must contend with this inward pressure and must be explained in terms of it. Stars are no exception.

Stars burn by converting mass into energy. This energy, flowing outward, maintains a star's hydrostatic equilibrium by pushing back against the gravitationally infalling matter from the star's mantle. It is also, once it clears the star completely, responsible for the *solar wind*. But that is not the end of the story. This outward pressure of a star pushes against the whole cosmos, and the cosmos pushes right back. If we travel out from a star, we will find a location where the outward pressure of the star is exactly equal to the vacuum pressure. This radius could be thought of as a star's *gravitational event horizon*; gravitational, because it is the location where the spacetime pressure gradient of the star is equaled by the pressure of the cosmos as a whole. The star has no direct gravitational influence beyond the point at which its pressure gradient ceases to exist. It is usually referred to as the *heliopause* and that is the term I will use as well.[1] Using the inverse square law, we can calculate the total surface area of the heliopause. Since we already know the vacuum pressure, we can calculate the total pressure exerted on this sphere. This pressure, pushing back against the star, cannot be exceeded by the outward pressure of the star itself. It is difficult to overstate the importance of this point. This limit to the pressure of a star dictates nearly all of its characteristics.

As the supermassive protostar we are considering col-

---

1   Later in the book this picture becomes more complex, but for now it is reasonable—if only as a practical matter—to think of the heliopause as the edge of the solar system.

lapses under the collective gravitational pull of its constituent hydrogen atoms, its pressure gradually increases, eventually reaching the point at which mass/energy conversion can begin. As mentioned, nuclear fusion is not the mechanism governing this conversion, and I will leave open for the moment exactly what is going on. For now, it is enough to refer generically to some as-yet-undefined type of mass/energy transformation that pushes out against the gravitationally infalling stellar mass.

Mass/energy conversion begins as soon as the pressure somewhere in the collapsing mass is minimally sufficient to trigger it. At first, this is clearly going to be at the very center of the new star, since that is where the pressure is the highest and first reaches the minimum necessary value. But once the process begins, the star's cosmological equilibrium begins to take over.

Even after the star begins burning, additional hydrogen from the protostellar cloud continues falling into the star, increasing its mass. According to the standard model, this increasing mass increases the core pressure, which in turn increases the rate of hydrogen fusion. That increased rate of fusion is sufficient to maintain the hydrostatic equilibrium of the growing star, at least up to a critical mass. After that point, the star becomes so massive that no rate of burn can balance the gravitational pull and the star collapses in on itself to become a black hole. Only hydrogen clouds smaller than this critical mass can form stable stars. The supermassive hydrogen clouds we are examining here are thought to have collapsed into the black holes that occupy galactic nuclei. However, there is another possibility.

Heliosphere

The complexities of the heliosphere are only indirectly relevant to the theory being described in this chapter. But because the heliosphere does govern the spacetime pressure values that are actually present, and because it could cause confusion to ignore it completely, we need to examine it here before moving on.

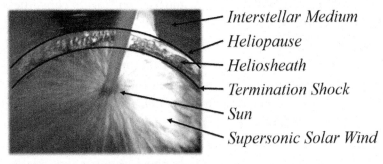

— *Interstellar Medium*
— *Heliopause*
— *Heliosheath*
— *Termination Shock*
— *Sun*
— *Supersonic Solar Wind*

Figure 3.1:   Heliosphere
The incline of the cookie sheet introduces gravitational resistance to the flow of water and is (along with the friction introduced by the sheet itself) analogous to the near-constant vacuum pressure of the interstellar medium. The fast flow of water radiating from the center out to the termination shock corresponds to the supersonic flow of spacetime from the star. The turbulent, foamy region beyond the termination shock corresponds to the heliosheath, and the outermost extent of the water corresponds to the heliopause. Beyond the heliopause is the interstellar medium.

If there were no interstellar medium, the spacetime flowing out from a star (the solar wind) would dissipate smoothly out to infinity, its pressure and velocity decreasing in accordance with the inverse square law at all distances. Instead, the interstellar spacetime, near its equilibrium value (the vacuum pressure), pushes back against the solar wind and causes an abrupt drop in velocity and abrupt increase in pressure on the surface of a vast sphere (latest estimates put its radius at ~84 AU) called the *termination shock*. Beyond the termination shock is a region of turbulent spacetime flow, called the *heliosheath*, which ultimately abuts the interstellar medium at the heliopause. This phenomenon can be captured, with surprising fidelity, by nothing more complicated than a water faucet and cookie sheet (**Figure 3.1**).

The major shortcoming of this analogy is that, unlike the solar wind, the water moves on a two-dimensional surface and is not constrained equally in all three dimensions; the air pressure above the water provides far less resistance than the cookie sheet below it. For that reason, the pressure at the termination shock does not exert nearly as much pressure against the fast flow of water as its solar analog exerts on the fast flowing solar wind. In a three-dimensional solar system, the pressure of the solar wind, pushing against a spherical termination shock, translates into a very significant pressure exerted back on the star itself.

For our purposes here, it is necessary only that we make note of the fact that the pressure of interstellar space (the vacuum pressure) pushes back against the star in a less than perfectly straightforward manner, not in a single step. The specifics are certainly interesting and worthy of study, but are incidental to the theory I am presenting here.[2] What is important is that the interstellar medium, because it exhibits a virtually constant pressure (the cosmological constant), means that the deceleration of solar winds and the pressure characteristics of various stars' heliospheres will exhibit a constant behavior from one star to the next. That is, though the stars themselves vary tremendously and the sizes of their heliospheres vary accordingly, their respective termination shocks and heliopauses will reflect the *constant pressure of the vacuum, not the variability of those stars.* In the discussion that follows, it is this constant behavior that is decisive, not the fact that it occurs in three steps (termination shock, heliosheath, heliopause). Therefore, for the sake of simplicity, I refer in the following sections to the *heliopause* alone rather than to the entire process, even though it might be argued that the termination shock is more directly responsible for the pressure exerted on a star.

Stellar Evolution

When the pressure in the center of a new star is high enough to trigger mass/energy conversion, the liberated energy begins pushing out not only against the star's mantle but also against the whole cosmos way out at the heliopause. A complete picture of this phenomenon must include both its hydrostatic as

---

2   In Chapter 11 I discuss yet another complexity of the heliosphere, related to the phenomenon of coronal heating. It also does not fundamentally alter the theory described in this chapter, though it will be very relevant to any experiments designed to test it.

well as its cosmological equilibrium. As hydrogen from the protostellar cloud continues falling into the star, increasing its mass,
the rate of burn in the core cannot simply increase unchecked in
direct proportion to the increasing pressure. If it did, the outward pressure of the star would exceed the inward pressure of
the ambient spacetime at the heliopause (i.e., the universe as a
whole). There is, therefore, an upper limit to this outward pressure. Yet massive stars clearly burn much hotter and brighter
than smaller stars. So what gives?

Though, as described in the previous section, it is not a
simple one-step phenomenon, the heliopause, or cosmological
equilibrium, of a star can be understood as a vast sphere with a
radius that reflects the distance at which the outward pressure
of the star is balanced by the inward pressure from the ambient spacetime of the cosmos. The relevant characteristic of this
huge sphere is its pressure per unit of surface area. This sphere
defines the location at which the pressure of the star is equal to
the pressure of the cosmos in general, and that pressure is just
the equilibrium pressure of spacetime itself. For every unit of
surface area on the heliopause, there is a corresponding unit of
surface area on the star. The total pressure on any two corresponding units must be equal. This results in a low pressure over
a very large area on the heliopause, and a very high pressure over
a very small area on the star. The inverse square law can be used
to quantify this proportional relationship.

If we start way out at the heliopause with the vacuum
pressure, and use the inverse square law to calculate backwards,
back toward the star, we can figure out how much pressure can
be exerted on any region of space (**Figure 3.2**). We can do this
because any sphere between the star and its heliopause must
have a total pressure that is equal to that of the heliopause. And
that means if we know the radius of the sphere in question, we
can calculate exactly how much pressure can be exerted on any
chosen unit of surface area on that particular sphere (at that particular radial distance from the star). Moreover, if we continue

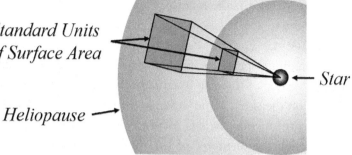

Figure 3.2: Heliopause
The inverse square law requires that any standard unit of surface area between the heliopause and the star exert the same pressure.

selecting smaller and smaller spheres, we will eventually find one that exhibits a very interesting characteristic.

The inverse square law—as applied to this phenom-enon—dictates that the pressure on any region of space *decreases* as the square of the distance from the star. Viewed from the op-posite perspective, it also dictates that the pressure *increases* as the square of the distance from the heliopause, and it is this op-posite perspective that is decisive. As we move from the helio-pause toward the star, the size of the standard unit of surface area on any chosen sphere decreases at the same exponential rate that the pressure increases, eventually becoming infinitesi-mal. Because the pressure per unit area must remain constant, even as that unit area shrinks exponentially, there comes a point at which that area approaches zero. As it turns out, the point of maximum allowable outward pressure of a star per unit area— the location at which that unit area is as close to zero as is physi-cally possible[3]—is located within the star but at a considerable distance from the star's center of gravity. It is *not* located at the very center of the star. As you might imagine, this has some as-tonishing consequences.

We can think of this strange point of maximum allow-

---

3 Most likely, the smallest "physically possible" point refers to the diameter of a proton.

able pressure as a shell within the star. Inside of this shell is the core. Outside of it is the mantle. Every single point on the shell corresponds to and balances a unit of surface area on the heliopause of the star. For that reason, the shell and not the core is the site of maximum pressure anywhere in the star. The pressure in the very center of the star is actually somewhat lower than the pressure on the shell, some distance from the center. Moreover, the pressure on this shell is identical in all stars regardless of mass, though the diameter of the shell *is* proportionate to the star's mass. The shell represents the location at which any point is exactly balanced by the cosmos as a whole. According to both the inverse square law and the equilibrium state of spacetime, any such point must always exert the same pressure.

A critical fact emerges from this reasoning. The shell (I will refer to it as the *neutrogenic shell* for reasons that will soon become apparent) exerts a spherically symmetrical force on the star's core, and that means the pressure in the core is the same everywhere. The core does not become denser as we approach the center—there is no pressure gradient—and that means the core does not exert its own gravitational pull. If you are still uncomfortable with spacetime pressure gradients and gravity, you can instead recognize that the shell's symmetrical force flattens the spacetime geometry inside the core; and no curvature means no gravity. For many, though by no means all, applications, traditional spacetime and the spacetime of this book are theoretically equivalent. If the core does not exert its own gravitational pull, then there is no upper limit on the mass of a star. The core can be a billion solar masses and still not collapse, because there is simply no gravity in there to collapse it. Still, the mass of the star dictates the diameter of the neutrogenic shell and the shell *does* generate the star's gravitational field. So at least in that respect mass is still proportionate to gravity. But because the gravitational force is not focused on the center of the star, instead being distributed evenly across the entire surface area of the neutrogenic shell, the star does not collapse no matter how big it gets.

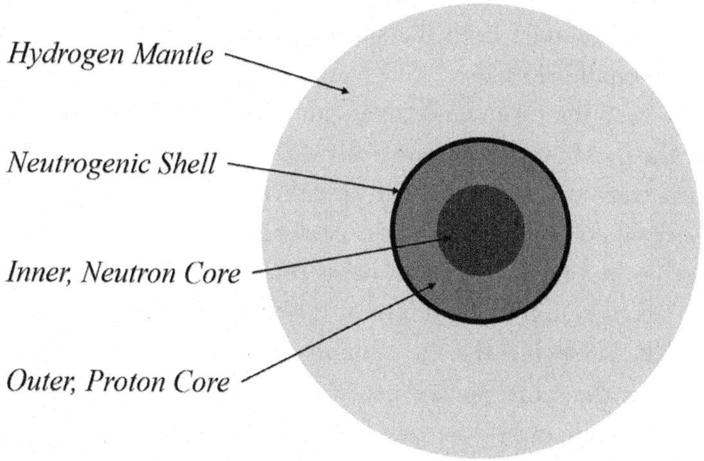

Figure 3.3:   Stellar Anatomy
Anatomy of a main sequence star. The neutrogenic shell exerts a very high and symmetrical pressure on the core. This pressure simultaneously relaxes (ionizes) the protons and neutrons, making atoms superfluous, and eliminates any pressure gradients (gravitational fields). The pressure of the shell is equal in all stars regardless of mass; only the diameter is variable.

The supermassive black hole currently occupying the core of the Milky Way galaxy got its start as a galactic star.

The Neutrogenic Shell

We now have good reason to believe that the pressure exerted by a star emanates from a spherical shell located at a distance from the core that is proportionate to the star's total mass. The shell is generated by the gravitational pressure exerted on it by the star's mantle (**Figure 3.3**). And because only a certain specific amount of mantle matter is required in order to trigger the mass/energy conversion we are about to investigate, any matter that is not necessary to maintain this hydrostatic equilibrium will remain in the star's core. The larger the star, the smaller the fraction of it that must be located above the shell, and the larger the shell can become. The mass of a star, therefore, dictates only the diameter of the shell, not its pressure per unit area. That pressure, as we have seen, is a universal constant.

Now we need to know exactly what is happening on that shell in order to maintain both the star's hydrostatic as well as cosmological equilibrium.

Of the three questions with which we started this chapter, the most important one dealt with the uniform mass of neutrons everywhere in the universe. We have since discovered a universal constant (directly derived from the cosmological constant) in the form of a shell that is responsible for maintaining a star's dual equilibria. It does not take much imagination to realize that this shell is the site of neutron creation. The neutrogenic shell has the same surface pressure in all stars and all neutrons have the same mass—a mass, like the proton's, that is dictated by the pressure under which it is created.

When a proton from the stellar core migrates onto the neutrogenic shell, the pressure there is so high that the number of partons in that particle no longer represents an ideal balance between the pressure of each parton and the pressure exerted by the particle as a whole. In particular, the ambient pressure on the shell *decreases* the ideal number of partons, causing a very specific number of them to migrate out of the proton. On the shell, the inherent repulsion of the partons briefly takes over. Once liberated, the partons do what they have wanted to do since they were trapped in the equilibrium condition of a proton immediately after the Big Bang: they expand. As they expand, they push down against the neutrogenic shell and up against the mantle, as well as the rest of the universe. These liberated partons, expanding by a factor of c^2, account for the energy of a star. Nuclear fusion has nothing to do with it. The particle that is left over after these few partons have been liberated reflects the equilibrium conditions on the neutrogenic shell. A proton has been transformed into a neutron.

Once a neutron is created, it remains within its equilibrium range as long as it stays inside the shell within the core of the star. Inside the core, free neutrons are completely stable and are under no obligation to form complex atoms. Only when the ambient pressure drops below a neutron's equilibrium pressure must it seek out a proton in order to maintain its stability. At core pressure, neutrons and protons mill around randomly, more or less indifferent to one another. The core does not gradually fill with atoms of progressively greater complexity creating onion-like layers of different elements. It does not heat up in successive collapses as it fuses progressively heavier elements. Rather, the core gradually fills with neutrons that migrate into the center, pushing the remaining protons up into the shell where they are converted into neutrons. Once this equilibrium state commences, little or nothing changes until the star leaves the main sequence.

One important question that arises from these ideas involves the relative masses of protons and neutrons. Current theory and experiment have shown that a neutron is somewhat *more* massive than a proton, and yet I have just argued that a neutron is actually somewhat *less* massive. I point this out now simply to alert the reader that this discrepancy will be addressed and that the explanation of this phenomenon is very relevant to other aspects of the theory. However, I have not yet presented enough information to explain it in detail in this chapter. For now, it suffices to say that mass is a complex relationship between the *quantity* of spacetime in a thing and the *behavior* of that thing— recall the distinction between intrinsic and extrinsic mass. Since protons and neutrons behave differently, the quantity of spacetime is not the only consideration when calculating their masses. By way of foreshadowing, the instability of neutrons means they are much more energetic (they move faster) at SEP, and their great convective velocity results in a type of *nuclear mass dilation*. That is the reason it is possible for a neutron to be composed of less spacetime and still weigh more than a proton. Indeed, their higher extrinsic mass is the reason neutrons gravitate to the centers of stellar cores, pushing protons into the shell. Another major and very unexpected consequence of this observation—and one to which I will devote considerable attention in later chapters—is that a proton, possessing more partons than a neutron, cannot be among a neutron's nuclear decay products.

Stellar Lifespan

If what I have said so far about the neutrogenic shell were the end of the story, something very curious and contrary to experimental evidence would have to be the case. We have seen that the pressure on the shell is a universal constant. That would seem to imply that the rate of neutrogenesis per unit area of any shell is also a universal constant. But if that were true, then large stars would live longer than small ones and exactly the opposite has been observed. Massive stars burn through their hydrogen in only a few million years, whereas stars much smaller than our Sun have been around since stars first formed, twelve to thirteen billion years ago. This is puzzling because the ratio of a sphere's volume to its surface area increases as its diameter increases. This implies that a greater percentage of a small star's protons is burning on the shell at any time. If the shell must maintain a constant pressure, it seems that large stars must take longer than small ones to burn up their protons.

The answer to this puzzle has to do with the other major equilibrium condition in a star—its hydrostatic equilibrium. A star's neutrogenic shell, by liberating partons that gradually expand, generates an intense spacetime pressure gradient and hence a powerful gravitational field. Indeed, this pressure gradient *is* the star's gravitational field. The larger the shell the more powerful the field, and the more powerful the field, the less mass must be located above it in the star's mantle in order to generate the necessary pressure to trigger neutrogenesis on the shell. Because of this variation in gravitational field strength, the same quantity of matter has a greater effect in a large star than it does in a small star. Put simply, the same quantity of mass is heavier on a large star than on a small one. As a result, the ratio of mass in a star's mantle to the mass in its core is inversely proportionate to the total mass of the star. Large stars have relatively thin mantles, while small stars have relatively thick ones. Consequently, the spacetime liberated from protons on the neutrogenic shell has to fight its way past much more mass in order to escape from a small star than it does to escape from a large one. To put it another way, the fraction of the equilibrium pressure on the shell of a given star that is contributed by the mantle is inversely proportionate to the star's mass.

In a large star, it is primarily its cosmological equilibrium that maintains the shell's pressure. In a small star, the hydrostatic equilibrium is dominant. Essentially, the liberated spacetime in a small star is trapped under the massive mantle right next to the shell and it expends a great deal of energy to free itself from the star. This state of affairs means that small stars only burn a tiny fraction—compared with large stars—of their hydrogen per unit area in order to maintain their shells' pressure. Therefore, small stars live much longer than large ones, despite having a lower ratio of core mass to shell surface area.

Gamma Ray Bursts and Nucleosynthesis

So far, we have been discussing the dynamics of what are referred to as *main sequence stars*. Such stars burn protons on their neutrogenic shells and gradually accumulate neutrons in their cores. As mentioned, nuclear fusion is not a relevant phenomenon, and these stars do not burn at different temperatures depending on which elements they happen to be fusing. Our sun, for example, has always burned and will continue to burn at an almost perfectly constant temperature until it begins its death throes, solving the Faint Young Sun problem in astrophysics.[4]

There is an obvious tipping point that pushes a star off the main sequence—namely, the moment in its evolution at which the diameter of its neutron core becomes equal to the

---

4   According to the current nuclear fusion model of stellar evolution, the Sun has been gradually warming since its formation. This is a problem because one or more unlikely scenarios must be assumed in order to explain how a star, at ~70% of the sun's current intensity, could have supported the life we know existed on earth as early as 3.5 billion years ago.

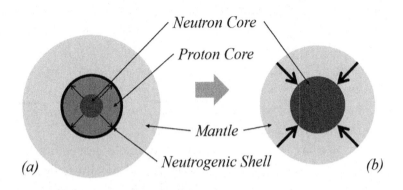

Figure 3.4:   Gamma Ray Burst 1
A main sequence star (a) is stable and has a gradually expanding neutron core. When all of the protons are converted to neutrons, the shell vanishes (b) and the mantle is pulled violently onto the core's surface.

diameter of its neutrogenic shell. This is when interesting things start to happen. In the supermassive stars we are considering here, the protons in the core are converted to neutrons fairly quickly because of the low ratio of mantle matter to core surface area. When the core runs out of protons, the shell simply vanishes. After all, the shell is nothing more than the locale at which protons are converted into neutrons. No protons means no shell. When the shell vanishes, there are no longer any expanding partons to either push down against the neutron core or push up against the infalling mantle. This moment (**Figure 3.4**), though brief, triggers the most spectacular phenomenon in the universe. With the disappearance of the shell, the neutron core is, in essence, *exposed*. That is, it instantly begins behaving as a supermassive *neutron star*.

A neutron star of ten million solar masses possesses more energy than anything since the Big Bang itself. The instant the shell disappears, our newly minted neutron star pulls the mantle down onto its surface with cataclysmic ferocity, sending a tremendous shock wave down into the star. The mantle matter rebounds off the surface and is catapulted into space (**Figure 3.5**), while the shock wave bounces off the center and back to the surface. When it hits the surface of the neutron core, it rips

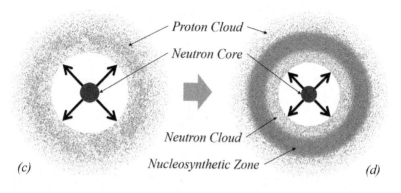

Proton Cloud

Neutron Core

Neutron Cloud

Nucleosynthetic Zone

(c) (d)

Figure 3.5: Gamma Ray Burst 2
After it hits the surface of the supermassive neutron core, the hydrogen mantle rebounds (c) into space in the form of a dense cloud. The shock wave from the collapse of the mantle then bounces off the center of the star and back to the surface, ripping off a large quantity of neutrons (d) and catapulting them into the proton cloud, resulting in the nucleosynthesis of most of our galaxy's complex elements.

off a significant fraction of the core's outer skin and sends it flying out into space right into the receding mantle matter. The neutrons from the core's skin and the protons from the mantle are mixed together in copious amounts, creating most of the complex atoms currently found in our galaxy. What happens next is even more spectacular.

Only some certain fraction of the neutrons ripped off the core will find happy homes within stable atoms. The rest—possibly the majority—either remain completely exposed to space or find themselves in various unstable neutron-rich isotopes. In either case, there is only one possible fate for all of these extra neutrons: *decay*. Over the course of the next few minutes, all of the neutrons that did not end up in atoms will decay all the way down to the level of undifferentiated spacetime (**Figure 3.6**). Recall that neutrons, having less intrinsic mass than protons, cannot decay into protons, an issue I will address in much more detail later. Incredible as it sounds, a quantity of neutrons that can be measured in solar masses is completely converted from mass to energy in just a matter of minutes. In normal stars, this

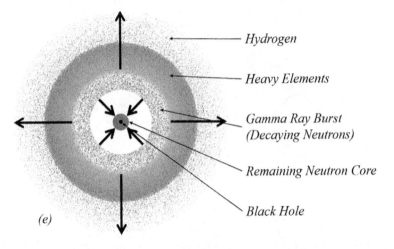

Figure 3.6:   Gamma Ray Burst 3

Any neutrons that did not find their way into stable atoms will decay in just a few minutes, resulting in a colossal explosion (GRB), the force of which compresses the center of the core all the way down to the level of undifferentiated spacetime, creating a black hole. Outside of the GRB, the newly created atoms are blasted out into the young galaxy.

event is what we know as a *supernova*. In supermassive galactic stars, it is known as a *gamma ray burst*.

The cloud of decaying neutrons is roughly spherical and so there are two interesting regions of the explosion, both inside and outside of the sphere. Inside the sphere, the force of the blast is focused directly onto the very center of the neutron star. If the blast is strong enough (as it always is in a galactic star) it will collapse some fraction of the star all the way down to the level of spacetime, crushing the partons and creating a black hole in the center. If it is not strong enough (as in much smaller stars), it will simply leave the neutron star behind. Neutrons are *not* created by smashing electrons (which are not discrete particles of matter) into protons (which already possess more intrinsic mass than neutrons to begin with). Outside of the neutron sphere, the newly created atoms are blasted with tremendous force out into the galaxy. It is this rapid nucleosynthetic process (similar to the current r-process), and not nuclear fusion, that accounts for the abundances of various elements in the universe.

I said the cloud of neutrons around the star was *roughly* spherical. In fact, the mass tends to concentrate more in the galactic plane than around the poles. This happens because as the mantle collapses onto the surface of the neutron core, it spins down toward the equator in order to conserve angular momentum. As a result, the subsequent GRB has a slight bias in the plane of the galaxy and is not entirely spherical. But it is not, as the current model argues, concentrated into two narrow jets emanating from the poles. That theory came from the inability of the standard model to accommodate anything large enough to generate the power of a spherical GRB. If it were concentrated in two polar jets, most of the complex atoms created in the process would be blasted away at right angles to the plane of the disk, significantly impoverishing the host galaxy and making our metal-rich solar system, for example, much harder to explain.

GRB Pulses

I just described what could be called a generic GRB. However, astronomical observations have shown that GRBs have a wide variety of energy signatures typically coming in a series of pulses. There are several possible candidates for these pulses that, depending on the mass of the parent star, will be more or less important in any particular example.

When the first cloud of neutrons explodes, the blast will inevitably send yet another shock wave into the remaining neutron core. That shock wave will also rebound off the center, bounce back to the surface, and rip off another layer of the core's skin. This second cloud of neutrons could explode even more violently than the first because, unlike the first cloud, it will not find any protons with which to form stable atoms. All of the elements have already been blasted away by the first explosion. How many of these neutron blasts, shock waves, neutron expulsions, and subsequent explosions a GRB can sustain almost certainly depends on its mass (like much else concerning stellar phenomena). The size, strength, and speed of formation of the supermassive black hole at the center of the neutron core will also place an upper limit on the number of pulses. As the black hole swallows the core—a phenomenon known as a *quasar*—additional blasts and shock waves will be quickly attenuated.

It might seem at first that the pulses just mentioned would have to be at least fifteen minutes apart, since that is the time needed to account for two consecutive neutron decay events. However, once the skin of the neutron core is exposed, the neutrons near the surface begin decaying immediately. By the time the shock wave from the first blast tears a second cloud from that skin, the neutrons are already well on their way to decaying. They have not completely decayed yet because their "decay clock" runs slower in the extreme gravitational field of the star; neutron decay rate is related to the pressure they are under. Once blasted away from the star, this second batch of neutrons decays much more quickly than the first because their decay is already well underway. Moreover, because all of the neutrons in this entire phenomenon are subjected to the same conditions, the actual moment of decay will be much the same for all of them. The concept of a *half-life*, as we will see, is not a matter of quantum uncertainty, but of a lack of knowledge regarding the true state of the system in question. Therefore, it is reasonable to expect each successive pulse to be much closer together than the expected fifteen minutes.

Another cause of some of the pulses (and these are not mutually exclusive) is the successive decay of various unstable isotopes. The first big blast is caused primarily by free neutrons, but there are many nuclides that decay within only seconds or minutes of their formation. If we consider the sheer quantity of such nuclides that are created when the neutron skin is thrown into the proton mantle, it is inevitable that, as these nuclides decay in reverse order of stability, the ensuing explosions would appear as a series of energetic gamma ray pulses. The strength and duration of these pulses will depend very sensitively on the exact ratio of neutrons to protons that were present during this rapid nucleosynthetic process. They will also depend on how far into the receding mantle matter the neutrons are flung. If the proton and neutron clouds are mixed together extensively, then, all else being equal, a lower ratio of unstable nuclides can be expected than if, for example, the neutrons are thrown only halfway into the proton cloud and are forced to make whatever they can of the few protons at their disposal. The strength of the ensuing explosion, in turn, dictates the force of the subsequent shock wave impinging on the remaining neutron core. That force dictates the power of the next explosion. And on and on and on. Needless to say, the possibilities are practically endless and so it is no surprise that GRBs come in so many varieties.

Here is yet another consideration. Some GRBs (as well as some supernovae) have a strong hydrogen spectral line, while others do not. If the neutron skin is catapulted all the way through the proton cloud, virtually every proton will be captured to form heavy atoms. If, on the other hand, the neutron cloud penetrates only half of the proton cloud (as in the diagram above) the leading edge of the GRB (or supernova) will be composed entirely of hydrogen. In all of the variations we are considering, the mass of the galactic star is decisive. In time, it should be possible to categorize these differences and use them to determine the relative masses of the parent stars.

Helium Abundance

The last question this chapter set out to answer concerns the high percentage of helium in the universe. Now that we have supermassive stars that are prodigious nucleosynthetic engines, the mystery is easily solved. In addition to the galactic stars I described above, it is certain that many first generation "normal" stars were thousands to millions of solar masses, much larger than the current theory permits. Not only would helium—because of both its simplicity and stability—be a major atomic product of the initial bombardment of the proton cloud by the neutron cloud, but helium would also be created (via the alpha decay process) in massive quantities by the subsequent decay of all the unstable nuclides. It would also, because of its binding energy, survive the GRB in relatively large quantities along with other stable atoms such as iron, carbon, and oxygen. In general, it is the combination of these three events—rapid nucleosynthesis, radioactive decay, and the subsequent GRB—that explains the abundances of elements in the universe. Once again, nuclear fusion is not a relevant phenomenon either in stars or anywhere else. The binding energy curve from helium to iron creates the illusion that stars are powered by releasing that energy in successive fusion events. That theory certainly seemed plausible, but it is just not the case (a fact I will demonstrate in a different way in Chapter 5).

Experimental Verification

The supermassive galactic stars that die in GRBs should still be visible from earth at extreme red shifts (around ten or eleven) corresponding to an epoch roughly thirteen billion years ago. Indeed, as the first luminous objects created after the Big Bang, they mark the very edge of the visible universe. They have been classified by astronomers as active galactic nucleus (AGN) galaxies and are currently explained as supermassive black holes that are actively consuming matter swirling around them in large accretion disks. True, such phenomena (typically called *quasars*) do in fact generate tremendous energy, and it is also true that the collapse of a galactic star leads to a supermassive quasar as the black hole consumes the remainder of its neutron core. Still, some fraction of these AGN observations should be intact galactic stars. Exactly what that fraction is depends on the relative longevity of galactic stars and quasars, and that question forces us to consider a rather bizarre possibility.

It is well known that the life span of a star drops precipitously as its mass increases. For a galactic star of ten or a hundred million solar masses, this implies a disturbingly short life—exactly how short must await further research. If that turns out to be true, these objects will be hard to catch in the act. If one is found, it might be worth the expense to train a telescope on it permanently on the assumption that it will explode in a GRB in a reasonable time frame. The current AGN theory, like the current GRB theory, is hamstrung by the notion that galactic stars are physically impossible. Since we now have reason to suspect that this is untrue, these huge stars need to be among the primary targets of astronomers' telescopes.

4

Astrophysics

In the previous chapter we looked at the basic dynamics of stellar evolution, particularly as it applies to supermassive galactic stars. The lessons learned from those extinct giants are applicable to the smaller stellar phenomena that are still with us today. All stars, regardless of mass, are characterized during their main sequence lives by their neutrogenic shells—the distance from the center of the star at which cosmological equilibrium is reached. The size of any such shell is determined by the mass of the star in question. The death of a star, in turn, is dictated by the manner in which the star responds to the disappearance of its neutrogenic shell, which occurs when the core has exhausted its supply of protons. In the case of a supermassive galactic star, the result is invariably a GRB followed by a quasar and a supermassive black hole. The gravitational force exerted by the core on the mantle is also decisive for the lives and deaths of all other stars once they leave the main sequence.

In addition to smaller, typical-sized stars, we will also look into the objects left behind in their wake. Quasars and black holes are the main products of galactic stars. Smaller stars leave behind *neutron stars, white dwarfs, nebulae, black holes*, and a variety of other exotic objects. In connection with such objects, we will have an opportunity to delve more deeply into the phenomena and forces that accompany their formation.

All main sequence stars have a few things in common. They all have neutrogenic shells that generate an equal outward pressure per unit area. They all convert protons into neutrons of equal mass on that shell. They all have gradually enlarging neutron cores. Their overall properties (heat, magnitude, gravity, longevity) differ only because their masses differ. The fraction of a second or third generation star that is composed of helium and other trace elements has no effect on the star's life, and is not evidence of anything the star is doing now.

In the core, neutrons are at their equilibrium pressure, making atoms superfluous. Any helium that is caught in the core of a new star will quickly *dissociate* into its constituent nucleons, with the neutrons migrating to the center, and the protons ultimately finding their way to the shell. In the mantle, heavier elements are, like the hydrogen, merely circulated by the upwelling spacetime plasma from the shell. As far as a main sequence star is concerned, the mantle is nothing but dead weight. Its chemical composition is irrelevant and evidence only of the composition of the cloud from which it condensed. Because of the intense upwelling, nothing from the mantle ever makes it all the way to the shell and, therefore, no new elements are formed in the mantle until after the star leaves the main sequence.

Very Large Stars

There is very little theoretical difference between the galactic stars—and their subsequent rapid nucleosynthesis, GRBs, quasars, and black holes—and very large stars. Only the terminology is different. For very large stars we say *supernova* instead of *GRB*, and we refer to the cloud of ejecta as a *nebula* rather than a *galaxy*. All that differs is the scale. **Table 4.1** summarizes the congruity.

The main difference between the two phenomena is related to the masses of the gas clouds (mainly hydrogen) from which they originally coalesced. In the case of a galactic star, the cloud is so large that the fraction of it that does not end up in the star is left over as a significant fraction of the nascent galaxy. It is available to form billions of normal stars and is the ultimate destination for most of the complex atoms that are ejected from the GRB. The formation of galactic stars is restricted to the ep-

Galactic Star	*Very Large Star*
Gamma Ray Burst	Supernova
Galaxy (note: most of a galaxy is not ejecta from the star, but nearly all the ejecta is part of the galaxy)	Nebula
Lifespan of centuries to millennia?	Lifespan of hundreds of thousands to millions of years
Millions of solar masses	~100 solar masses
Quasar (active galaxy)	Quasar
Major source of complex elements in the universe	Secondary source of complex elements

Table 4.1:   Star Terminology
A galactic star is, theoretically, an extreme example of a very large star.

och of extremely high hydrogen density immediately following the Big Bang.

Very large stars, by contrast, are essentially local phenomena not implicated in anything as grandiose as an entire galaxy. Their supernovae, via shock waves, do trigger star formation and their nebulae certainly contribute to the chemical richness of their host galaxies. But they are not the anchors of galaxies themselves and do not have billions of star systems orbiting them after they die. If they did, they could also be thought of as galactic stars.

In view of the similarities between these stars, this is a good opportunity to address matters I gave only a cursory review in the previous chapter, specifically, the nature of black holes. That in turn will give us a good opportunity to look more closely at the nature of gravity.

Black Holes

A black hole (BH) forms when the blast from either a GRB or a sufficiently powerful supernova compresses a part of the neutron core all the way down to the level of spacetime itself. In practice, this means that some fraction of the partons inside the neutron core is put under so much pressure that the gradient characterizing these subnucleonic particles is destroyed. They are crushed into a homogeneous fluid-like state not unlike the condition at the moment of the Big Bang. The fraction of the core that succumbs to this intense pressure instantly begins behaving as a single entity. It does so because spacetime, once it is liberated from its partons, is perfectly homogeneous. The resulting object has some very unusual properties.

The first thing to notice is that a highly compressed mass of spacetime, according to this theory, is violently explosive. Indeed, such a mass—though a much larger one—was originally responsible for the Big Bang. It wants nothing more than to expand to its equilibrium pressure. Yet black holes are enduring entities. How can that be? It is possible because black holes, unlike the Big Bang, are not expanding into the void, but into normal space composed of spacetime at its equilibrium pressure. That means a black hole, just like stars and every other expansive phenomenon, must strike a balance between its own ambitions and the steady resistance provided by the vacuum pressure. Black holes are essentially held together by the entire cosmos. In one respect, they are a frozen moment of Big Bang aching to explode but thwarted by the collective mass of the whole universe. Had the Big Bang tried to explode into normal space, it would have become nothing but a colossal black hole.

What this means is that a black hole is nothing more than an intense spacetime pressure gradient, and a spacetime pressure gradient is nothing other than a gravitational field. Hence, a black hole is, right down to its very center, gravity itself. There is nothing else there. No quantum singularity. No rip in spacetime. No wormhole. No matter, as it is usually conceived. Black holes are made of the fundamental stuff of the universe, spacetime, and spacetime behaves as a gravitational field when it exhibits a pressure gradient. There is nothing else there to explain. Moreover, there is no sharp distinction between a black hole and the rest of the cosmos. The much discussed *event horizon* is simply the radius at which light can no longer escape—quite likely the innermost termination shock of the object. From the perspective of the black hole, the event horizon does not mark an important boundary. It is nothing more than one pressure region on the way to and from the extremes at its center on the one hand, and its heliopause, billions of miles away, on the other. Examining a black hole anywhere inside of this enormous region (including within the EM event horizon and at the very center) would reveal nothing more than a pressure gradient dictated by the inverse square law. At no point would it make any sense to say, "The black hole begins here."

When a black hole forms, it immediately begins consuming the remainder of the neutron core that surrounds it. Whether astronomers call this a *quasar* seems to depend on how energetic it is, but whatever we call it, it is nothing more than a mass of neutrons swirling around and into a newly minted black hole. There are two interesting aspects of this phenomenon. First, because the gravitational field is so strong (the spacetime pressure is so high), the rate of neutron decay slows dramatically. Viewed relativistically, we would say that this is an extreme example of *gravitational time dilation*. Viewed from the theory I am advancing here, we would say that the high pressure, analogous to that of a stellar core, is sufficiently close to the equilibrium value of a neutron to decrease its decay rate. Either way, the neutrons do not immediately explode, but instead decay slowly as they are swallowed by the black hole. We could think of a quasar as a *toroidal* (donut-shaped) neutron star orbiting the black hole. Its decay, though slow, is responsible for the intense gamma rays and x-rays observed from quasars.

The second important aspect of a quasar is the manner in which it accelerates the black hole as its neutrons are consumed. The hydrogen gas from the protostellar cloud starts the phenomenon spinning as it falls into its parent star. It is accelerated further by the collapse of the mantle onto the neutron core. It is accelerated most of all by the consumption of the neutron core in a quasar. This series of conservations of angular momentum gets the black hole spinning at tremendous speeds. It is the great angular velocity of a black hole that enables me to demonstrate empirically that the theory I am advancing here is correct. If a black hole were a simple stationary sphere, it would be very difficult to observe the behavior I am about to examine.

The angular motion of a black hole causes it to bulge around its equator, because that is where the centripetal acceleration is the greatest. As a result, the gravitational field is strongest in its equatorial plane, known as the *accretion disk* if the black hole is busily consuming something (e.g., a companion star, its neutron core, a hydrogen gas cloud, or any other unfortunate passerby). This phenomenon is already reasonably well understood. What is less well understood is the other important feature of a black hole, namely, its *relativistic polar jets*. As we have seen, a black hole is violently explosive, but is held in check by the whole cosmos. However, it does expand, though very slowly as a percentage of its total mass. If a black hole were completely stifled by its cosmological equilibrium, normal stars would be stifled as well. After all, black holes are even more explosive than stars. We know that normal stars liberate a great deal of spacetime. Therefore, black holes evaporate at an even faster rate.

As a black hole evaporates, there are two important regions: its equatorial bulge and its polar jets. At the poles of a black hole—at its axis of rotation—the centripetal acceleration is zero, and that allows spacetime to expand without any resistance from the rotation of the BH itself. Everywhere else, spacetime is spun out toward the equatorial bulge. The relativistic jets, then, are simply evidence of how desperately the black hole wants to expand. If the BH did not spin, the whole object would exhibit the same behavior as the jets, though of course that would make it impossible to observe. If we superimpose the angular momentum profile onto its intrinsic explosiveness (**Figure 4.1**), we get a shape that resembles a top: intense regions

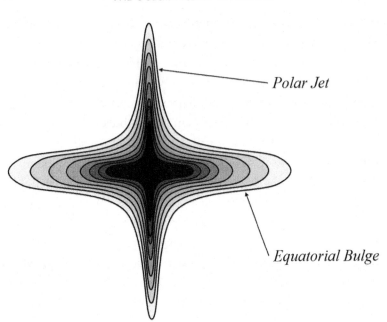

Polar Jet

Equatorial Bulge

Figure 4.1:   Black Hole
Superimposing a black hole's intrinsic explosiveness onto its centripetal acceleration profile yields a shape that resembles a top. The gravitational zones are most intense at the poles and equator, but considerably more so at the equator.

at the poles and the equator, though considerably more intense at the equator. This picture provides us with the necessary information to explain one of the more peculiar phenomena in the universe.

It is typically assumed, because they are the most powerful sources of gravity in the universe, that black holes are mutually attractive. That is, if they came close enough they would try to consume one another. However, according to the theory I am developing here, black holes must in fact be mutually *repulsive*. This is so because BHs are made of nothing but spacetime far above its equilibrium pressure. According to this theory, spacetime is always self-repulsive under such conditions, when it is dominated by its finite pole. There are no exceptions. Hence, black holes must also repel one another. Sound crazy? As it turns out, there is incontrovertible empirical evidence for this implausible-sounding claim.

Individual black holes are difficult enough to find, given their blackness, so binary black holes should be even rarer. If my theory is correct, they will be extremely rare indeed, because as soon as they form they will drift off in opposite directions. However, there is a place in the universe where binary black holes are fairly common: in the cores of merged galaxies. When two galaxies—each of which already contains a supermassive black hole at its core—merge, the black holes are forced into the new core by their gravitational pull on the merged galactic disk. Their pull on the disk is so great that even though they are mutually repulsive, they are inexorably drawn to the center of gravity of the galaxy. In this respect, they are actually *pushed* together by their common attraction to the disk, rather than *pulled* together by their attraction to one another. To prove this, we need only look at a galaxy where such a merger has occurred.

If black holes were mutually attractive, they would tend to line up along their most intense regions, that is, along their equators. The accretion disk of a black hole clearly shows where the object's gravitational field is the strongest. Hence, a pair of black holes, if attractive, ought to share the same equatorial plane. If, on the other hand, binary black holes are mutually repulsive, we would expect the larger of the two to tilt the smaller one roughly forty-five degrees onto its side (**Figure 4.2**) such that the most intense region of the big one (its equator) is lined up with the least intense region of the small one (a region roughly halfway between its equator and pole). So which of these scenarios is actually observed?

In every known case, the latter configuration is observed. Known as *X-shaped galaxies*, merged galaxies that contain binary black hole systems—in which the BHs are close enough to the same mass for the phenomenon to be detected—always exhibit the ~45° tilt just described. Pictures from the Hubble telescope show the polar jets of binary BHs intersecting in an X-shape, which can only mean that they have tilted to avoid lining up

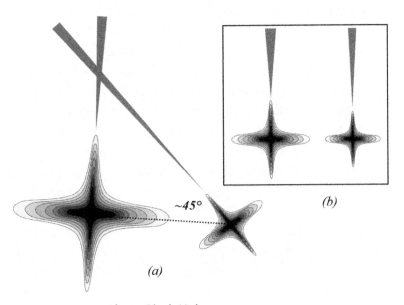

Figure 4.2:   Binary Black Holes
Because black holes are composed of nothing but high pressure space-time, they are highly explosive and mutually repulsive. Therefore, when they are forced together in the core of a merged galaxy (a) the larger one tilts the smaller one so that its equator lines up with the least intense region (around 45°) of the smaller one. If black holes were mutually attractive (b), we would expect them to line up along their most intense gravitational zones.

along their equators. This repulsiveness is anything but a subtlety; the energy required to force a black hole out of the primary plane of a galactic disk is staggering. The BH must not only fight against its gravitational pull on the galaxy, but also against the angular momentum of the disk. Because galaxies spin, it takes a tremendous amount of force to pull them out of their preferred rotational plane. Nevertheless, this is exactly what happens.

When the smaller of the two BHs is turned on its side, its equatorial plane defines a secondary galactic plane. At least part of the merged galaxy is gravitationally attracted to this secondary plane, creating a strange lobed shape that seems to defy both gravity and angular momentum. According to the latest astronomical research, approximately seven percent of all spiral galaxies are X-shaped. We should assume, however, that there are far more cases of central black holes turned on their sides than are actually observed. This, because usually the largest of the BHs will so overwhelm the others that no secondary galactic plane is visible. Some galaxies exhibit gravitational ripples that suggest the presence of at least one relatively small secondary central black hole.

With the possible exception of the hydrogen emission spectrum, I consider the preceding description of the mutual repulsiveness of black holes to be the most compelling direct empirical evidence yet for the theory being developed in this book. If black holes are repulsive and are also composed of spacetime (the fundamental stuff of the universe), then every other concept presented here falls into place in a perfectly logical manner. Consider that it is a bit of a mystery under the standard model that the singularity from which our cosmos is hypothesized to have emerged did not simply remain a singularity. Gravity would seem to be insurmountable under such conditions, and yet the Big Bang was violently explosive. This theory makes perfect sense of that phenomenon.

Also, consider that it is the intrinsic repulsiveness of spacetime that generates the equilibrium condition within a proton or neutron, driving its convective circulation. Further, spacetime, occupying the seemingly empty vastness of space, resists compression, thereby causing the cosmological equilibria of all stellar phenomena, one of which gives rise to neutrons of equal mass everywhere in the universe. Finally, it was the extreme repulsiveness of spacetime that first created partons (granules)—the basis of all matter. In chapters to come, I will present similarly convincing evidence for the intrinsic *attractiveness* of spacetime when it falls below its equilibrium pressure—when its infinite pole becomes dominant.

Spiral Galaxy Rotation (Dark Matter)

Now that we have some familiarity with spacetime and

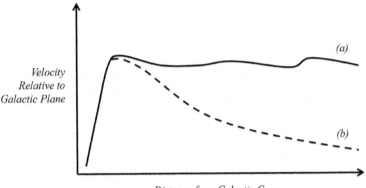

Figure 4.3:   Galactic Velocity Curve
If galaxies behaved according to Newtonian predictions (b), the velocity of objects, relative to the galactic plane, would steadily decrease the farther they are from the core. Instead, it has been observed that objects maintain a nearly constant velocity (a) regardless of their distance.

the manner in which it generates gravitational fields, we can turn our attention to another of the great unsolved mysteries of the universe: the curious rotational characteristics of spiral galaxies. Back in the 1930s, a physicist named Fritz Zwicky discovered that objects in spiral galaxies do not seem to observe Newton's laws. In the 1960s, physicist Vera Rubin took up his work and discovered that objects far away from the center, unlike those in our solar system, do not slow down in proportion to their distance from the core (**Figure 4.3**).

If our solar system behaved in this way, Neptune's orbital velocity (5.4 km/sec) would be at least as fast as Mercury's (48 km/sec), nearly nine times as fast as its true value. So far as Newton is concerned, that would exceed the escape velocity of an object at that distance from the Sun and send it flying off into interstellar space. Nevertheless, that is exactly how it appears to be with our galaxy as a whole. Objects near the rim somehow manage to orbit as rapidly as those near the core without flying off into intergalactic space. This has prompted at least one physicist to speculate that Newton's laws might change in relation to the velocity of the object under consideration.

Most physicists, to their credit, are hesitant to discard Newton's laws without a very good reason, but the alternative they have conjured up is no less peculiar. In order to keep the objects at the rim of the Milky Way moving as fast as they do, there must be a very powerful gravitational field that pulls in the opposite direction to the galactic core. Indeed, to account for the motion of our galaxy, the calculated field strength implies a quantity of matter roughly ten times as great as the whole visible galaxy. Unfortunately, when astronomers look they find nothing out there to generate such a field. Therefore, physicists reason, there must be a species of particle that is virtually undetectable, invisible, and only weakly interacting with others of its kind, but which nonetheless exerts a strong gravitational pull. This *dark matter*—hypothesized to be made of WIMPs (weakly interacting massive particles)—the theory goes, exists as a gigantic halo surrounding the galaxy that exerts exactly the right gravitational counterforce to keep the galaxy rotating the way it does.

If you're scratching your head and knitting your brow, you are not alone. No direct evidence exists for these WIMPs. Their predicted properties are just whatever is necessary to explain this unexplained phenomenon—not necessarily a bad idea in itself. Unexplained phenomena are great for science; they present an opportunity for discovery. The problem here is that these particular particles are way too convenient. To hold a galaxy in place without tearing it apart, this halo of matter must mold itself into an impossibly unlikely geometric configuration. Also, because galaxies rotate at different velocities and come in different sizes, the quantity of dark matter must exactly balance a specific galaxy's angular velocity and total mass. That means the quantity of dark matter must be intimately related somehow to the galaxy for which it is responsible. On top of all that, it has to be virtually impossible to detect since, when we point our telescopes at the place where this stuff should be, no one's home.

Thankfully, there is a perfectly reasonable explanation for galactic rotation that does not require us to either banish Newton or accept the existence of dark matter. As I have shown, all stellar phenomena (stars, black holes, neutron stars, quasars) liberate spacetime in one way or another, either through neutrogenesis, evaporation, or neutron decay. All of this spacetime is liberated by objects that are themselves orbiting the core of the Milky Way at a virtually identical velocity. That is, unlike our solar system, the orbital velocity of all objects in the galaxy is roughly the same and so *angular momentum* increases as the distance from the core increases. That, in turn, means the *centripetal force* required to hold the object in its orbit must also increase. The farther an object is from the galactic core, the harder it pulls against whatever force (I'll get to that next) is holding it in its orbit. It is easy to see why this is such a confounding problem. The farther an object is from the galactic center, the harder it pulls against the core, despite the fact that gravity ought to decrease the farther one gets from the core. As far as galaxies are concerned, Newton's laws seem to have been turned upside down. So, what's the answer?

The centripetal acceleration of any galactic object is related to its orbital radius. By mass, most of these objects are stellar objects, busily churning out spacetime via neutrogenesis, evaporation, or neutron decay. That spacetime, in turn, is liberated into the galaxy with a velocity proportionate to the centripetal acceleration of the object that liberated it. As we saw with black holes, spacetime is very much affected by centripetal acceleration, creating their equatorial bulges. Therefore, spacetime liberated by any stellar object will tend to flow toward the rim of the galaxy at a speed proportionate to the centripetal acceleration of its source. That, in turn, means that the velocity of the spacetime flow at any point in the galaxy is directly proportionate to the distance of that point from the core. Finally, we already know that spacetime resists compression above its equilibrium value. Consequently, as spacetime is accelerated off the

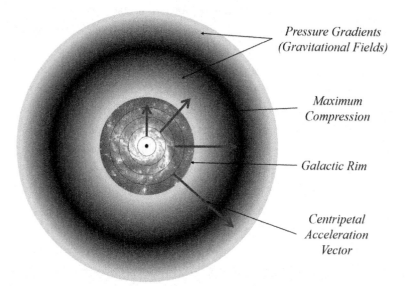

Pressure Gradients
(Gravitational Fields)

Maximum
Compression

Galactic Rim

Centripetal
Acceleration
Vector

Figure 4.4:   Spiral Galaxy Rotation
Spacetime accelerated off the rim of a spiral galaxy is compressed as it attempts to move into the intergalactic medium. The resulting pressure gradient creates gravitational fields both inside and outside the ring of maximum compression. This phenomenon, not dark matter, is responsible for galactic rotation as well as gravitational lensing.

edge of the galactic disk, it presses against the cosmos as a whole and, as always, the cosmos pushes right back. This push-back by the cosmos against the flow of spacetime along the disk establishes the cosmological equilibrium of a spiral galaxy. Essentially, spacetime, flowing off the disk, is bottled up and compressed as it attempts to move into intergalactic space. That compression is most intense where the spacetime flow has the highest velocity, namely, near the rim where its source object had the highest centripetal acceleration. As a result, a spacetime pressure gradient (**Figure 4.4**) is created. It is strongest just outside the rim and gradually diminishes in the direction of the core, as well as way out beyond the rim. A pressure gradient means a gravitational field. It is this phenomenon, not dark matter, that holds the galaxy together.

The evidence for this model is overwhelming. Notice that

no matter what the rotational velocity of a given galaxy, no matter how rapidly or slowly it spins, and no matter how massive it is, the strength of the resulting gravitational field will always be exactly calibrated to hold it together. This is because the centripetal accelerations of the sources of spacetime are proportionate to their angular velocities, and the intensity of the spacetime gradient is, in turn, proportionate to centripetal accelerations of its various stellar sources. These variables, whatever they happen to be, always find a stable cosmological equilibrium. The spacetime flowing off the edge of the disk pushes against the cosmos in proportion to the angular velocity of the galaxy, and that is what determines the intensity of the gravitational field (the spacetime pressure gradient). Notice also that the intensity of the gravitational field at any point in the galaxy is proportionate to the radius at that point, meaning that the field strength decreases smoothly toward the core. A giant mass of dark matter would tend to pull the galaxy into a ring or donut shape unless its physical distribution and consequent gravitational pull just happened to correlate exactly with the disk shape we actually observe, and that would be very hard to explain. Neither do we have to explain how exactly the right quantity of dark matter happens to be present to generate the proper gravitational field for any particular galaxy.

Another piece of evidence: Draw a line from the galactic core through the earth and on to the rim (**Figure 4.5**). If we measure the Doppler shift of starlight anywhere along this segment, we find that it is directly proportionate to the difference between the velocity of the spacetime flow at that point and its velocity here at earth. Starlight is red-shifted anywhere along the segment between the earth and the core and blue-shifted between the earth and the rim. Moreover, the extent of the blue shift increases as the star in question approaches the rim. This happens because the light from blue-shifted stars must flow upstream against the spacetime current and is compressed in the process, shortening its wavelength. Meanwhile, light from

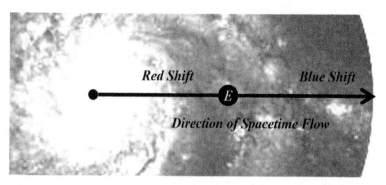

Figure 4.5:   Red and Blue Shift
Starlight reaching the earth is red-shifted if its source is between the earth and the galactic core, and blue-shifted if it comes from a star between the earth and the rim. The flow of spacetime toward the rim of the galaxy, not the relative motions of the stars, is primarily responsible for this Doppler effect.

red-shifted stars is stretched. These Doppler shifts have little to do with the relative motions of the stars. Stars near the rim are not moving much, if at all, toward the earth, despite their blue-shifted light.

Finally, this galactic gravitational field is shaped like a large flattened out donut with the thickest part just beyond the rim. In essence, it is a huge circular convex lens that, not coincidentally, is exactly the necessary shape to account for the *gravitational lensing* that astronomers have observed.

Frame Dragging

When the above theory is tested, it will be discovered that the gravitational field I have been describing is not quite strong enough to hold the galaxy together. That is because there are actually two distinct phenomena at work. The first is the spacetime pressure gradient and resultant gravitational field. The second is related to the *flow* of spacetime. The pressure gradient, of course, is created by the flow, but the flow has an effect all by itself. If we view the flow of spacetime as it is liberated by the various stellar objects and spun off toward the rim, the motion is different depending on whether the observer is inside or outside of the galaxy. From inside, the flow seems to make a beeline straight for the rim. From outside, the spacetime flows toward the rim, but also in a circular path right along with the movement of the galaxy as a whole. Objects in a spiral galaxy possess both types of motion. Again, if you are more comfortable with Einstein you can think of this as a very large and pronounced example of *frame dragging*. The gravitational field explains the fraction of galactic motion that is *through* space, but the circular motion of the spacetime flow is needed to explain the component of its motion that is *with* space. Essentially, the circular part of the flow sweeps objects along in its currents, and that is why the gravitational field does not need to be strong enough by itself to explain everything.

In addition to explaining the rotation of spiral galaxies, this same phenomenon is also responsible for the large-scale behavior of galactic clusters. Just as stars have centripetal accelerations that are proportionate to their angular momenta, so too do galaxies. When galaxies begin orbiting one another in huge clusters, spacetime is liberated in a direction and at a velocity that is related to their motions. Hence, huge intergalactic gravitational fields are generated as galaxies swirl around one another across millions of light years. But unlike the fields I described above, these intergalactic fields are created by entities that are fairly discrete—at least by comparison to the enormous empty regions between them. The Milky Way, by contrast, contains a roughly continuous distribution of matter. As a result, the gravity between clusters will be uneven and complex, exhibiting the behavior of colliding and interacting waves and filaments rather than a smooth field. Galaxies will tend to pass *through* gravity waves left behind by other galaxies, suddenly jerking one way or the other for no apparent reason. Averaged over the entire cluster, these jerks and jolts tend to maintain the coherence of the group, but in a very complicated manner.

Cosmic Microwave Background

Superclusters of galaxies, as they move through space, generate weak but truly colossal gravitational fields and waves that propagate through the endless intergalactic voids that occupy most of the cosmos. These waves create slight variations in the pressure of spacetime at the largest cosmic scales and are responsible for the differences in the intensity of the cosmic microwave background (CMB) radiation. Contrary to the current theory, the CMB is not an echo of the Big Bang. Rather, it is a weather map of high and low pressure regions of spacetime. The prevailing theory has it that the CMB has gradually cooled since the Big Bang to its current value of 2.7 Kelvins. If that were true, then the pressure of the universe would also have been gradually decreasing. But that would imply that the cosmological equilibrium of early stars would have been different from that of today's stars. That would mean that neutrons created in the early universe would have to be smaller than those being created now. If the universe had, via higher spacetime pressure, pushed back against early stars harder than it is pushing today, then the pressure per unit area on those early stars would have been higher. A higher pressure on the neutrogenic shell would decrease the number of partons per neutron that constitutes an equilibrium condition. Clearly, old neutrons are not smaller than new neutrons.

The spacetime, just after the Big Bang, that was liberated from the filaments of partons—those that did not form protons—rapidly decompressed (in the second rapid expansion period) until it reached the equilibrium value that is still present to this day. That equilibrium value is the cosmological constant itself and varies only slightly. Measured twelve billion years ago, the CMB would have been 2.7K just as it is now. This is so because the universe never actually had any need to "cool down." Most of its energy (including even its kinetic energy) was trapped within protons in the form of matter. Other than the first split-second and then again during the second rapid expansion, the cosmos was never particularly "hot." Protons were not hotter back then just because they were new. By the time the first stars began to form, the CMB had already reached its current temperature. The slight variations we see today are the result of cosmic-scale spacetime weather patterns. Any patterns that were present during the early universe were long ago wiped clean by the turbulent spacetime flows that have taken place in the interim. Finally, the fractal shape into which the cosmos fractured at the end of the first rapid expansion period is sufficient to explain both the large scale isotropy and small scale anisotropy of the universe. The CMB is not necessary to explain the observed distribution of matter in the cosmos.

Cosmic Expansion (Dark Energy)

The problem of cosmic expansion, and particularly of its acceleration, is simultaneously the most difficult and simplest question of cosmology. Difficult, because it depends on knowledge of the fundamental substance and, for that reason, naturally comes at the end of our quest for the truth. Simple, because, armed with that truth, the answer is very straightforward.

Spacetime is liberated by all stellar phenomena. At the same time, the ambient spacetime of the universe resists compression above its equilibrium pressure. Therefore, the only way to make room for the spacetime liberated by these stellar phenomena is for the universe to expand. Since it is expanding into the void, which, as I have shown, does not provide any resistance, *nothing* impedes this expansion; the rapid expansion of the Big Bang being the other prominent example. And if a force (that of spacetime decompression) is applied to a mass (the cosmos), that mass is accelerated according to the simple equation $a=F/m$. I wish there were more to it, but that is pretty much the whole story. Still, the ease with which the theory explains this perennial head-scratcher is further evidence of its power.

Clearly, gravity will not arrest the motion of the cosmos.

When all the atomic objects have disintegrated into undifferentiated spacetime, there will not be anything left in the universe that is attracted to a pressure gradient. In any case, there will not be any pressure gradients either. Instead, the momentum of expansion will eventually return the universe to the void according to $x/\infty = 0$.

Big Rip

All stellar phenomena drive the acceleration of cosmic expansion. When the last of these (most likely a supermassive black hole) is completely exhausted, there will be no significant sources of spacetime left to fill the increasingly nebulous universe. Yet the momentum of cosmic expansion will cause the universe to go on expanding for billions (perhaps trillions) of years (though it will now be decelerating rather than accelerating). Combined, the lack of new spacetime and the ongoing expansion will cause the universe to undergo a major transformation; the pressure of space will drop below the equilibrium value of spacetime. It will be stretched over time to ever increasing negative energies. Negative pressure spacetime is roughly equivalent to the current notion of *antimatter*: it pulls out against positive pressure phenomena, including atomic matter. Any remaining planets, asteroids, dust, gas, and the like will be pulled apart, gradually at first, but with increasing intensity. Atoms depend on the pressure exerted by their protons on their electronic shells. As the ambient pressure drops, it becomes increasingly difficult for a proton's polar jet to concentrate the spacetime in its vicinity to a sufficiently high pressure to balance the low external pressure. Eventually, protons begin simply dissociating themselves from their atoms—the proton drip line begins migrating toward the strip of stability. In a sense, the radioactive decay clock (more on this in subsequent chapters) of all atomic matter speeds up until even the most stable nuclei come apart.

When nuclei dissociate, the neutrons quickly decay (the ambient pressure is still far too high to stabilize them outside of an atom), leaving only protons behind. It is likely that these protons will survive for many billions of years, until the energy of the negative pressure finally achieves an absolute value equal to that of a star's neutrogenic shell. When that happens, partons will begin migrating out of their protons in proportion to the decreasing ambient pressure. It is conceivable that every possible number of partons—from a complete proton, to a neutron, all the way down to just a handful—will characterize a standard particle at various stages of this gradual decay process. As the pressure continues to drop, a smaller and smaller number of partons will represent an equilibrium condition, and I can see no reason why this process would not be more or less continuous. Eventually, the very last parton will decompress, leaving our universe as nothing but an expanding sphere of negative pressure spacetime.

In Chapter 1, I showed that the attraction of points in space (the coherence of spacetime) is related to their density. Therefore, as the density drops over the course of eternal expansion (we have now entered the realm of infinity again), their mutual attraction decreases as well. Over eternity, spacetime is once again dissociated into simply space and time (four infinite degrees of freedom) and is restored to its pristine state of nothingness. The paradox of infinite and finite geometries is returned to its extreme finite pole, the void, setting the stage for another cosmic cycle.

Large Stars

The primary difference between a large star[1] and the very large stars we have seen so far is that the supernova blast of the former is not powerful enough to compress any part of its neutron core into a black hole. Partons may be severely

---

1   If the theory being presented in this book is correct, it will significantly alter our understanding of astrophysics, leaving the definition of a *large star* yet to be determined. Currently, it is believed that a star must be at least two solar masses in order to be a black hole candidate. The ideas presented here do not depend on the exact figures, but might indeed help make such classifications more accurate.

stressed, but their pressure gradients remain intact. As a result, the neutron core is simply left behind in the center of the resulting nebula. The current theory of neutron star formation argues that the pressure (something called *electron degeneracy pressure*) of a collapsing large star crushes electrons into the protons of the metallic core, resulting in neutrons. As I have shown, this is an unworkable notion on several different fronts.

First, electrons are epiphenomena; they have no independent existence as discrete particles of matter. They are not the sorts of things that could be crushed into another particle. Second, neutrons possess less intrinsic mass than protons. To create a neutron, partons must be removed from a proton. Adding something to a proton, even if that were possible, would not create a neutron. Third, we should be very skeptical that such a haphazard process could create neutrons. Only the extremely precise conditions on a neutrogenic shell, regulated by the cosmological constant itself, can give rise to the perfectly uniform neutrons we actually find in nature. The chaotic collapse of a star is far too messy a process to do the job. Finally, even if the collapse of a star could create neutrons out of protons, the ensuing energy release (in the form of liberated partons) would exceed that of even a GRB and would utterly destroy the core, leaving nothing behind. The *metallic core* concept simply does not make sense.

Neutron Stars

A neutron star is a neutron core that has been stripped of its mantle, as well as its neutrogenic shell, during a supernova. As a result, it is under less pressure than it was during its main sequence existence. Neutrogenesis is not occurring above it, pushing down against the star or up against the cosmos. Yet a neutron star does not simply explode, despite the manifest instability of its only constituent (neutrons). How does that happen? As always, it depends on the star's cosmological equilibrium.

As we will see in the next chapter, when a neutron decays it gives up all of its partons. It does not decay into a proton or an electron. Protons have more intrinsic mass than neutrons and cannot be among their decay products. At SEP, neutron decay is a very violent process, because there is little resistance from equilibrium spacetime to such an explosion. On the surface of a neutron star, where the pressure is extremely high, the decay rate of a neutron is greatly slowed. As a neutron decays, its partons expand, pushing down against the star's surface and up against the rest of the cosmos, thus establishing the cosmological equilibrium of a neutron star.

As expected, the star's gravitational field is the same thing as its spacetime pressure gradient, the strength of which is proportionate to the total *surface area* of the star, not directly to the star's total mass (though its mass helps determine its surface area). This is so because only the neutrons on the surface decay. Within the star, neutrons are at their equilibrium pressure and behave much as they do in a normal stellar core. Now, because the ratio of a sphere's surface area to its volume increases as the sphere shrinks, a neutron star appears more massive than it really is. Its gravitational field strength will always be proportionate to its surface area, rather than its volume. Like an individual neutron, it possesses a relatively high ratio of extrinsic to intrinsic mass; and that ratio will increase as the star continues to decay. In effect, the star will appear to become denser and denser as it shrinks, almost as if it is collapsing in on itself.

Correlatively, small neutron stars appear denser than large ones. This happens because the rate of neutron decay per unit of surface area remains constant (because of the cosmological equilibrium) even as the ratio of that surface area to the total mass of the star increases. It appears, therefore, that each unit of stellar volume exerts a greater and greater gravitational pull (is denser) as the star shrinks. In fact, all neutron stars have the same *intrinsic* density (number of particles per unit volume) and they are merely a case (like galactic rotation) in which gravity and mass have a complicated relationship. This *gravitational illu-*

sion must be taken into account when a neutron star is weighed.

Finally, as the star decays and its surface area increases relative to its total volume, the decay of the star accelerates. The smaller it is, the faster it decays. Since the star must always exert the same force per unit of surface area in order to maintain its cosmological equilibrium—no matter how small the star has become—the fraction of the star's total mass that is decaying on the surface increases as the ratio of surface to volume increases. Therefore, smaller neutron stars are disappearing faster as a fraction of their total mass than larger ones.

Like black holes, the angular velocity of a neutron star is dramatically increased as it conserves angular momentum during its formation. As a result, many neutron stars spin with rotational periods of anywhere from seconds down to milliseconds. Such extreme conditions cause a neutron star to mimic certain behaviors of a black hole. In particular, spacetime liberated during neutron decay is spun down toward the star's equator, generating two distinct gravitational zones: an equatorial bulge (where centripetal acceleration is greatest) and polar jets (where centripetal acceleration is zero). The polar jets and accretion disks of neutron stars are virtually identical to those of a black hole. But perhaps the most striking aspect of a pulsar is its incredibly powerful magnetic field, making now a good time to examine exactly what a magnetic field is.

Stellar Magnetic Fields

While a gravitational field is a spacetime gradient, a magnetic field is a spacetime *flow* or *current*. In a simple bar magnet (**Figure 4.6**) spacetime is physically pulled in through the low pressure end and pushed back out of the high pressure end. It circulates around the magnet in the characteristic pattern associated with its force lines.

It is unfortunate that with a fifty-fifty chance of getting it right, by convention, we have decided that *positive* refers to the *negative* pressure side of a magnetic field while negative refers

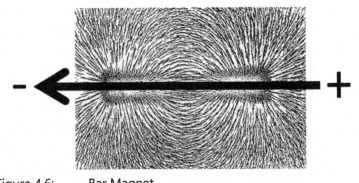

Figure 4.6:   Bar Magnet
Spacetime is physically pulled in through one side of a magnet and expelled from the other side. Currently, the poles of a magnet are arbitrarily
denoted by *north* and *south*, but because they are the result of spacetime
pressure, it would be more accurate to call them *positive* and *negative*.

to the positive side. As we will see, this is also true of electrical
charges in atoms and molecules. A water molecule, for example,
has a negative pressure region on the hydrogen end and a positive pressure region on the oxygen end. That is what accounts
for the hydrogen bonds of water. Unfortunately, again by convention, the hydrogen end is considered *positive* and the oxygen
end *negative*. As we have seen, an electron, though it may be an
epiphenomenon, is a positive pressure region on the electronic
shell of an atom. Moreover, the electrons created in beta decay
(typically by the sudden release of partons from a neutron) are
nothing but shock waves—also positive pressure regions. Finally, protons actively evacuate spacetime from their immediate
vicinities making them negative pressure phenomena.

I know, I know; what difference does it make? It's just
nomenclature, right? However, if mathematics and computers
are to be used to implement this theory in a coherent and comprehensive way, and if future science students are to be treated
with even a shred of compassion, negative and positive throughout the physical sciences will have to be reversed. We cannot
change what the words themselves mean and we cannot change
how mathematics deals with the sign of a number.

To establish a spacetime current we need both a high and

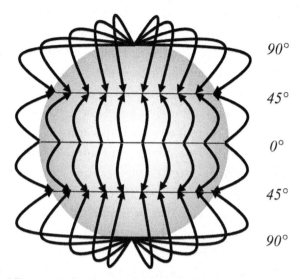

Figure 4.7: Solar Magnetic Force Lines
Magnetic field lines on the Sun originate from the equator and the poles and terminate at the 45° latitudes. Sunspots are most visible around the 20° and 30° latitudes because the twisting of the force lines pulls the ends together.

low pressure region. In any spinning star, neutron or otherwise, the spacetime liberated either by neutrogenesis or neutron decay is spun down toward the equator, creating a low pressure zone *between* the poles and equator and high pressure zones *at* the poles and equator. We can see exactly where this low pressure region is on our own star by the location of *sunspots*. The spots indicate where spacetime is flowing back into the star from primarily the equator, but also the poles (**Figure 4.7**). They are dark and relatively cool because they are pulling energy back down under the surface. They fluctuate around about the 45° lines because, as we saw with binary black holes, that is where the spacetime pressure is the lowest.

Now if the flow of spacetime looping up from the equator to the 45° lines were smooth, we would simply observe two uniformly dark regions or stripes roughly halfway between the sun's equator and poles. However, because the Sun spins, the equator is moving twice as fast as the 45° lines and so the source of spacetime is moving twice as fast as its destination.

The Coriolis force twists the equatorial end (the positive end) of the magnetic current relative to the 45° end (the negative end), tightening up the flow like a steel cable or stick of licorice. The same phenomenon holds from the 45° lines to the poles only in reverse—the 45° lines twist up the current relative to the poles. In lieu of a smooth spacetime flow, we end up with a number of discrete, highly concentrated magnetic force lines gradually being twisted to the breaking point. Once these force lines get going in earnest, they rapidly reach a pressure that exceeds the pressure that prompted them to form in the first place. That is, the positive equatorial end spins like a tornado pulling in even more spacetime than is needed to simply equalize the pressure difference between the equator and 45° lines. To put it another way, each force line, because there is no uniform flow, is concentrated by a factor equal to the surface area associated with that line. Each force line must balance the pressure of the entire region in its neighborhood, not just the pressure immediately beneath itself.

When the positive end of the force line begins to dramatically exceed even the high local pressure on the equator, it starts to wander—a truly bizarre phenomenon. Exactly where it wanders depends on the local pressure, the movement of other force lines, and, as always, it seeks out lower pressure regions. Meanwhile, the negative end near the 45° line, by accepting spacetime from the equator, raises the local pressure as well and must also wander in search of a lower pressure region. Combining these two wandering ends, we get a magnetic arc that crawls around the surface of the sun, each end in search of a lower pressure region, but each dependent on the other to maintain a powerful pressure differential. That is, the positive end must stay positive and the negative end negative. If the negative end wanders into a high pressure region or simply cannot reorient itself fast enough to avoid raising the local pressure, the *magnetic attraction* will suddenly disappear. When that happens, all the spacetime (and associated particles swept up in the current) in the magnetic arc will be blown off into space. The attractiveness of the negative end will have been destroyed. This is called a coronal mass ejection.

To complicate this picture even more, the twisting of the equatorial end continues to intensify as long as the arc exists, gradually exerting a greater and greater force pulling the two ends together to minimize the stress. When a rubber band is twisted, the tension in the rubber increases and pulls the ends of the band toward one another. On the sun, the twisting magnetic lines also pull their ends toward one another. Indeed, by the time sunspots and their associated magnetic loops are most visible, they have already moved a great deal from their places of origin (equator and 45° lines) and tend to cluster between the 20° and 30° latitudes, essentially splitting the difference. But there is a great deal of randomness involved because of the interactions between adjacent force lines and other fluctuations in local spacetime pressure. As a result, there is always a nontrivial probability of finding the ends of the force lines almost anywhere on the surface. Sometimes a positive end—one that is connected to a negative end in the northern hemisphere—will migrate, simply because of local conditions, into the southern hemisphere. It does this, as always, in an effort to find a region of lower pressure. It can find itself in the opposite hemisphere as its negative end, simply because, when it started its migration, the twisting had not yet become severe enough to overcome local fluctuations. In that case, a force line will actually straddle the equator from one hemisphere to the other. Or, if an arc maintains a strong pressure differential, the two ends can migrate together way above or below even the 45° lines. In most cases, however, the ends get closer and closer together as the torsional force increases, eventually putting the ends into the same pressure zone, destroying the attraction and snapping the arc.

Another piece of evidence for this concept, over and above the location of the spots, comes from the fact that the Sun exhibits two major cycles: one of eleven years and the other of twenty-two years. Of these, the eleven-year cycle is much more intense than the twenty-two year cycle. If we consider the manner in which the force field lines are twisted up by the Coriolis force, we would expect lines emanating from the equator and terminating at the 45° latitudes to be twisted up twice as fast as those originating from the poles; the equator moves twice as fast the 45° latitudes. Because spacetime from the poles is much less intense than that from the equator, we should expect the twenty-two year cycle to be far less intense as well.

The main solar cycle lasts roughly eleven years. During that cycle, sunspots reach a maximum, fade, reform, reach a new maximum, and then fade again. We can assume that the extremes of this cycle represent minimum and maximum stresses of the magnetic field lines. If we look at the Sun when spots are at a minimum, one thing we *cannot* infer is that there is little or no flow of spacetime from the equator to the 45° lines at that time. We can infer only that the flow has not yet been twisted up tightly enough to be visible. It takes time for the Coriolis force to separate the flow into lines and then sharpen the ends of those lines. Active sunspots indicate a time when the lines are well formed but not yet stressed quite to the point at which they begin to snap. The disappearance of spots indicates a time during which the lines have been twisted to the breaking point and are being replaced by a smooth flow that will, during the next cycle, be twisted into a new set of force lines.

Pulsars

If we extrapolate from the discussion above to the behavior of pulsars, we see a very compelling picture. By comparison with a pulsar, the Sun is a soft, slow, lumbering affair. It is spread out over a huge volume and rotates only about once a month, and yet the solar cycle, though far from perfect, is still fairly regular. A pulsar, by contrast, is compact, dense, and very fast. In general, we should expect any behavior exhibited by such an object to be considerably less variable—more mathematically perfect—than a comparatively sloppy mess like our sun. The extreme angular velocity of a pulsar combined with its powerful source of gravity (neutron decay) implies an almost incomprehensible pressure difference between its equator and 45° lines. That disparity is half of what drives the magnetic field.

The other half is the Coriolis force, which also driven by rotational velocity, rapidly twists the magnetic lines into strands that are extremely dense. These two dynamics taken together generate an incredibly strong magnetic field, as well as an exceedingly short solar cycle. The field lines are twisted up very quickly and to very high energies. However, they resist breaking until they have reached a much higher energy than those on the Sun because they are responsible for balancing a much higher pressure differential. Finally, when they do break, they release a great deal of energy (their pulses) in a very short span. The energy released is primarily derived from the angular momentum of the star, which is tapped to twist up the field lines. As a result, the magnetic field exerts a kind of friction that gradually slows the star's rotation.

There is also evidence that every *other* pulse from a pulsar is somewhat more intense than the ones in between (**Figure 4.8**). If this can be confirmed, it would suggest that the short cycle causes the relatively weak pulses, while the short and long cycles combined cause the relatively strong pulses.

Another point to notice is that if this theory is right, the pulse of a pulsar is not coincident with its rotational period, just as the solar cycle is not coincident with the sun's rotation. The only reason a pulsar would pulse on each rotation is if it had an asymmetry on one side, like a lighthouse, that was only detectable when it faced us. The currently accepted theory is that the magnetic field of a neutron star looks much like the Earth's. Since the Earth's field has poles that are not lined up with its axis of rotation, it is assumed that we can only observe pulsars from which the magnetic poles rotate through our line of sight.

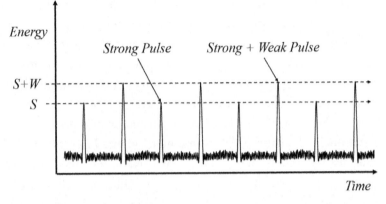

Figure 4.8:   Pulsar Pulses
It is sometimes possible to distinguish pulses of two different intensities from a pulsar. This is likely the result of both the long and short stellar cycles.

However, it is very unlikely that the Earth's magnetic field is generated the same way as a neutron star's. The Earth does not liberate spacetime. It is more likely that the Earth's field is the result of the iron core not rotating in exactly the same plane as the mantle. That is, the solid core of our planet does not track the *precession of the axis* of the liquid mantle and thin crust, but instead continues rotating in the same plane no matter what the rest of the planet does. If all of this is true, the orientation of a pulsar does not determine whether or not we can observe it.

Now, though the sun's cycles (11 years and 22 years) are much longer than its rotational period (25 days) there is no reason to assume the same is true of a pulsar. The dynamics that drive the birth and death of magnetic field lines depend on the intensity of the pressure differential and the ability of the force lines to withstand twisting. It remains to be discovered exactly what that might mean for pulsars, but I have a hard time imagining it means they rotate hundreds of times faster than they pulse. There is no doubt they spin very fast, but probably not that fast. As with their gravity, things are not always as they appear with neutron stars.

Variable Stars

For even smaller stars, things start to get really interesting. In these stars, even a supernova is not possible. When the shell in a medium-sized star disappears, the mantle, as before, collapses onto the neutron core. But instead of rebounding out into space—that is, instead of being completely blasted out of the star's immediate gravitational influence—it merely bounces up a bit and then returns to the shell. Meanwhile, the shock wave the mantle imparts to the core rebounds off the center and tears off some fraction of the core's skin, bombarding the mantle with neutrons. However, because the mantle has not been ejected from the star's surface, nearly all the neutrons find protons with which to form atoms. As with supernovae and GRBs, many of these atoms are unstable isotopes that quickly decay, and the primary product of that decay is alpha particles. As a result, the regular flashes observed from such stars have strong helium EM signatures. These flashes are certainly energetic, but not nearly enough to destroy the star. Something else interesting happens as well.

During the brief absence of the neutrogenic shell, mantle matter is free to fall right onto the surface of the core and occupy the region that was recently vacated by the neutrons that were stripped off by the rebounding shock wave. This mantle matter is proton-rich and therefore rejuvenates the star, if only for a while. The shell forms again under the pressure of the mantle that has not been blasted away from the star (though it is now richer in heavy elements) and neutrogenesis on the new protons in the core begins anew, essentially putting the star temporarily back on the main sequence.

This same cycle recurs over and over: the shell disappears; the mantle collapses creating a shock wave; the shock wave bounces off the center and back to the core's surface; the outer skin of the core is propelled into the mantle, creating more heavy elements; radioactive decay on the unstable isotopes causes an intense helium flash; proton rich mantle matter rushes into the void left by the removed neutron skin; the shell reforms; the star burns until the new protons are exhausted; the process is then repeated. These regularly flashing stars are known as *cepheids* and because their flashes are of such uniform brightness, astronomers use them as standard candles to calculate cosmic distances.

Eventually this process becomes unstable. Though it takes a very long time, the mantle will slowly become saturated with heavier and heavier neutron-rich atoms. As the mantle becomes increasingly neutron-rich, fewer of the neutrons stripped from the core will be able to find stable homes. Meanwhile, the mantle matter will have fewer and fewer protons to contribute to the next cycle. Consequently, the flashes become more frequent and more intense. More intense because more of the new atoms are neutron-rich. More frequent because the rejuvenating mantle matter is increasingly proton-poor, which means the shell will collapse with greater frequency. Through a series of intense explosions, the mantle will be thrown off piecemeal creating a planetary nebula until there is not enough mass in the mantle to sustain neutrogenesis on the shell. The leftover mantle will cling to the neutron core, leaving behind a *white dwarf* (see below).

The value of cepheids as standard candles is related to the strict relationship between a star's luminosity and its variable period; the brighter the star, the longer the period. This can be explained by considering the intensity of the shock wave imparted to the neutron core by the collapsing mantle. In a more massive star, the shock wave is more energetic, causing a larger fraction of the core's skin to be stripped away during the rebound. This leads to a larger vacancy on the surface of the core for proton-rich mantle matter to occupy, and that means a larger star will be reinstated to the main sequence for a longer period than a smaller one. Apparently, the higher rate of neutrogenesis in a large variable star is *less* important than the total quantity of protons trapped under the newly formed shell.

White Dwarfs

White dwarf stars are extremely dense, which argues against their being composed of normal atomic matter. Even a solid lead sphere of the same size would not exert the gravitational attraction of a white dwarf. The only reasonable possibility is that they are actually small neutron stars with a thick atmosphere of heavy elements. Because white dwarfs were not created in supernovae, blasted clean by the explosion, it is not surprising that they would retain such a blanket of normal matter. Further evidence that white dwarfs are cloaked neutron stars comes from the fact that the former, like the latter, appear denser as they become smaller. That makes no sense unless their gravitational fields are generated by neutron decay on the surfaces of neutron cores. The currently accepted theory argues that white dwarfs are composed of something called *degenerate matter*, which is basically normal matter that has been compressed to a density just barely above the electron degeneracy pressure. In fact, the concept of degenerate matter is a phantom of quantum theory, which, as we will see later, has little to do with physical reality. Let's look at the reasons for this.

The pressure in the cores of all main sequence stars is the same and that pressure is within the equilibrium pressure range of neutrons. Therefore, atoms do not exist within stellar cores. Nor do they exist anywhere else where the pressure meets or exceeds this core pressure. If the pressures associated with degenerate matter were applied to real atoms of, for example, oxygen or carbon, those atoms would dissociate into their constituent nucleons and form a new main sequence star. Taken together, these observations lead to the following conclusion. If the pressure is high enough to trigger neutrogenesis, it is also high enough to dissociate any normal matter into its constituent nucleons, regardless of the binding energy. If normal matter (composed of both protons and neutrons) is so dissociated, neutrogenesis will always be the result. Therefore, if such pressures are implied by some phenomenon (e.g., white dwarfs) and yet neutrogenesis is *not* occurring, normal matter (degenerate or otherwise) cannot be implicated.

Also, all stars create neutron cores, regardless of their size or life cycle. If there is not a neutron core at the center of white dwarfs, then where did the neutron core from the parent star go? Neutron cores are large massive objects. They do not simply vanish without a trace. Moreover, we have seen that the relationship between mass and gravity is anything but straightforward.

Red Giants

The flashes emitted by a cepheid variable are related to the mass of the star. Larger stars emit brighter flashes at longer intervals than smaller stars. As we consider smaller and smaller stars, the flashes become weaker and more frequent. Based on the above theory, this relationship makes sense. The absolute magnitude of the flash (just outside the neutron core) is related to the intensity with which the core pulls the mantle down onto its surface. A smaller core exerts less gravitational force than a larger core, and therefore provides fewer neutrons per cycle to fuel the helium (alpha particle) flash. Furthermore, a smaller star has a higher ratio of mantle to core mass and that means anything generated by the core must fight its way past a relatively large quantity of matter before it has any visible effects on the surface. These two factors explain why there is an exponential rather than a simple linear relationship between the intensity and period of the flashes and the star's mass. The weak core and thick mantle combine to subdue the flashes in smaller stars.

Cepheids are driven by the same mechanisms that create supernovae[2]. The only difference is that the gravitational force of the core is insufficient to propel the mantle into space. In a

---

2   Supernova impostors are almost certainly the transitional objects between standard supernovae and the largest cepheids.

sense, a cepheid is a series of tiny supernovae that are too weak to destroy the star. I mention this congruity because it is important to view all variations of stellar evolution as a smooth continuum from supermassive galactic stars all the way down to tiny brown dwarfs. Because there is a continuous range of masses, there can be no sharp distinctions between any two stars of only slightly different sizes. Therefore, to understand stars smaller than cepheids, we must explain the transition between their behavior and the behavior of stars like our Sun without introducing anything fundamentally new.

As the mass of a cepheid decreases, the variable period and intensity of the flashes also decrease. Eventually, the flashes will become so weak and so frequent that they are no longer detectable. Essentially, they are completely absorbed by the mantle. By the time we get to a star as small as our sun, it does not make any sense to treat each cycle as a distinct phenomenon. The disappearance and reappearance of the neutrogenic shell happens so rapidly and is so weak—more like a strobe light than a cepheid—that we can think of it as a vibrating porous shell that stirs up the surface of the neutron core, mixing neutrons and protons just beyond its surface. Imagine accelerating and weakening the cycles of a cepheid thousands of times until the individual pulses became indiscernible. The shell would simply vibrate or buzz, churning up the neutrons and protons on either side of it, mixing them together to form heavier elements.

Now, a star's neutrogenic shell generates its gravitational field. When that shell weakens, so does its gravitational force, and though neutrons are leaking out of the core, they are snatched up immediately by protons in the mantle long before they can decay. Unlike on the surface of a naked neutron star, they contribute little or nothing to the gravitational field. And because neutrogenesis, albeit more slowly, is still occurring on the shell, the upwelling force of liberated spacetime continues to push the mantle away. As a result, the star as a whole puffs up to many times its original size becoming a red giant.

For a while at least, a new equilibrium condition forms between the far more nebulous mantle and the much weakened and vibrating neutrogenic shell. Unlike in a main sequence star, this equilibrium state evolves over time. As neutrons leak out of the core, the core shrinks further, weakening the gravitational field and causing the mantle to become increasingly diffuse. Eventually, the mantle becomes so diffuse and distant that there is insufficient pressure on the shell to sustain even a reduced rate of neutrogenesis and the star dies. It leaves behind nothing but a white dwarf and a planetary nebula. By the time neutrogenesis ceases, the mantle is far too distant and the neutron core far too small to trigger any sort of collapse. With the death of the star, the heliopause is greatly weakened, exposing the nebula to the steady galactic winds that flow toward the outer rim. Over the eons, the heavy elements in the nebula are distributed throughout the galaxy and made available to future solar systems. Meanwhile the white dwarf slowly decays until all of its potential energy (in the form of its neutrons' partons) is converted into the kinetic energy of cosmic expansion.

The Kuiper Belt and Oort Cloud

So far, we have seen that our Sun generates two different gravitational fields. The familiar one in its immediate vicinity holds the planets in their orbits. The second one is generated by the sun's centripetal acceleration around the galactic core and does its small part to hold the Milky Way together. Beyond those two, there is a third and possibly a fourth field I have not yet described.

The pressure gradient between the Sun and its heliopause is created by the decompression of partons that have been liberated from protons on the neutrogenic shell. The force of the field at any radial distance is given by the inverse square law and is related only to the *pressure* of spacetime at that location. It has nothing to do with the *flow* of spacetime, known as the *solar wind*. This wind is the result of the fact that the pressure at any distance from the star, inside the heliopause, must remain constant even as the Sun continues to churn out newly liberated spacetime. The only way to accommodate the new spacetime is for the existing spacetime to flow away from the star into interstellar space. If it simply flowed away smoothly, there would be no additional phenomenon to explain. However, the solar wind, just like a proton's polar jet, stops abruptly at a point that marks its cosmological equilibrium. Described by the notion of *termination shock*, the fast moving solar wind runs up against the relatively slow moving interstellar medium, essentially slamming into it as if into a wall.

This collision of solar wind and interstellar space has the effect of driving up the pressure of the heliopause, and because the pressure inside the heliopause is already relatively high, the only place for this pressure to go is out beyond it. As the pressure relaxes out beyond the heliopause, it generates a distinct secondary gravitational field. The energy for this field does not come directly from decompressing partons as it does for the primary field. Instead, it comes from the *kinetic energy* of the solar wind. If we measure the orbital characteristics of anything out beyond the heliopause—typically referred to as the *Oort cloud*—we will discover that its gravitational attraction to the Sun is stronger than is predicted by the inverse square law. If we instead measure its attraction to the heliopause, the inverse square law will apply once again. Making such an observation—using a powerful telescope—is among the easiest and most direct ways to confirm this entire theory.

Further complicating this picture is the stepwise fashion in which the solar wind is decelerated. It appears that there may be no fewer than three termination shocks, of decreasing pressure, between the Sun and the interstellar medium. As I discuss in more detail in Chapter 11, the coronal heating problem is best solved by recognizing that the solar wind, immediately upon leaving the stellar surface, is moving at a relativistic velocity and slams hard into a radius defined by the corona, dramatically driving up the temperature and pressure at that innermost termination shock. The second termination shock is the better understood one, located approximately 50-70 AU from the sun, and gravitationally implicated in the behavior of objects in the Kuiper Belt. The final termination shock, if it exists, is located way out at the inner boundary of the Oort cloud, governing the orbits of objects (e.g., long-period comets) hypothesized to be located there.

5

Atomic Nuclei

By now it is clear that the theory I am presenting in this book is an extension of Einstein's Theory of Relativity. Indeed, if there is any merit to what I have been saying here, this is the theory he spent the last thirty years of his life trying to find. Had he recognized that spacetime is not merely the mathematical stage on which events play themselves out, but also the real, three-dimensional substance of those same events, he very well may have succeeded. Be that as it may, the essence of any such theory is, as Einstein knew, contrary to the various quantum theories that plagued him, but which nonetheless dominated twentieth century physics.

Spacetime is geometric and *realistic*, whereas quanta are probabilistic and *positivistic*. These two visions of reality differ fundamentally, and clearly I have come down in favor of the former. From a scientific perspective there is nothing wrong with this approach; nature has absolutely no respect for the time and energy we expend pursuing dead ends. However, from a practical standpoint, nearly everything we think we know about nuclear physics comes from quantum theory. So much so, that relativity effects (the effects of spacetime pressure differences or gravity) are currently taken to be negligible within the atomic nucleus, when in fact they are decisive. As a result, a spacetime theory of nuclear physics simply does not exist. By necessity, then, the following theory of atomic nuclei is completely novel, based entirely on the models of protons, neutrons, and space-time built up in previous chapters, as well as on raw empirical data. Quantum theory will play no part in it. I mention this, not as an apology, but simply to prepare the reader to ingest some wholly unfamiliar fare.

Hydrogen

Toward the goal of understanding the atomic nucleus, there is nothing more fortunate than the fact that a single proton behaves as an atom of hydrogen. From the previous chapters, we now know everything we need to know about protons to describe their behavior in as much detail as necessary to completely capture their essence as atoms. Specifically, we now know:

1. Partons are tiny subnucleonic spacetime gradients that still possess the extreme pressure of the Big Bang.
2. Protons are made of partons that are in direct physical contact along their surfaces.
3. Partons circulate in a convection current, driven by the contrast in pressure between the partons on the surface and those in the core.
4. Spacetime is drawn in through the proton's north pole and expelled from its south pole as a highly focused jet.
5. The complex rotational pattern of a proton is governed by the geometry of any one of several different series of derivative axes, the purpose of which is to maintain a constant, symmetrical pressure between the proton and its electronic shell.
6. The electronic shell is the distance at which the proton's south polar jet achieves cosmological equilibrium with the ambient spacetime.
7. An atomic electron is a high-pressure bump on the electronic shell, where the polar jet hits the ambient spacetime—a phenomenon explained by the concept of termination shock.

There is not a single aspect of this entire phenomenon that is the least bit murky. Everything from the spacetime of which a proton is composed to the dynamics of hydrogen's EM spectrum is fully explained, without gaps, leaps of faith, or *ad hoc* assumptions. We also have a complete understanding of the ambient spacetime (its equilibrium conditions) in which protons exhibit their behavior. And because nothing is missing from this picture, it is a relatively straightforward, if not always simple, proposition to describe the interactions of protons and neutrons in atomic nuclei.

Gravity in Atomic Matter

In previous chapters I explained how various astronomical objects generate gravity. Black holes, main sequence stars, and neutron stars liberate spacetime through evaporation, neutrogenesis, and neutron decay, respectively. Spiral galaxies (as well as elliptical ones, for that matter) spin spacetime off of their edges, compressing the intergalactic medium. As spacetime decompresses, it creates a pressure gradient, and hence, a gravitational field. However, I still have not explained why a pressure gradient is attractive in the first place, or how normal matter, which does not liberate spacetime, can be gravitational. It is now time to remedy that omission.

Looking at a hydrogen atom, we can see that the pressure inside the electronic shell is always lower than the pressure of the ambient spacetime (**Figure 5.1a**). The proton concentrates the spacetime in its immediate vicinity into its polar jet, and blasts it away toward the electronic shell. As a result, the pressure of the electron reflects the difference in pressure between the atom and the surrounding space. However, the electron is not a discrete particle of matter, and continues to exist only so long as the process that creates it continues unabated. The constant pressure of the electron, in any energy state (series of derivative axes), is the result of the constant convective velocity of the proton. In a sense, the electron is created anew every instant by the proton's jet, and that means it must also be in a constant state of decay. The polar jet cannot very well maintain an elec-

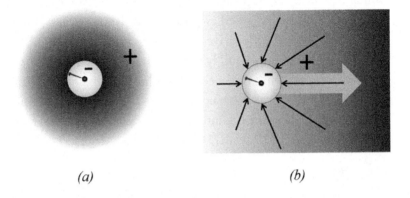

(a)   (b)

Figure 5.1:   Gravity in Atomic Matter
The high pressure spacetime, blasted against the electronic shell by the proton's south polar jet (*a*) decompresses outside of the atom's termination shock according to the inverse square law, creating the atom's gravitational field. And because the pressure within the electronic shell is symmetrical and negative relative to the ambient spacetime, it pulls spacetime preferentially from high pressure regions (*b*), pulling the atom farther into a gradient (gravitational field).

tron of constant pressure if that electron is not simultaneously giving up its excess spacetime. If it did not, it would balloon up to enormous proportions in no time at all. Therefore, the high-pressure spacetime on the electronic shell decompresses away from the atom according to the inverse square law, creating a gradient. That spacetime gradient is the atom's gravitational field. Phenomenologically, it is virtually identical to the secondary gravitational field generated by the sun, out beyond its termination shock, though much stronger because of the power of the proton's polar jet.

Still, a spacetime gradient only explains how an object *generates* a gravitational field, not why an object is *attracted* to such a field. Looking again at our hydrogen atom (**Figure 5.1b**), we see that its internal pressure is lower than that of the ambient spacetime. This is the case because the proton draws spacetime in and blasts it back out, evacuating the region around itself and compressing it up against the electronic shell. I have also shown that the pressure in the atom is symmetrical, a condition resulting from the complex rotational pattern of a series of derivative axes. Now, spacetime resists either compression above or decompression below its equilibrium value, and its resistance increases as this compression or decompression increases. That is, the greater the disparity between its actual and ideal pressures, the more energetically it resists it.

If the spacetime surrounding the atom is of a uniform pressure, then it makes no difference to the atom whether it pulls it in from one direction or another. Indeed, if the ambient pressure is uniform, the proton will draw in spacetime equally from all directions—the atom will experience weightlessness. However, if the atom is within a pressure gradient, the low-pressure atom will be biased in the direction of the higher pressure region. This is so simply because, as noted, the greater the contrast in pressure, the greater spacetime resists it. This means an atom will tend to pull spacetime preferentially from the higher pressure region, causing the spacetime to move toward the atom from that region. When spacetime moves toward the atom, the atom must move in the opposite direction, farther into the pressure gradient. As I have shown, black holes, unlike atoms, do not have low-pressure zones and are, therefore, repelled by gravitational fields. However, since they generate very powerful high-pressure gradients, they are attractive to all normal (atomic) matter. It is only because atoms possess a lower pressure than their surroundings that they are attracted to, rather than repelled by, pressure gradients.

At first blush, it may seem that the internal pressure of an atom has something to do with the *magnitude* of its gravitational attraction, but that is not the case. Even if the pressure within a given atom is extremely negative—far lower than in a hydrogen atom—it is not more attracted than a hydrogen atom to a pressure gradient. This is so because it is only the *difference* in ambient pressure from one side of the atom to the other that causes the atom to move into the gradient. It is not the absolute intensity with which an atom draws in spacetime that determines its attraction, but rather the disparity in attraction across the atom's breadth. And because the pressure inside an atom is symmetrical, this difference is determined entirely by the gradient itself, not the atom. As a result, a lead ball and a feather both fall at the same rate, because they are both falling through the same gradient. On the other hand, the strength of the field *generated* by an object *is* related to the intensity of the pressure gradient it forms on its surface.

Neutron Decay

The second member of the nuclear club is a rather peculiar character. As we have seen, a neutron is created on the neutrogenic shell within a star. A small number of partons is removed from a proton so that the internal pressure of this new particle reflects the extremely high ambient pressure on that shell. Within the stellar core, neutrons are stable and are not required to capture protons to form atoms in order to maintain their equilibria. Indeed, within the core, neutrons and protons exhibit very similar behaviors. They circulate at whatever rate is necessary to alternately compress in the core and then allow to decompress on the surface, their constituent partons. Yet the pressure is so high that neither particle spins fast enough to create an electronic shell; that is why stellar cores and neutron stars are so dense, and also why a stellar core does not have a gravitational field (the uniform pressure is dictated entirely by the neutrogenic shell). Instead, they propel themselves about, more or less randomly, like miniature jet engines. Other than their rate of convection (neutrons are somewhat faster at core pressure), there is no simple way to tell them apart. Things only get interesting when the star falls off the main sequence and ejects its neutrons. At SEP, neutrons are unstable, with a half-life of roughly ten minutes. Time is always running out on free neutrons.

The first thing to notice is that neutrons are exactly the same as protons, except with slightly less intrinsic mass (slightly fewer partons). Still, it is this difference in intrinsic mass that makes the particles behave as they do. There is no simple property in either particle that answers to the concept of *electric charge*. When a proton's south polar jet pushes up against its electronic shell, the shell (via its cosmological equilibrium) pushes back with an equal force. This is the origin of the "equal but opposite charge" of electrons and protons, but it is clear now that no independent reality can be ascribed to this notion. Electric charge is an *epiphenomenon*, not an explanatory tool, and neutrons are no more "neutral" than protons. Again, within a stellar core, where they are stable, neutrons behave much the same as protons, and neither particle has an electric charge. To understand how the mass of a neutron governs its behavior, we must look closely at the manner in which it decays at SEP. To do that, we must revisit the equilibrium conditions of elementary particles.

In Chapter 2, I argued that just after the Big Bang the universe fractured into filaments of partons. The asymmetric pressures of partons in the interiors and those on the surfaces of those filaments prompted them to exhibit a large number of convection currents; the filaments began boiling. A proton is formed each time a very specific number of partons begins circulating together near the surface. That number is precisely calibrated to create a particle in which the total pressure exactly balances the pressures of its constituent partons. Moreover, the total pressure of the particle implies zero contribution from the surrounding space, because protons formed in the void, not in normal space (spacetime at the vacuum pressure). By continuously turning itself inside out, the explosive force of the partons is directed into the proton's core, rather than out into free space. This amazingly elegant and dynamic process transforms a nuclear bomb into a stable equilibrium state. It also explains how a proton can possess enough energy to continue spinning for billions of years without running out of gas.

To see how a particle composed of circulating partons might decay, we need only consider what would happen if it possessed too many or too few of them. For example (though I seriously doubt this ever occurs in nature), what would happen if a proton *gained* a few extra partons? At first glance, it might appear that such a particle would be even more stable than a proton. With a surplus of partons, it possesses a higher total pressure than is needed to hold itself together. The partons should be even less able to escape than in a standard proton. But there is a problem with this reasoning. With more total pressure than it needs, the particle can allow its partons to expand a great deal before the coherence of the overall particle is threatened. And because it *can* allow them to expand, it *does* allow them to expand; partons are so explosive that they can only be held in check if it is absolutely necessary for equilibrium. Once the partons start expanding, there is nothing to put a stop to it. The particle does not need to spin fast enough to recompress its partons in the core as fast as they decompress on the surface. No matter how much the partons expand and the particle as a whole bloats, it still possesses more total pressure than it needs. Therefore, the partons go right on expanding and the particle as a whole goes right on bloating. Now, though the particle does not have any net angular momentum, that is only true of the particle as a whole. The individual partons are a different story. As the particle bloats the individual parton orbits (within the convection cells) get larger and larger, and yet their convective velocity must remain roughly constant. It is not long before their centripetal accelerations exceed their mutual attraction and they fly off into space and explode. The particle decays.

The opposite condition, in which a few partons are *removed* from a proton, does occur naturally. Specifically, it occurs on the neutrogenic shells of all main sequence stars, and neutrons are the result. But whereas a particle with too many partons has more total pressure than it needs, a neutron has too little total pressure to hold itself together (**Figure 5.2**). As partons circulate through a neutron's core, their explosive force is more than the particle can absorb. With each circuit, partons emerge from

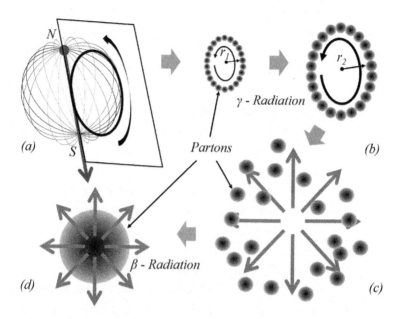

Figure 5.2: Neutron Decay

Though a neutron, like a proton, has no net angular momentum (a), that is only true because all of the individual parton orbits (convection cells) balance one another. Individually, partons experience angular momentum. As both the orbital velocity and convection cell radius of the partons increase (b), so too does their centripetal acceleration, increasing the intensity of the south polar jet, causing gamma radiation. Eventually, their centripetal acceleration exceeds their mutual attraction (c), and they fly apart, destroying the neutron. The partons then expand rapidly (d) by a factor of c^2, causing a shock wave known as beta radiation.

the south pole slightly larger than they were during the previous circuit. The particle as a whole simply cannot compress them fast enough to keep them from expanding. Because the partons are less compressed with each orbit, there is a much larger contrast in pressure from the surface to the core than there is in a proton. This pressure differential is what drives the convective circulation, and that is why neutrons spin so much faster than protons.

As the partons expand, the particle bloats and the pressure differential increases, further accelerating the convection. When this happens, the south polar jet pushes harder and harder on the ambient spacetime, and that means the ambient space-time pushes harder and harder back against the neutron's core, greatly stressing the particle. To get an idea of just how franti-cally a neutron spins, instead of emitting the benign EM waves of a proton, a neutron emits highly energetic gamma rays as it decays. The too-large particle discussed above slows down out of complacency, while a neutron speeds up in a panic. Eventually, as the partons expand and the particle bloats, a neutron meets much the same fate as a too-large particle would: the centripetal acceleration of its partons exceeds their mutual attraction and they fly apart and explode. This explosion—the expansion of the neutron's partons by a factor of c^2—generates a powerful shock wave and is known as *beta radiation*.

Combining this description of neutron behavior with the theory of gravity discussed earlier, we can see why neutrons are heavier than protons, despite the fact that they possess fewer partons. The strength of an atom's gravitational field is related to the pressure on its electronic shell. As the spacetime that is com-pressed against the shell decompresses outside of the particle, it creates a pressure gradient. That pressure, in turn, is determined by the vigor with which spacetime is compressed by the particle and fired at the shell. Finally, that energy can be determined by measuring the intensity of the object's EM emissions, since those emissions are generated by the south polar jet of said object.

From this we can see that the gravitational field gener-ated by a neutron is considerably more powerful than that of a proton, because gamma rays are far more intense than anything emitted by a proton. The tremendous rotational velocity of a free neutron, therefore, can be thought of as an example of *nu-clear mass dilation*. Once again, gravity and mass have a complex relationship.

One final observation about neutrons is needed before we move on with the discussion. As mentioned, neutrons con-tinue to accelerate as they decay because the contrast in pres-sure between the surface and core is continuously increasing.

That means free neutrons can never settle into a stable rotational pattern; that is, they, unlike hydrogen, cannot benefit from the symmetrical absorption and emission of spacetime afforded by the geometry of some particular series of derivative axes. Consequently, neutrons (outside of atoms) do not have stable electronic shells. Only when spacetime is absorbed and emitted at a constant rate can the polar jet terminate at some stable radius from the particle. With neutrons, the pressure generated by the polar jet dissipates chaotically all the way from the south pole outwards; there is no stable termination shock, and therefore, no electron. Similarly, the low pressure near the particle itself is not contained by the well-defined region within an electronic shell. Instead, the low pressure drops off turbulently as the distance from the core increases. Taken together, these two facts mean that free neutrons do not exhibit any *electrostatic repulsion*, either from each other or from other particles. This is the origin of the notion that neutrons have no electrical charge. It is also the reason neutrons can so easily capture protons and be captured by protons to form atoms.

Deuterium

In addition to generating a powerful spacetime pressure gradient and an intense EM signature (gamma rays), the frantic rotation of a neutron creates a very deep low-pressure zone in the immediate vicinity of the particle. The intensity of this low-pressure region is, like every other nuclear property, determined by the particle's rate of convection. The more vigorously spacetime is evacuated, the lower the pressure becomes, and the lower the pressure becomes, the more attractive it is to other nucleons—protons and neutrons alike. In the high-pressure environments that promote nucleosynthesis—either a supernova or any of the other stellar processes discussed in the previous chapter—protons are completely *ionized*. They are under so much pressure that they are not required to spin with enough vigor to generate an electronic shell. Nevertheless, their relatively relaxed convection still propels them hither and yon, more or less randomly, sending them careening into whatever happens to be in their vicinity. If neutrons are present, the protons, lacking an electronic shell, can propel themselves right into the low-pressure region around that particle. If that happens, they become trapped there.

A proton propels itself like a tiny jet engine by drawing spacetime in through its north pole and expelling it from its south pole. If the ambient spacetime has a high pressure it does not resist, indeed it welcomes, the decompression implied by the action of the north pole. However, if the ambient pressure is low, near or below its equilibrium value, spacetime begins to resist the tugging of a proton's north pole. This resistance to being stretched pulls the proton into the low-pressure zone, because low-pressure spacetime pulls back against the proton as the proton attempts to stretch it. If the pressure is very low, as it is around a neutron, this force can be incredibly powerful. Indeed, it is the basis of the *strong nuclear force*. Once a proton is locked into a neutron's low-pressure zone, it is next to impossible to pull it away. This is the proton capture process.

One proton and one neutron is an atom of deuterium, a completely stable isotope of hydrogen. The obvious next question is, Why on earth is a neutron stabilized by this arrangement? From what I have said so far, it is fairly clear what a deuterium nucleus looks like (**Figure 5.3**). The attraction of the proton to the low-pressure region around the neutron comes partly from the suction generated by the north pole, and partly from the propulsion generated by the south pole. Together, these forces ensure that the proton is aimed directly at the center of the atom. Meanwhile, in order to maintain the low-pressure region to which the proton is attracted, the neutron must continue spinning much as it did before it captured its proton. Finally, the proton must orbit the neutron in order to maintain a symmetrical region of low spacetime pressure between itself and its electronic shell. As with protium, a complex series of derivative axes and corresponding energy states characterize its orbit. The

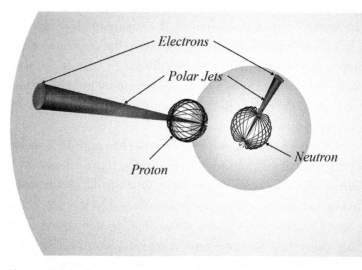

Figure 5.3:   Deuterium
In an atom of deuterium, the neutron is stable and continues to spin, creating an intense low pressure region to which the proton is attracted. The proton orbits on the neutron's electronic shell, evacuating spacetime and maintaining the atom's electronic shell and low core pressure.

difference now is that the proton does not merely spin, but orbits the neutron core. All atomic nuclei have neutron cores with protons orbiting them. The two particles never mingle together into anything resembling the amorphous blob depicted in physics and chemistry textbooks.

The most striking and disconcerting aspect of this arrangement of nucleons is that both particles vigorously *evacuate* spacetime from the nucleus. Such behavior dramatically drops the pressure in the core to very intense negative pressures, well below SEP, exactly the opposite of a stellar core, the place neutrons are most stable. I must admit, as the implications of this arrangement began to sink in, I nearly gave up on this entire project. Up to this point, most aspects of this theory seemed to fit together pretty well, but then all of a sudden it led to a scenario that appears completely implausible. On the one hand, there is no other reasonable way to explain an atom. The south polar jet of the proton must be oriented toward the electronic shell in order to achieve the atom's cosmological equilibrium, as well as the inward pressure implied by the strong nuclear force. Yet surely such a low core pressure is exactly the opposite of what neutrons need to maintain their equilibria. So what in the world is going on in there? Why would an extremely intense negative pressure have the same effect on a neutron as the extremely high positive pressure in a stellar core?

It is here that the other, somewhat less familiar, aspect of spacetime becomes dominant, specifically, its resistance to *decompression below* its equilibrium value. Our cosmic epoch is dominated by high-pressure phenomena—stars, black holes, cosmic expansion, partons—because of the ongoing decompression of the Big Bang. Negative pressures are a bit alien to us. There are no large-scale negative pressure (antimatter) phenomena in our universe, because any such region would immediately be repressurized by the surrounding space. Only in the tiny pocket at the core of an atomic nucleus, protected from the outside world by the protons, can a negative pressure be sustained for any length of time. And because the energy of spacetime is equal to the absolute value of the Lorentz Factor associated with its pressure, it is possible to generate enough energy to keep a neutron compressed using either positive or negative pressure. Though, admittedly, it is not perfectly obvious at first why negative pressure would not instantly tear the neutron apart.

While examining the manner in which a neutron decays, I showed that its convective circulation invariably increases its core pressure. This happens because, at the high convection rate needed to keep its partons compressed, its polar jet pushes extremely hard against the ambient spacetime (evidenced by its gamma emissions), and that in turn increases the pressure on the core, expanding the particle and contributing to its eventual decay. But look what happens inside an atomic nucleus. With the pressure of the core reaching extreme negative values, the spacetime circulating through it is well below its equilibrium value rather than above it (**Figure 5.4**). Consequently, instead

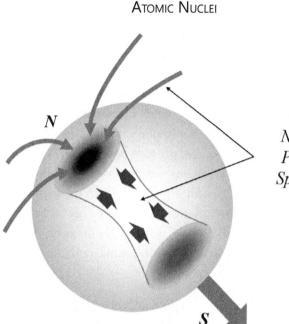

Figure 5.4:   Atomic Neutron
When the ambient spacetime pressure is negative—as it is in an atomic
nucleus—it pulls in against the interior walls of the neutron's core like a
vacuum pump. Rather than puffing up the particle and causing it to decay,
the energy associated with negative pressure spacetime (antimatter) actually holds the particle together. A stellar core pushes down on the surface
of a neutron while an atomic nucleus pulls against its core.

of pushing against the inside of the core, puffing up the neutron like a marshmallow, it pulls in against the inner walls like
a vacuum pump, holding the particle together. Notice also that
the spacetime expelled from the south pole receives very little
push-back from the ambient spacetime, leading to little or no
increase in pressure within the neutron's core. The proton pulls
the spacetime away, greatly decreasing the pressure on the neutron's electronic shell.

        None of this implies that a neutron would be stable in
the void, despite the fact that it could (with no upper limit on
its convective velocity) circulate well above the speed of light. In
that case, the absence of spacetime (below its equilibrium pressure), pulling the particle together, would leave the partons free

to expand at a greater rate than the entire particle could counteract, no matter how fast it circulated. Spacetime exerts a force
both above and below equilibrium and that force is necessary,
in one form or another, to stabilize the neutron. That is why
neutrons did not form in the void, immediately after the Big
Bang, along with protons. Only one equilibrium condition for
partons exists in the void, and protons have already claimed that
honor. So we see that neutrons are stabilized in stars by an extremely high ambient pressure pushing down on their surfaces,
while they are stabilized in atomic nuclei by an extremely low
pressure exerted on the inside walls of their cores. Stars push
them together from outside, while atoms pull them together
from within.

The Strong Nuclear Force

Perhaps the strangest aspect of the force that holds nucleons together is that it increases rather than decreases with the
distance between the nucleons. This is considered odd because
forces, as they are currently conceived, involve the exchange of
force particles (e.g., gluons) between their corresponding mass
particles (e.g., hadrons). It stands to reason that the farther these
force particles are required to travel, the weaker and less numerous they become. Gravity and electromagnetism, as expected,
both decrease in strength as the distance increases, though neither has anything to do with the exchange of particles (i.e., photons or gravitons). The theory I am developing here renders this
curious aspect of the nuclear force perfectly comprehensible.

The first thing to notice about our emerging picture of
deuterium is that the proton and neutron are not attracted to
each other by anything that is going on between the particles
themselves. Instead, the two particles team up to create a very
low-pressure region, and it is that region, not one another, to
which both of them adhere. The force that holds the proton in
place comes both from its south polar jet, pushing against the
electronic shell, as well as the suction generated by its north

pole. Neither of these is focused specifically on the neutron, but on the region of low pressure in the center of the atom. The neutron, it is true, is the only reason such a low-pressure region can exist, but that does not imply that the proton is attracted specifically to the neutron. The neutron can continue its highly energetic convective motion in such a low-pressure region because its equilibrium pressure (whether positive or negative) was originally established in the extreme environment on a star's neutrogenic shell. A proton, by contrast, hardly moves at all (is entirely ionized) when subjected to the pressure in either an atomic or stellar core. What all of this means is that the vigor with which a nucleon circulates is related to the equilibrium conditions under which it formed. A neutron is very energetic even at the low pressure in an atomic core and is, therefore, able to generate a very low-pressure region to which a proton is attracted. The proton, though attracted to this low-pressure region, cannot, by itself, maintain such a region, because the high energy there renders the proton virtually motionless.

Consequently, there is a very specific distance from the neutron where the pressure is simultaneously high enough to permit the proton to continue circulating and low enough to be attractive to that proton. To move closer to the neutron, the proton must increase its convective velocity, since that is how a proton propels itself forward. However, the faster the proton spins, the more vigorously it evacuates spacetime from the nucleus, and the lower the core pressure becomes. As this pressure drops, it becomes increasingly energetic, offering powerful resistance to any further stretching. This energy, by pulling against their cores, stabilizes both the neutron and the proton, causing both of them to slow down. When the proton slows down, its convective velocity decreases and it moves back away from the core.

Correlatively, if the proton slows and moves away from the core, it evacuates spacetime less vigorously and the core pressure begins to rise. When this happens, the neutron begins to panic, causing it to increase its convection rate, decreasing the core pressure. This lower core pressure is more attractive to the proton and it moves back to a lower orbit. Taken together, these dynamics result in a very specific equilibrium state for a deuterium atom. The proton must keep the core pressure low, but not so low that it loses its convective power. The neutron, in turn, must balance its desire to keep the pressure as low as possible against its need to keep the proton at a high enough convective velocity to continue assisting. In general, this balance of forces determines the orbital geometry of all nuclides.

It is clear that the power of the strong nuclear force comes from both the nucleon's south polar jet pushing against the electronic shell and the suction created by the north pole. Nothing (i.e., gluons) is directly exchanged between the nucleons themselves. Rather, the neutrons are responsible for creating the necessary conditions for both particles, acting in concert, to generate a low-pressure zone to which each is individually attracted.

Nuclear Magnetic Moment

Normally when we think of two objects orbiting one another, we can imagine two masses connected by a string and then set to spinning. The force holding the two masses together is transmitted by the string, and the orbiting system possesses angular momentum in the plane of its rotation. The Earth-Moon system is a very good example. However, the conditions in atomic nuclei are very different from this familiar model. In particular, there is no analog in deuterium to the gravitational string that holds the Moon and Earth together. The nuclear force is not transmitted along a line between the nucleons. Instead, it is distributed evenly over the entire interior surface of the spherical electronic shell. The nuclear force, therefore, is largely a *pushing* rather than *pulling* force, and that push is balanced by a two dimensional surface located *outside* of the particles, rather than a one dimensional string stretched *between* them. If we consider all the simple circular orbits that a proton might occupy and draw in the angular momentum vectors associated with those orbits, we discover that, like a lone proton, they sum exactly to zero. As a result, the angular momentum of a proton, whether alone in protium or paired with a neutron, is zero . . .almost.

Superficially, the notion of a *nuclear magnetic moment* is very simple and straightforward. It is nothing more than a measure of the wobble (angular momentum) of an atom that results from asymmetries in its nucleonic orbitals. Not surprisingly, only atoms with odd numbers of protons and/or neutrons exhibit a magnetic moment. Deuterium is lopsided, and therefore, possesses a magnetic moment. The best way to picture this phenomenon is to think of the circus stunt in which motorcyclists ride their bikes (nucleons) on the inside of a spherical metal cage (electronic shell). If two cyclists "orbit" exactly opposite one another, the cage will not wobble (ignoring gravity, which is not relevant for nuclear behavior). If, on the other hand, only one cyclist is involved, the cage will have to be fastened securely to the floor in order not to shake and roll all over the tent.

The picture becomes muddier as we add more cyclists, though the principle is always the same. Three cyclists, for example, can, if they remain equidistant and within the same orbital plane, prevent the cage from wobbling. But if their orbital plane itself begins to orbit around a secondary axis, a wobble will develop. No matter how the entire three-member orbital is rotated, it will always be lopsided. From this example, we can see that a magnetic moment might come from a single nucleon, causing the wobble all by itself, though it might also come from the wobble of a derivative axis. This added complexity makes it virtually impossible, even with complete knowledge of the nucleonic configuration, to determine, simply by eye-balling the atom, exactly where a given component of a wobble comes from. Moreover, an atom will tend to compensate for wobbles in one orbital by *tuning* one or more different orbitals to balance it out, at least as much as possible. Since different orbitals have nothing obvious to do with one another, these sorts of extreme subtleties will only become evident with the help of high speed computer simulations. Absent that, it would be like trying to determine, simply by looking at them, which of several different electric fans, when switched on and placed on the same metal table, will spontaneously begin resonating together.

I mention magnetic moment here, not because it is particularly helpful in determining nuclear configurations, but because I argued above that nucleonic orbitals have zero angular momentum. Clearly, many atoms, as a whole, do exhibit angular momentum in the form of their magnetic moments, so it would appear that we have a problem. We can resolve this by considering the difference in magnitude between the observed magnetic moment and the hypothetical values that would be present if the nucleonic orbitals exhibited the same sort of angular momentum that is observed in other orbiting systems.

If, for example, the two protons in helium (**Figure 5.5**) were joined by a nuclear "string" tied between them, the atom as a whole would exhibit an extreme bias in the direction of its angular momentum vector, perpendicular to the protons' orbital plane. Almost no force in the universe would be able to push the atom out of this preferred orientation, and yet helium clearly does not exhibit any such bias.

Magnetic moments manifest themselves on the electronic shells as wobbles of an entire atom, but these fluctuations are many millions of times weaker than the forces in the nucleus. For comparison, imagine the circus stunt again. If the cyclists are whizzing around at thousands of miles per hour, the magnetic moment of the entire cage, were it proportionate to that of an atom, would amount to a wobble of only a tiny fraction of a millimeter, rather as if the cage were millions of times more massive than the motorcycles. The cyclists do indeed cause this wobble, but are not themselves affected by it. For that reason, we can say that nucleonic orbitals have an *effective* angular momentum of zero, though the angular momentum of an atom, measured on a scale that is several million times more sensitive (what we might

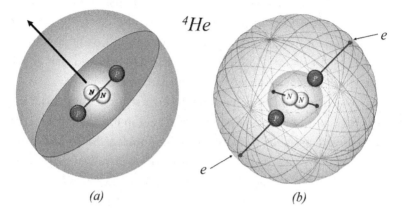

^4He

(a)   (b)

Figure 5.5:   Helium 4
The strong nuclear force is not like a string tied between the nucleons. If
the protons in helium were attracted specifically to one another (a), their
orbital would be locked tightly into one particular plane by their extreme
angular momentum. Instead, the strong force is balanced by a two dimensional surface (the electronic shell) located outside of the nucleons
(b), allowing the nucleonic orbitals to be governed entirely by spacetime
pressure variations inside the shell.

call the *chemical* or *electromagnetic* scale), is not always exactly
zero. This is important because, as with hydrogen, the series of
derivative axes that characterize an atom's orbital configuration
depend on the protons possessing no angular momentum of
their own. Only in that way can their rotational patterns be dictated entirely by the pressure variations within their electronic
shells. If orbitals were locked into a particular plane, their behavior would be completely different than is actually observed.

Mass Defect

There are two concepts that dominate our current understanding of atomic nuclei: *mass defect* and *cosmic abundances*.
The latter refers to the relative distribution of elements throughout the universe. The former deals with the fact that multinucleonic atoms are always lighter when weighed as a unit than their
constituents are when weighed separately. It is assumed that this
mass defect is related to something called *binding energy*, the

force holding nucleons together. If nuclear fusion actually were a natural phenomenon, it would release the energy contained in the mass difference between the parent and daughter nuclei according to $E=mc^2$. Indeed, it is currently believed that this is where the energy of a star comes from.

Among the more unexpected consequences of this theory is that an intense negative pressure region in the neutron core of an atomic nucleus powers the strong nuclear force. We know the nucleus is negative because if it were positive it would, like a black hole, be repelled by gravitational fields. We also know that neutrons require pressures analogous to those in a stellar core in order to remain stable. That means the energy of the spacetime in an atom is not only negative, but is extremely negative, with an absolute value roughly equal to the high pressure in a stellar core. Only in that way can neutrons be stabilized. Moreover, the geometric configuration of nucleons in deuterium requires that they both vigorously expel spacetime from their immediate vicinities in order to propel themselves toward the center of the atom, as well as maintain the atom's electronic shell (its cosmological equilibrium). In brief, everything points to a deeply negative core. In Chapter 3, I argued that nuclear fusion has nothing to do with the energy released by stars. Instead, partons are released from protons on a star's neutrogenic shell, creating neutrons of equal mass everywhere in the universe. Now I will show that nuclear fusion is not only absent from stars, but does not occur anywhere else either. Fusion is not a natural phenomenon and, unfortunately, no such process will ever be used by man to generate electricity.

The strong force is related to the vigor with which nucleons evacuate spacetime from their atomic nucleus; their convective circulation is responsible for both the positive pressure of the electronic shell as well as the negative pressure in the core. The negative pressure core is irresistibly attractive to both protons and neutrons and it can be sustained at such a low pressure for two reasons.

First, neutrons can remain energetic at extremely low (or high) pressures, enabling them to continue spinning even under extreme conditions that would render protons virtually motionless (completely ionize them). Second, orbiting protons expel enough spacetime from the core so that the south polar jets of the neutrons do not exert excessive pressure on their cores, puffing them up and leading to their decay. Though neutrons are energetic (compared to protons) in the equilibrium state of an atom, they spin much more slowly than do free neutrons; the contrast in pressure from their surfaces to their cores is not constantly increasing, forcing them to accelerate. As a result, an atomic neutron creates less positive pressure with its south polar jet and less negative pressure in its immediate vicinity than it did when outside of the atom. And as I have shown, the measured mass of a free neutron is high exactly because of the extreme energy of its convective circulation. When the neutrons are slowed by the equilibrium condition in an atom, they generate a weaker gravitational field, and that is the reason for the mass defect associated with the strong nuclear force. To summarize, neutrons are relaxed by the extremely low pressure in the atomic core, decreasing their convective velocity, which in turn, decreases the intensity of their gravitational field, reducing their extrinsic mass.

Now, the energy of negative pressure spacetime has, obviously, never been considered before. So far as the standard model is concerned, energy is energy. When it is released, it always pushes out from its source; that is, it is always conceived as positive pressure energy. However, negative pressure energy *pulls in* against the surrounding ambient spacetime just as it pulls in against the core of a neutron; it is *endothermic*. Therefore, in a positive pressure environment—such as the one characterizing the current cosmic epoch—negative pressure cannot actually be *released*. Only if the ambient spacetime were already stretched to significantly negative values would the exposure of that space to a deeply negative region have any significant effect. Imagine a fishing net that is completely slack. Pulling anywhere on the mesh will not have any effect on the rest of the net. But imagine if the net were already stretched. Pulling on it under those conditions would transmit a negative pressure wave throughout the net. So far as negative pressures are concerned, our cosmos is completely slack. As a result, the only way to tap into the relatively small differences in binding energies between various nuclides would be to release that energy into a negative pressure environment. Clearly, stars do not fit the bill.

Even so, it is worthwhile to conduct a thought experiment to see how this might work. Suppose we try to fuse three helium atoms into one carbon atom, *in a negative pressure environment*. Again, this makes no sense at all in a positive pressure environment. Helium exhibits a lower mass defect than carbon, which means it generates a more powerful gravitational field per neutron. Another way to think of this is to say that the convective vigor of helium's neutrons, compared with those of carbon, is slightly closer to the extreme state in which free neutrons are found. In carbon, the neutrons are more relaxed. That, in turn, means that the negative pressure, per neutron, in the core of a helium atom is more intense. The depth of the negative pressure core (again, per neutron) is proportionate to the strength of the atom's gravitational field. When we fuse the three helium atoms together, some of this negative energy is released and pulls in against the already taut (negative) spacetime in the atoms' vicinity. The resulting carbon atom has a higher mass defect, which means a lower electronic shell pressure (weaker gravitational field) per neutron. The absolute core pressure in carbon is somewhat lower, and the electronic shell pressure higher, than in helium (that is why its neutrons are more relaxed), but each of the six neutrons contributes less to that low pressure than it did while in its original helium atom. This implies that there is something about the geometric arrangement of the neutrons (discussed in the next chapter) in a carbon atom that enables the same six neutrons to simultaneously increase the core pressure, while decreasing the convective vigor of each of them. A small fraction of the negative pressure energy from the three helium atoms has been released in this fictional fusion reaction.

Notice that if this process could somehow be sustained in a stellar core, it would be radically endothermic. The total energy associated with the negative pressure in three helium atoms—the energy per neutron—is greater than the energy in a single carbon atom, even though the absolute pressure in the carbon core is somewhat lower. But because this energy comes from negative pressure, the exposure of a stellar core to a fusion reaction would absorb energy rather than release it. Negative pressure is equivalent to the traditional notion of antimatter. When matter and antimatter are brought together they *equilibrate*, but the positive pressure energy released (in a simple shock wave) is trivial by comparison to the quantity absorbed. In essence, negative pressure is a positive pressure sinkhole, and because stars are very obviously positive pressure phenomena, it is impossible for fusion to play a role in their energy production.

Current efforts to generate a self-sustaining hydrogen fusion reaction have revealed that more energy must be added to the system than is ever retrieved from it. This failure is not evidence of a technological hurdle that is yet to be surmounted or a mistake made by the researchers. Instead, it is strong evidence that, as I have argued, fusion is endothermic and not a natural phenomenon.

So what exactly does the mass defect of an atom have to tell us? The mass defect curve (**Figure 5.6**) shows a dramatic increase in the stability of neutrons, starting with a free neutron and ending with oxygen. Beyond that (e.g., between oxygen and iron), the differences are relatively trivial but still instructive. What is most interesting about this curve is that there is not a simple relationship between the number of nucleons and the mass defect; simply adding nucleons does not increase it. As has been suggested by the *nuclear shell model*, these discrepancies are likely the result of the underlying nucleonic geometry. Now that

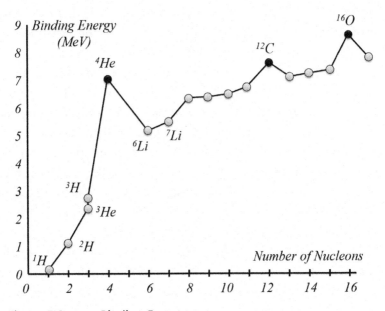

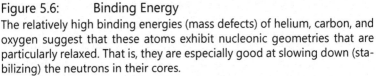

Figure 5.6:   Binding Energy
The relatively high binding energies (mass defects) of helium, carbon, and
oxygen suggest that these atoms exhibit nucleonic geometries that are
particularly relaxed. That is, they are especially good at slowing down (stabilizing) the neutrons in their cores.

we have a good understanding of nucleons, we can use these
discrepancies to determine what does and does not constitute a
geometrically relaxed nucleus.

6

Multinucleonic Atoms

Atoms

In much the same way the atomic properties of hydrogen helped us understand deuterium, the latter will help us understand the rest of the periodic table. Thus far, I have argued that the strong nuclear force is the result of a deep negative pressure region within the neutron core of an atom. This negative pressure has a roughly equal but opposite value as the high pressure of a stellar core. A star pushes on the surface of a neutron while an atom pulls in against its core, and either process can stabilize the particle. The strong force, therefore, is not a force of attraction between nucleons, but rather an attraction by both protons and neutrons to the low-pressure region at the core of the atom.

Atomic protons are arranged in orbitals and are aimed directly at the center of their host atom. In this manner they simultaneously evacuate spacetime from the neutron core, as well as maintain the atom's electronic shell. As always, the orbital characteristics are governed by various series of derivative axes, the effect of which is to maintain a low, symmetrical pressure within the electronic shell. Finally, we know that the effective nuclear magnetic moment of a nucleus is negligible by comparison to the strong nuclear force. The strong force is not like a string tied between the particles, but is instead distributed evenly over the interior surface of the electronic shell. Hence, orbital geometry is unaffected by the angular momenta of the nucleons. What we need to know now is how the nucleons are arranged to give rise to the chemical properties of their atoms.

Magic Numbers

In a simple atom like deuterium, the absence of angular momentum in the proton orbital is not immediately obvious (so long as the atom is not part of a molecule). Since there is only one proton, it has nothing to run into, and so even if it were held in one particular orbit, the atom might still remain stable. However, in more complex atoms with dozens of protons buzzing around at high speeds in very close proximity, the lack of angular momentum is critical to an atom's orbital configuration. Try to imagine six protons, all with circular orbits and in the same shell, somehow managing to avoid one another. It is inconceivable. Without angular momentum, protons are not required to "orbit" a nucleus at all. Indeed, simple spherical orbitals are the exception. In most proton shells there are too many protons for them to orbit the nucleus in anything resembling a circle. Now that we know protons have no effective angular momentum, we are free to consider these other possibilities. Our first clues come from the unusually high mass defects of both helium and oxygen, indicating that the neutrons in both of these nuclei are unusually relaxed by comparison to their free state.

In helium-4, we have two protons evacuating spacetime from a nucleus occupied by two neutrons. What we need to know is how the protons respond to one another now that there are more than one of them. In this case, the obvious intuitive answer turns out to be the right one: they are located on opposite sides of the nucleus and move in roughly circular orbits (**Figure 6.1**), though the requirements of their derivative axes (just as in hydrogen) determine exactly what paths they take. Note: even with only two protons, the derivative axes become immeasurably more complex, and only a computer simulation will be able to disentangle them all. Still, we know that such axes are present in multinucleonic atoms, both because the cosmological equilibrium conditions are the same, and because the discrete EM spectra of such atoms, though different, mirror that of hydrogen.

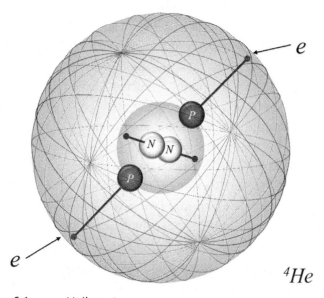

Figure 6.1: Helium 4

Neither protons nor neutrons are attracted specifically to one another. Instead, they respond to the pressure variations of the entire phenomenon in order to maximize the efficiency of the nuclear force.

Now, though the obvious answer is the right one in this case, it must be explained in detail so that we can make sense of atoms that are less obvious. First, notice that the protons, by themselves, do not exhibit anything that we might call *electrostatic repulsion*. This idea comes from the concept that protons have something called *positive charge*, and that like charges repel. As I have argued at length, the dynamics of attraction and repulsion are always related to pressure differences and these differences are due to complex relationships, rarely obvious or straightforward, between various objects and phenomena. Nothing in nature simply possesses, without further ado, a positive charge, whatever might be meant by the enigmatic term *charge*.

We can see this if we simply imagine what would happen if both protons in helium tried to occupy the same side of the atom. With both polar jets pointing in the same direction the atom as a whole begins accelerating in the opposite direction. That, in turn, undermines the nuclear force in several ways. It decompresses the nucleus on one side at the expense of the other side, decreasing the pressure on the far side and weakening the protons' jets. It saps the energy of the protons, converting the inward-pointing nuclear force into an acceleration of the atom as a whole. Finally, with both jets on the same side, the spacetime in the region around the nucleus is unevenly evacuated, creating a strong pressure gradient. Combined, these disequilibrium conditions strongly pull the protons to opposite sides of the nucleus. But notice, none of them has anything to do with protons being inherently repulsive. The very same dynamic keeps neutrons in the core evenly spaced, though it has been claimed that they have a *neutral charge*. In general, there is no meaning to the notion that particles carry a particular charge. How they behave toward one another always depends on the whole scenario.

What we learn from helium is that the protons tend to point at the core and arrange themselves evenly on their shell. They do this because pointing directly at the core maximizes the efficiency of spacetime evacuation, while being evenly spaced decreases pressure variations. Together, these two factors maximize the nuclear force per proton. In a sense, the two protons leverage one another, pushing in opposite directions so that none of their efforts are wasted (except the trivial fraction that gives atoms, though not helium, their magnetic moments) accelerating the atom as a whole. And, inasmuch as neutrons are virtually identical to protons, they also arrange themselves evenly and point directly at one another. Interestingly, helium is one of the few atoms in which protons can be arranged in this ideal manner. The inflexible facts of geometry force most atoms to settle on a less than perfect compromise.

Notice that in helium the protons are evenly spaced, but *also* located exactly opposite one another on a diameter of the shell. For atoms with one, three, four, or five protons in their outermost shell (e.g., lithium, boron, carbon, and nitrogen)

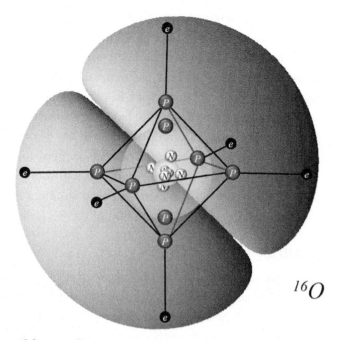

^{16}O

Figure 6.2:   Oxygen

Because the strong force does not generate any effective nuclear angular momentum, it is reasonable to consider more than two protons in a particular orbital. And based on the relatively high mass defects of both helium and oxygen, we know that nucleons seek an equidistant and diametrically opposed configuration. In oxygen, these dynamics dictate an octahedral valance shell with protons at the vertices. It is clear from this arrangement why oxygen has a dual hemisphere electronic shell geometry.

this ideal condition cannot be met. But it can be met in *oxygen*, which has *six* protons in its outer shell. The six vertices of a regular octahedron are diametrically opposed *and* equidistant when transcribed on a sphere (**Figure 6.2**). This is the clue we needed in order to understand how protons are arranged. Both helium and oxygen are unusually stable (doubly magic) because each of them has a proton configuration in which the protons are evenly spaced and directly opposite one another. And, as we have just seen, geometry makes this a rare combination. The first two magic numbers, therefore, are *two* and *six*, which just happen to add up to eight in oxygen. Eight is not a magic number by itself, because protons arranged at the corners of a cube are not both equidistant and diametrically opposed.

To review, the simple arrangement in helium, combined with its extraordinary stability, led us to the mechanisms that govern proton distribution. That, in turn, suggested a geometric arrangement that is rare, present in both helium and oxygen, and unusually stable. Finally, the fact that proton orbitals do not possess angular momentum opened the door to considering more than two protons (six, in the case of oxygen) in a given shell. Combined with the insights below, we will soon have the necessary tools to piece together the nuclear configurations of the entire second period (Li through Ne) of the periodic table.

The Neutron Core

Strictly speaking, this section of the book is premature; only a computer simulation, faithfully employing the spacetime theory being developed here, can definitively answer specific questions about the neutron configurations of atoms. Thankfully, the speculations that follow do not have to be entirely accurate in order to illustrate the overarching principles at issue. For my limited purposes, it is enough to describe the various forces at play, how they interact, their general consequences, and what is required, moving forward, to make these predictions in a more systematic and defensible way. That said, and in full view of the provisional nature of this discussion, it still makes sense to offer the most likely scenarios that current research permits.

The most pertinent insights we have into the geometries of neutron configurations come from the detailed nuclear binding energy data that physicists have cataloged, along with observations related to the nuclear stability of nuclides (**Figures 6.3 and 6.4**). According to the best research to-date, there are magic numbers at 2, 8, possibly 14, 20, 28, and 50 (and higher numbers for heavier atoms).

If we combine all of our knowledge of nuclear binding energies, nuclide stabilities, principles derived from the nuclear shell model, as well as the requirements of the theory I am devel-

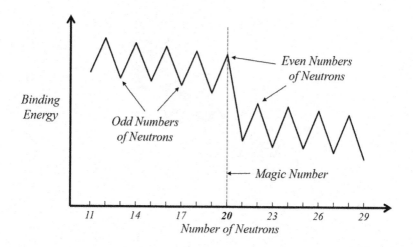

Figure 6.3: Incremental Neutron Binding Energies
Holding the number of protons constant, this graph shows: 1) the overall gradual decrease in binding energy as the neutron number increases; 2) that even numbers of neutrons have higher binding energies than odd numbers, resulting in the graph's saw tooth shape; and 3) a sudden significant drop in binding energy immediately following the "magic number" 20.

oping in this book, we come up with the neutron configurations represented in the diagrams in **Figures 6.5-6.9**. Up through 14 neutrons, the three shells are full when they contain 2, 6, and 6 neutrons, respectively. I stopped at 14 because, as far as I am able to determine, the existing data will not allow us to decide whether the 15th neutron is the seventh member of the 3n shell (which would be full when it contains 12 neutrons located at the vertices of a regular icosahedron) or the first member of the 4n shell. Either option—a single 12-member icosahedral shell or two consecutive 6-member octahedral shells—could result in a magic number of 20. Again, only a computer simulation will be able to answer this question definitively.

The reason a computer simulation is critical here is that the spacetime pressures generated by the various shells have very subtle and complex effects on adjacent shells and, by extension, the rest of the atom. Further complicating matters are

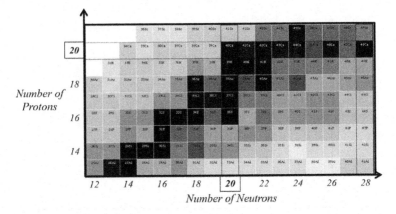

Figure 6.4: Nuclide Stability

Though the relationship is far from perfect, there is a tantalizing correlation between binding energies, magic numbers, and nuclide stability. There are many more stable species with even, rather than odd, numbers of neutrons (and protons), and there is a spike in the number of stable species at both Z=20 and at N=20. Note: darker shading indicates longer half-lives, and black indicates entirely stable nuclides.

the differing geometric conditions of each shell; interior shells are smaller and more constrained than exterior shells. Hence, an octahedral shell may be ideal in certain respects, but if it simply won't fit in the center of the atom then, *ipso facto*, there isn't one there. The following discussion is just one example of the complexities that a computer simulation could help resolve.

The entire neutron core constitutes one of the two main poles—the protons being the other one—of an atom. The forces at play between these two poles are balanced according to the principles discussed in the previous chapter; the neutrons attempt to keep the pressure as low as possible, but not so low that the protons lose their convective vigor and cease evacuating spacetime from the nucleus. The balance, thus achieved, is unique for every single nuclide. Recall, the mass defect of the neutrons reflects the degree of relaxation afforded by the entire atom. So, if we consider, for example, the same 20-member neutron core, but in several different atoms (e.g., Ca-40, K-39, Ar-38, Cl-37) we will discover slightly different binding energies (mass

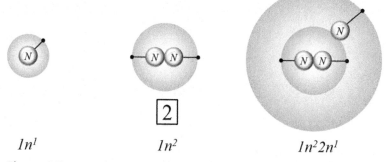

$1n^1$ $1n^2$ $1n^2 2n^1$

Figure 6.5: Neutron Cores 1

Neutron configurations are more difficult than proton configurations to determine without a computer simulation because, unlike protons, they are not directly implicated in an atom's chemical behavior. Magic numbers (including 14, because it has an octahedral outer shell) are indicated in boxes.

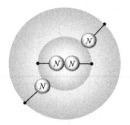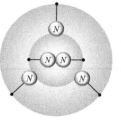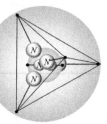

$1n^2 2n^2$ $1n^2 2n^3$ $1n^2 2n^4$

Figure 6.6: Neutron Cores 2

Neutron configurations four through six.

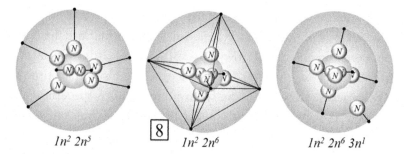

$1n^2 2n^5$ $1n^2 2n^6$ $1n^2 2n^6 3n^1$

Figure 6.7: Neutron Cores 3

Neutron configurations seven through nine.

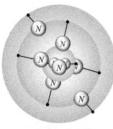
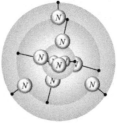
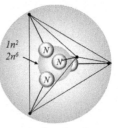

$1n^2\ 2n^6\ 3n^2$ $1n^2\ 2n^6\ 3n^3$ $1n^2\ 2n^6\ 3n^4$

Figure 6.8:   Neutron Cores 4
Neutron configurations ten through twelve.

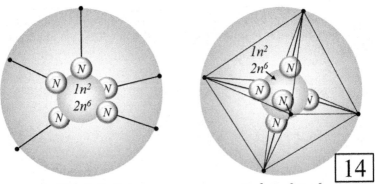

$1n^2\ 2n^6\ 3n^5$ $1n^2\ 2n^6\ 3n^6$

Figure 6.9:   Neutron Cores 5
Neutron configurations thirteen and fourteen.

defects) in each one. Specifically, for the same neutron core, the binding energy (of the neutrons) will increase, on average, as the number of protons increases. This happens because the extra protons can absorb the lower pressure more easily, thus allowing the core to spin a bit faster and evacuate more spacetime in the process. However, exactly how much more spacetime the protons can absorb depends on equally subtle variables (e.g., geometry) in the proton shells.

Trying to understand all of these complex relationships, using theory alone, quickly becomes intractable. By contrast, a computer simulation will enable us to tease apart the relative contributions and intricate interactions of all of the following elements:

1. Nucleonic Geometry—so far as the inherent stability of an orbital is concerned, six is better than two, which is better than four, which is better than three, which is better than one. In practice, however, each of these has advantages and disadvantages in certain contexts.

2. Neutron-Proton Ratio—for a given number of neutrons, there is an ideal number of protons, in terms of both binding energy and nuclear stability. However, this general rule is often violated when specific nucleonic geometries either promote or frustrate stability.

3. Shell Filling—only a simulation, balancing all of the forces, can uncover the extremely subtle reasons why, and exactly where, ideal (octahedral, icosahedral) nucleonic shells must be periodically punctuated by less than ideal 2-member shells in order to reduce the intensity of the negative pressure.

4. Inter-orbital Resonance—refers to any complex harmonic relationship between two or more orbitals (proton and/or neutron) that increases or decreases the overall binding energy of the atom.

While any one of these phenomena is comprehensible in theory and in isolation, the interactions between them are simply too complex to be disentangled without a supercomputer.

There is one other, somewhat unexpected, conclusion that we can draw about neutrons. It is currently believed that neutrons have no electrical charge, which is the same as saying they neither attract nor repel other particles, including other neutrons. However, it is clear that neutrons are even more attracted to low pressure regions than are protons, and neutrons are the particles most able to generate such regions. Therefore, when neutrons are expelled from a star (e.g., in a supernova), they will tend to cluster together, even before they encounter any protons, in an effort to create the deepest possible low-pressure region. By the time the neutron skin of a stellar core reaches the proton cloud, the neutron nuclei—what could be referred to as *neutronium*—of the resulting atoms have already been created. When these prefabricated cores come into contact with protons, they capture as many as are necessary to reach equilibrium or, failing that, as many as possible (often leading to unstable, neutron-rich isotopes). There is no reason to assume that neutrons wait until protons are present before they begin forming nuclei.

Proton Orbitals

In the previous chapter I discussed the equilibrium conditions that keep protons at a very specific distance from the neutron core. They must balance their attraction to the low-pressure core against their need to remain sufficiently energetic to keep that core at a low pressure. If they move too close, the pressure drops and the protons slow down and move away. If they move too far away, the pressure rises. This rise in pressure causes the neutrons to accelerate, dropping the pressure and pulling the protons back in. In practice, these equilibrium dynamics define a particular orbital radius for the protons.

Now, because protons must balance their attraction to low pressure against their own part in maintaining it, the most efficient arrangement is not always the best arrangement. That is, just because an atom has exactly the right number of protons to form a tetrahedral or octahedral valance orbital, it does not follow that it actually will. In many cases, such orbitals are too efficient, evacuating spacetime at a rate too fast and dropping the pressure too much to maintain the protons' convective circulation. Recall, protons, like neutrons, are stabilized (slowed) by low pressure, which means their convective vigor decreases as the pressure drops to intense negative values. If it drops too far, the protons' polar jets become too weak to evacuate spacetime. Indeed, they may even become too weak to hold the protons in the nucleus at all. As a general rule, protons will only maintain an orbital configuration that is minimally sufficient to keep the atom stable.

The Limits of Reductionism

The current dream of mathematical physicists is the development of a relatively simple set of equations that capture everything in the cosmos. That is never going to happen. The reason it will not happen is that the complexity of nature (contrary to the hopes of string theorists) is not contained within its fundamental substance. Instead, it arises bit by bit as that substance is configured into progressively more complex geometric configurations, the dynamics of which are *not mathematically related to one another*. Spacetime itself is very simple stuff; it resists compression or decompression in proportion to the variance of its current pressure from its equilibrium value (the cosmological constant). However, the simplest stable object made of spacetime is a proton, and protons are characterized by several different complex series of derivative rotational axes. There is no mathematical relationship between the simple properties of spacetime and the complex rotational pattern of a proton.

Contrary to the promises made by reductionism, a proton is an *emergent order*. Similarly, there is no way to extrapolate the curious behaviors of various platonic solids, such as tetrahedrons or octahedrons, from an individual nucleon. The reason these shapes make such efficient orbitals is that they aim all the nucleons that comprise them at the same point in space, while exploiting the most efficient geometric distribution. The negative pressure at that point is shared by all the nucleons that generate it, decreasing their workload and enabling them to relax. But, there is nothing about a single neutron that suggests this collective behavior; there is no mathematical relationship between a neutron and an octahedron. Like an individual proton, a multinucleonic atom is an emergent order, not mathematically derivable from its parts.

In both of the examples above, the mathematical discontinuity between simple constituents and composite objects rests with the absolute primacy of Euclidean geometry. By *absolute*, I mean exactly that: the relationships between points in three dimensions (geometry) transcend every other kind of order. Geometry cannot be derived from anything more fundamental, because it is that from which everything else is derived. Consider, the collapse of infinite space over eternity occurs because of the geometric tension between infinite and finite geometries. There is nothing more fundamental at our disposal that might form the basis of a still more fundamental (reductive) argument. Nothingness (three infinite degrees of freedom) itself dictates the properties of geometry, and in that regard it is not actually an assumption but a given. By *assuming* nothing, we are *given* geometry. If you want to wrestle with questions even more basic than those in this book, you might wax philosophical (or theological) on the ontology of *pi*, or some similarly irreducible absolute. To ask this question involves nothing less than asking why there is such a thing as *dimensionality* in the first place—why the universe happens to be three dimensional. By my theory, *pi* comes from nowhere, nothingness itself. On the other hand, Pythagoras may have been right: perhaps *God* is a more dignified name for infinity.

The only plausible way to work with this theory is not by deriving ever more complex equations, but with the aid of high-speed computer simulations, and even they will prove extremely challenging. Such a simulation will involve defining a three dimensional space and then assigning pressure and velocity (both magnitude and direction) values to each point in that space. The program will then evolve the system so the disparity in pressure between adjacent points is reduced. Emergent properties will reveal themselves naturally as the system evolves. In theory, this is a very simple process, though in practice it will be exceedingly difficult. To begin with, spacetime is a *perfect continuum*; there is no minimum distance (e.g., the Planck distance). If we continue

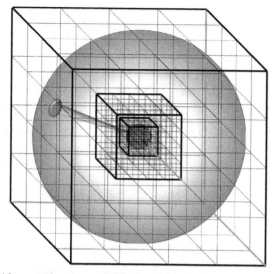

Figure 6.10: Simulator Grid
To capture both the large size of an entire atom as well as the detailed structure of a nucleon's individual partons, the grid used to define a point must be both large and fine—bad news for computational efficiency. Possibly, a graduated logarithmic grid, like the one pictured here, is an option.

to divide spacetime into smaller and smaller bits, we will never be done with it. Alternatively, if we divide it infinitely we end up with nothing, because that (the void) is exactly where spacetime came from. Only because spacetime is infinite is it something rather than nothing. As a result, our simulations will never be more than approximations.

How accurate these approximations are depends on the resolution of the grid or mesh (**Figure 6.10**) we use to define a point. Unfortunately, as the resolution of the grid is increased, so too is the computation time. This situation is very much analogous to the conundrum currently faced by researchers in quantum chromodynamics (QCD), though obviously the theory being modeled is completely different. Consider the difficulties that must be overcome to model even a single atom of hydrogen.

The ambient spacetime is a critical element of most phenomena, because that is the medium through which they establish their cosmological equilibria. In the case of hydrogen, the ambient spacetime powers the proton's polar jet, which in turn causes the particle to spin, and also establishes the atom's electronic shell. Therefore, the grid used in this simulation must include not only the proton itself, but also all the space around it, increasing the volume of the simulation by a factor of several billion. Yet we cannot reduce the resolution of the grid in order to compensate for all of this extra space. Each individual parton is not merely a simple point, but a complex pressure gradient upon which the behavior of the proton is completely dependent. So the resolution of the grid must be fine enough to capture the structure of the partons and large enough to encompass the entire atom. That implies a very large *and* very fine grid—a worst-case computational scenario. Many physical phenomena (e.g., stars) involve similarly gigantic contrasts in scale between their simple constituents and their composite behaviors.

There is one bit of potential good news. Protons are stable in the void and that means it is possible to simulate one (though not a hydrogen atom) without including the surrounding space. Such a simulation is critical because it will reveal how many partons are in a proton and how large a parton is. Only with that knowledge will it be possible to conduct simulations that are more complex. The answers to those questions will also determine how quickly, if at all, this sort of research will develop.

If nucleons are composed of relatively few partons, perhaps several hundred or a few thousand, then computer simulations will show great promise. If, on the other hand, partons are small and each nucleon contains millions or, God forbid, billions of them, it is quite likely that this approach will proceed very slowly. Though I do not know what the answer is, I have a terrible suspicion the number will be at the high end of the range.

Mock Simulations

Whether or not computer simulations ever keep their promise, it is important to bear in mind that they are still the only option for making systematic, detailed predictions. Because the reductive model is not capable of assimilating *emergent order* mathematically, we will never have a comprehensive set of equations that capture the essence of these complex phenomena. The best we can hope for, either mathematically or computationally, are synopses and approximations.

Now, clearly I do not have access to a spacetime simulator, but that does not mean I cannot say anything about the sorts of things it might uncover. Such a simulator will do nothing more than lend precision to the very same concepts I have been presenting throughout this book. It will show how far a proton orbits from its neutron in deuterium, how tightly it is bound, how nucleons are arranged in various atomic nuclei, how many partons are released from a proton during neutrogenesis, and how complex atoms generate their EM spectra, among many other things. Collectively, these findings will facilitate some very specific predictions about nature. In the meantime, it is perfectly reasonable to use the concepts I have been developing to offer some predictions about what the simulator might ultimately help us discover.

The way to proceed is to keep one eye on all the relevant objects and forces, and the other eye on the existing empirical data for the phenomena we want to describe. Working back and forth between the two, we can piece together a serviceable picture of at least the large-scale structure of multinucleonic atoms. A simulation, by its nature, would not proceed in a logical fashion from premises to conclusions. It would instead, over the course of many iterations, eventually settle into an equilibrium state that reflects the dynamic nature of the phenomenon in question. Indeed, nature itself does the same thing, balancing competing forces until a compromise is, or is not, found. That must also be our goal in these mock simulations.

What follows in the next few sections, therefore, are my own predictions about what the computer simulations will eventually show us. If you regard this as an irredeemably unscientific approach, I certainly will not argue with you. These speculations are meant only as examples, and are not intended to be the final word on nucleonic geometry.

Period Two

Three pieces of information are especially relevant to determining the proton configurations of the elements. The neutron configurations are always the same and, locked tightly in the neutron core, have nothing directly to do with the chemical properties of an atom. These three are:

1. Proton orbitals have an effective nuclear angular momentum of zero. What this means, in practice, is that multiple protons can inhabit the same shell without running into one another. It also means those orbitals need not revolve in simple circles. In some cases, a proton will "orbit" entirely on one side or in one isolated quadrant of a shell.

2. Protons do not always arrange themselves in the most efficient configuration to evacuate spacetime from the core. Protons must balance their own internal equilibria against the low pressure in the core. This means we need to look beyond simply the number of protons to determine how they are organized.

3. Related to #2, the additional evidence we need in order to understand proton orbitals comes primarily from their chemical properties. As a rule, whenever two different orbital configurations appear equally plausible, the one that best explains the atom's chemical behavior is preferable. This will become even more obvious during the discussion of chemistry in Chapter 8.

The diagrams in the following sections represent the nuclear configurations of elements three through ten on the periodic table. The neutron cores correspond to the most common isotopes of those elements. I have omitted the electrons for

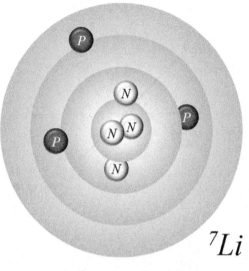

$1n^2\ 2n^2\ 1p^2\ 2p^1$

Figure 6.11:   Lithium-7

clarity but, as always, they are located directly outside of their corresponding nucleons. Also, the outermost electronic shells are obviously not drawn to scale. In reality, they are millions of times more voluminous than the nuclei.

Lithium

Lithium-7 (**Figure 6.11**) has two consecutive spherical proton orbitals, a full one and a valance orbital with only one proton. Hence, this atom is capable of forming one chemical bond. This element also illustrates the fact, discussed above, that protons do not always exhibit what might appear, on cursory inspection, to be the most efficient possible configuration. The three protons are not all located in the same shell. We know from boron (see below) that there is nothing wrong with having three in one shell, so there must be a reason that lithium does not do it that way. The only explanation for this apparent anomaly is that a single trigonal planar orbital, located just outside the neutron core, lowers the pressure too much for the protons to endure.

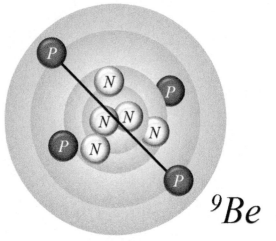

$$^9Be$$

$$1n^2\ 2n^3\ 1p^2\ 2p^2$$

Figure 6.12:   Beryllium-9

Put another way, the two inner protons are *almost* capable of stabilizing the neutrons by themselves. The 4-member neutron core is a very efficient arrangement all by itself, evidenced by the fact that ^{6}He (half-life=801 ms) is vastly more stable than ^{5}He (half-life=0.60 MeV), despite being more neutron-rich. The ^{7}Li valance proton merely picks up the slack. In a sense, four neutrons only need two-and-a-half protons to be stabilized, and so the third one is kept at a distance that halves its effect. This fact points to something else as well. Lithium is a *metal* because its valance shell is not as tightly bound to the atom as it would be if it were to exhibit the most efficient possible configuration.

Beryllium

Beryllium (**Figure 6.12**) is interesting because it has a full spherical valance shell, like helium, and yet still behaves as a metal. At first glance, this looks like a contradiction. However, from the example provided by lithium we can see that the protons are not packed into the core as efficiently as possible. They could exhibit a tetrahedral configuration but have settled instead on two concentric spheres. Therefore, the valance protons are

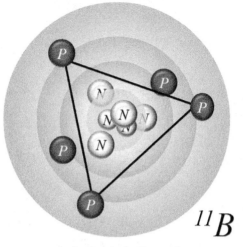

$$1n^2\ 2n^4\ 1p^2\ 2p^3$$

Figure 6.13: Boron-11

not as tightly bound to the atom as the two protons in helium (or in the other noble gases).

In general, when protons are not as tightly bound as possible they are capable of adopting a larger (relative to nonmetals and semi-metals) range of orbital characteristics. That makes them more susceptible to external forces, enabling them to resonate with and respond to incident waves and energy much more readily than nonmetals. That is what makes them good conductors of heat and electricity.

Boron

With boron (**Figure 6.13**), it begins to become clear that the inner, spherical orbital never accepts additional protons. More generally, a spherical orbital that is located outside of a filled proton orbital or the neutron core is, for all intents and purposes, inviolable. All of the noble gases have filled, two-proton orbitals in their outer shells, rendering them virtually inert. Inner, spherical orbitals of this variety (just outside the neutron core, a filled octahedral, or a filled icosahedral shell) are similarly impenetrable. A computer simulation will one day reveal

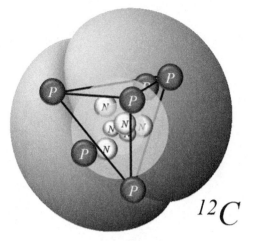

$$^{12}C$$

$$1n^2\ 2n^4\ 1p^2\ 2p^4$$

Figure 6.14:   Carbon-12

that this "six-two-six-two" alternation is necessary to keep the protons from evacuating spacetime too vigorously. Octahedral orbitals are very efficient (magic). Apparently, they need to be punctuated by two-proton spheres in order to prevent the pressure from dropping below their ideal convective range. In effect, the spherical shells push the octahedral shells apart, away from the core, lessening their effects.

Carbon

Carbon (**Figure 6.14**) is the first element on the table that clearly exhibits what we might call a *secondary* geometric structure. Specifically, the tetrahedral orbital spins in such a way as to create two electronic hemispheres. This is similar to the manner in which the octahedral shell in oxygen spins, also giving a dual hemisphere shape. In fact, beryllium also does this, though it is not obvious until it forms a chemical bond. Unlike oxygen, the four valance protons in carbon are also each capable of "spinning" in one particular quadrant. Hence, carbon can form one, two, three, or four chemical bonds.

This diagram represents the electronic shell geometry

in which the tetrahedron spins on its axis (perpendicular to the central sulcus), and which corresponds to two chemical bonds. Conversely, the beryllium diagram above shows the simple, spherical geometry of its monatomic state, not the hemispherical geometry it displays in its more common molecular configuration.

Nitrogen

There are a couple of interesting aspects of this atom's geometry that are clear right away. First, it is easy to see why nitrogen (**Figure 6.15**) is able to form three bonds, but of two different types. It has two features with two protons each, and one feature with a single proton. In Chapter 8, I will show how these features orient themselves in an ammonia molecule. Second, nitrogen's electronic shell geometry is identical to that predicted by quantum theory. Indeed, as I started creating these models, it did not take long for me to realize that all of these diagrams mirror the findings of quantum theory. Instead of denying the obvious, I used a software program based on the quantum wave function to generate the outermost electron shells of these graphics.

The idea that this confluence of theories could be merely a coincidence strikes me as patently absurd. What it suggests instead is that my theory reflects the unprecedented accuracy of the quantum wave function, but presents an alternative (far more physical and intuitive) to the Copenhagen interpretation of that function. It was never my intention to dispute either the wave function or, for that matter, any of the other mathematical descriptions of modern physics; if we consider nothing more than their astonishing accuracy, these formulas clearly capture something significant about the natural world. But by themselves these equations, however accurate, only capture the relationships between observable phenomena (they are positivistic). They do not say anything about the unobservable phenomena (reality) that underlie the parts we can actually see. My theory,

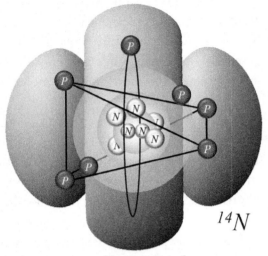

$$1n^2\ 2n^5\ 1p^2\ 2p^5$$

Figure 6.15: Nitrogen-14

on the other hand, is concerned exactly with explaining those unseen forces and objects that have prompted the creation of the mathematical expressions we already have.

   With all of this in mind, it is difficult to deny that the quantum wave function must have something of substance to say about the balance of forces in the atomic nucleus, since that is what gives rise to the electronic shell geometry. It is critical to bear in mind here that the wave function, like all mathematical expressions, is nothing but a symbolic representation of ratios between numerical quantities; by itself, it does not suggest any particular interpretation (e.g., the Copenhagen interpretation). It is very likely that this equation can be adapted to describe something for which it was not originally designed, but which may in fact lend it a more intuitive relationship to reality.

Oxygen

   It is commonly believed that oxygen (**Figure 6.16**) forms two chemical bonds because it is striving to achieve a noble gas electron configuration. However, if chemical bonds

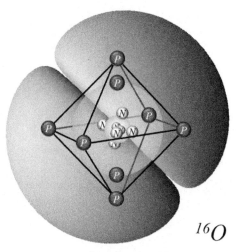

^{16}O

$1n^2\ 2n^6\ 1p^2\ 2p^6$

Figure 6.16: Oxygen-16

had anything to do with overlapping electron orbitals, it would seem that a water molecule, for example, would exhibit a linear rather than bent geometry. Oxygen's octahedral valance orbital spins on an axis perpendicular to the central sulcus, isolating three electrons on each side of the atom, and resulting in a symmetrical hemispheric arrangement. In fact, this picture of oxygen, though accurate for its monatomic state, conceals a fascinating ability—a *tertiary* geometric structure—that I will explain in Chapter 8, and which only becomes apparent with the full power of this theory.

Fluorine

Fluorine (**Figure 6.17**) has one, not seven, valance protons (and electrons). Perhaps the most pressing question this raises is, why does fluorine behave so differently from lithium or sodium, also with only a single valance proton? The answer points to the extreme difference between a proton located just outside of a full octahedral shell, on the one hand, and just outside a full spherical shell, on the other. In lithium, the valance proton is barely necessary and is kept away from the core to

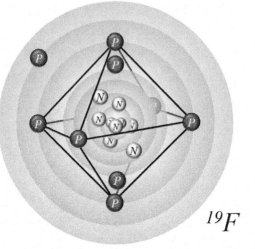

$$^{19}F$$

$$1n^2\ 2n^6\ 3n^2\ 1p^2\ 2p^6\ 3p^1$$

Figure 6.17:   Fluorine-19

lessen its effect. By contrast, the valance proton in fluorine is stressed nearly to the breaking point, forced to evacuate, all by itself, the spacetime pumped up to it by six protons just below.

Notice that the most common isotopes of both neon and fluorine each have the same ten-neutron core. Therefore, fluorine is not only required to do the same amount of neutron stabilization with one fewer proton, but it is required to do it with a far less efficient arrangement; a full spherical orbital, because of its symmetry, is more than twice as good as a single-proton orbital. What all this means is that fluorine is desperate for some assistance, and that explains its extreme *electronegativity* and chemical reactivity. Viewed psychiatrically, lithium is relaxed and easygoing, while fluorine is violently sociopathic.

Neon

Since we already know what helium looks like, neon (**Figure 6.18**) provides us our first example of the *periodicity* of the periodic table. Both of these gases have a filled two-proton spherical shell, which, as mentioned, is virtually impenetrable.

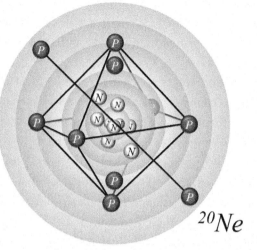

$1n^2\ 2n^6\ 3n^2\ 1p^2\ 2p^6\ 3p^2$

Figure 6.18:   Neon-20

Any additional protons must be added to a new shell, outside of it. The noble gases are largely inert because a spherical shell (just outside octahedral orbitals) is very tightly bound, making it extremely difficult (impossible, as far as I can tell) for other atoms to alter its geometry. The extreme behavior of a fluorine atom's valance proton is, in neon, focused on its nuclear counterpart rather than on an external atom. That explains why such spherical orbitals are so tightly bound. This can be contrasted with the situation in column two (alkaline earth metals) in which the two-proton valance shell is not as tightly bound. There, the protons are capable of adopting a double-lobed, hemispherical electronic geometry and, therefore, of making two chemical bonds.

Ionization

An atomic electron is not a discrete particle of matter. It is the point on an atom's electronic shell where a nucleon's polar jet reaches cosmological equilibrium. Since an atom cannot lose its protons, neither can it lose its electrons. *Ionization*, therefore, has nothing to do with stripping electrons off of an atom. If a nuclear proton is ionized (completely relaxed), the electron is not stripped, but simply ceases to exist. Nevertheless, the valance protons undergo a vaguely analogous process that explains this phenomenon.

Ionization refers to changes in chemical reactivity that correspond to changes in the energy states of an atom. The way to ionize an atom is to add energy, bumping it into progressively higher energy states. Each successively higher energy state corresponds to a slower series of derivative axes. Protons are stabilized by high pressure, and therefore, slow down when the pressure rises. When the valance protons slow down, they become less tightly bound to their host atom. This is not to imply that they are likely to drift away, only that they do not push as hard on their electronic shell when they slow down. And, since it is the shell that determines the strength of resistance of an atom to any sort of intrusion, highly ionized (more relaxed) valance orbitals are, all things being equal, more likely to form chemical bonds.

Ionization energy, therefore, is the quantity of energy needed to bump the valance orbital into the next slower series of derivative axes. Also in connection with ionization, as I will show in Chapter 8, in order to form a chemical bond, the valance protons must change their average locations, and that requires less energy when those protons are more relaxed (ionized).

7

Light

We have already seen in general how hydrogen and, by extension, the rest of the elements, generate their EM spectra. To evacuate spacetime from the region of space in the immediate vicinity of the nucleus, neutrons and protons orbit in a manner that minimizes the frequency with which their south polar jets pass through any point on their respective electronic shells. The resulting complex pattern is generated by a series of interdependent derivative axes, each of which is derived by rotating the poles of the previous one. This pattern is fairly straightforward in hydrogen, with only one proton. In multinucleonic atoms, usually with several nucleons in a single orbital, there is no way, absent a computer simulation, to figure out exactly which spectral line is associated with which axis or which nucleon. Nevertheless, given the ease with which this model explains hydrogen, we can be very confident that the same behavior, if more complex, takes place in all atoms.

Finally, each energy state of each orbital corresponds to an entire series of spectral lines, not to only one particular line, and no single orbital emits lines from two different energy states at the same moment. Even so, two different orbitals in the same atom may very well emit some of the same spectral lines at the same time. Indeed, such internal resonances between orbitals are likely to be fairly common.

From this model of the atom, we now know that an electron is not an independent particle of matter, but rather is the bump, the termination shock, on the electronic shell at the far end of a nucleon's polar jet. A *free electron* is a spacetime shock

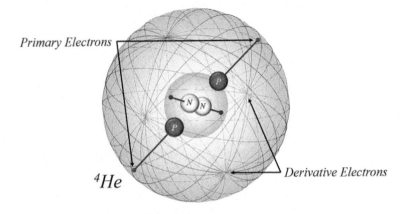

Figure 7.1:   Derivative Electrons
Not only the south polar jets themselves, but every one of the derivative axes creates bumps on the electronic shell. These *derivative electrons* are also responsible for light waves.

wave caused by any number of phenomena, including neutron decay, as well as others I will describe in this chapter and elsewhere. In addition to the primary bump on the electronic shell—the one we would naturally identify as *the* electron—there are smaller bumps (**Figure 7.1**) corresponding to every one of the derivative axes. This is so because each of these axes is responsible for rotating another axis, which itself sends the nucleon's jet through some points (the poles) more than others. We could then make a case that a hydrogen atom actually has dozens of *derivative electrons*, each of which corresponds in its intensity and orbital velocity to one of the atom's spectral lines.

Now, with this model in mind, it does not take much imagination to see how light is transmitted. As the bumps on the electronic shell orbit the atom, they impart disturbances to the ambient spacetime. The wavelength and amplitude of these disturbances are directly proportionate to the orbital velocity and intensity, respectively, of the bumps that cause them. There is no such thing as an *electromagnetic field*. The ambient spacetime is more than sufficient to transmit these disturbances. Moreover, the waves of energy are always created smoothly and continuously; there are no particle characteristics (quanta) to be found. I will demonstrate shortly where that illusion comes from. If you have the queasy feeling I have just reintroduced the *luminiferous aether*, you are not far off. Spacetime, in this incarnation, is exactly the substance the old Michelson-Morley experiments tried unsuccessfully to detect. For that reason it is worth taking some time to see why those experiments were unsuccessful.

Revenge of the Aether

The Michelson-Morley experiments failed for a very simple reason: the researchers assumed the aether would flow right *through* matter or be *dragged* by it, rather than flowing *around* it like a fluid. As I have argued throughout this book, spacetime resists compression, and the earth (as well as every other piece of matter) possesses a gravitational field in the form of a spacetime pressure gradient. As the earth moves through space, the ambient spacetime does not pass right through the planet; it does not pass through the magnetic field; it does not even pass through the earth's gravitational field. Instead, spacetime flows *around* the gravitational field, leaving the spacetime at the surface virtually stationary (**Figure 7.2**). This is true no matter how fast, or relative to what, the earth is moving. Hence, the aether experiment, which is designed to detect a difference in the speed of light parallel and perpendicular to the direction of motion, detects nothing at the earth's surface. The surface is *absolutely* stationary relative to the fabric of space and time itself. If we were to place the experiment in a moving vehicle (like an airplane or spaceship), it still wouldn't work, because spacetime does not flow unimpeded through solid objects. The pocket of spacetime inside the vehicle moves, like the air, right along with it. Clocks slow down on airplanes and spacecraft because the entire vehicle—and the spacetime within it—is compressed in the direction of motion, much as spacetime is compressed within a gravitational field. Spacetime does not flow through the craft.

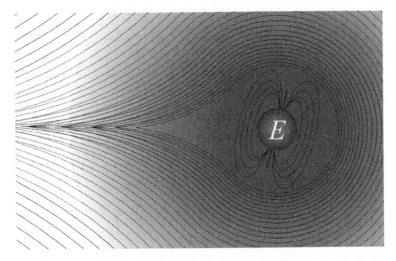

Figure 7.2:   Spacetime Flow Around the Earth
As the earth moves through space, the ambient spacetime flows around, not through, the earth's gravitational and magnetic fields. It also flows around the atmosphere and the earth itself. At the surface, the spacetime is absolutely stationary. The Michelson-Morley experiment depends on a difference in the velocity of the aether perpendicular and parallel to the earth's direction of motion. Therefore, the repeated failure of this experiment over the past century has not demonstrated the nonexistence of the aether.

Thankfully, we already saw nature's successful version of the Michelson-Morley experiment when we noted, in connection with galactic rotation, the Doppler shift of starlight both toward and away from the center of the galaxy. Spacetime, flowing toward the galaxy's rim, shifts stars into the blue if they are farther out than Earth and into the red if they are closer in. Though it is more than a century late, I believe this observation of the galactic-scale flow of spacetime (aether) at least partly vindicates Michelson and Morley, despite the fact they completely misconceived the substance they were looking for.

Odd as it sounds, it should be possible to create a spacetime flow within an evacuated vessel (a vacuum), using nothing more elaborate than a very powerful turbine (**Figure 7.3**). Since spacetime resists compression by matter, the blades of a fan ought to push it around just as they push around air. If a la-

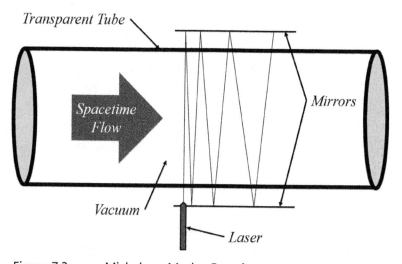

Figure 7.3:   Michelson-Morley Experiment
Placing a powerful turbine (to the left of this diagram) within an evacuated tube should generate a measurable spacetime flow. If the laser light is stretched when reflected back and forth between mirrors located outside of the tube, the aether will have been detected. It is important to keep the laser and mirrors outside of the tube so they are not warped by the spacetime flow.

ser beam is stretched when directed through the spacetime flow perpendicular to its motion, the aether (spacetime) will have been observed. I will not try to predict whether these challenges can be overcome, but it is certainly worth the effort to try. Even if there are technical constraints that make this experiment impossible, the astronomical observations remain convincing.

Back to the Future

It is impossible to overstate the significance of reintroducing the aether (in the form of spacetime) to the cosmos. All of twentieth century physics can be understood as an effort to conceive the universe in the absence of any medium through which light is propagated. Einstein's version of spacetime as well as the field theories of quantum mechanics (the dominant positivistic and mathematical media of physics) are necessary and meaningful only if the aether does not exist. Indeed, these theories were conceived explicitly in response to the failures of the Michelson-Morley experiment. If there really is a medium that pervades space, the basic assumption underlying all of modern physics collapses and the whole enterprise becomes a quixotic effort to explain a nonexistent fact. This is where we find ourselves today.

The counterintuitive, mind-bending complexities of both Relativity Theory and quantum mechanics issue from the effort to describe the universe absent its main feature, *physical spacetime*. This situation is analogous to the condition of astronomy during the reign of Ptolemy's geocentric universe. With its epicycles, deferents, equants, and eccentrics—all interrelated and introduced *ad hoc* whenever a new observation had to be explained—his model worked, more or less, but purchased its success at the cost of transforming a simple, elegant system into a horrendously complex monster. Quantum theory is the same sort of monster. And this analogy goes even deeper. Aristarchus, way back in ancient Greece, had already developed a rudimentary heliocentric model. But because the planets' orbits are slightly elliptical, his predictions (based on circular orbits) were less accurate than Ptolemy's, despite the fact that he was much closer to the truth. It was not until the revolutionary work of Kepler, who uncovered the subtle elliptical orbits of the planets, that the heliocentric model outperformed Ptolemy's.

Similarly, the aether theory predates relativity and quantum theory. But because spacetime behaves more subtly than the pioneers could have known, the extreme complexities of twentieth century physics were, like those of the Ptolemaic model, thought necessary to bring theory into line with observation. Only now, more than a century later, is there a model of the aether robust enough to outperform relativity and quantum theory.

What we should expect from this back-to-the-future scenario is that physics is suddenly going to become vastly simpler, just as it did after Kepler. A complex theory is not always proof of an underlying, complex reality. It is more often a symptom of desperately trying to force, in violation of Occam's Razor, a fundamentally flawed model onto facts that contradict it.

The failure to discover the aether was the result of assuming it passes right through or is dragged by matter, just as the failure to confirm the heliocentric cosmos was the result of assuming circular planetary orbits. The common sense models turned out to be right all along, but because they depend on subtleties that are far from obvious, complex *ad hoc* models supplanted them—at least temporarily. Now that we have our light-propagating medium back, we can easily restore physics to the simple, elegant model we all know in our hearts it should be. Therefore, to make physics *physical* again, we must reacquaint ourselves with the following common-sense statements of principle:

1. Light is never a particle and a particle is never a wave.
2. The two phenomena are unambiguous, mutually incompatible, and easily distinguishable.
3. Nothing in nature flip-flops back and forth from one to the other.
4. Nothing comes into or goes out of existence without a clear Newtonian explanation.
5. No phenomenon is intrinsically probabilistic.
6. As Einstein suspected, God does not play dice with the universe.

Derivative Axes, Revisited

The spinning bumps (electrons) of an atom's electronic shell impart waves to spacetime, resulting in light (defined as all wavelengths from gamma to radio). Decaying neutrons, for example, generate gamma rays as they rotate frantically in an effort to maintain their equilibria. More generally, anything that either spins or vibrates creates waves in spacetime and could be classified as light. The discreteness of light transmission is the result of an atom's derivative axes; only certain rotational velocities are permitted by the geometric demands of nucleonic spin as space-time is evacuated from the atom. In the chapter on protons, I briefly mentioned the three conditions of equilibrium, but did not go into much detail. Now that we have a more complete picture of an atom, we can further develop this notion.

When the proton in hydrogen spins, it pulls spacetime in through its north pole and evacuates it from its south pole. The distant end of the spacetime jet, as it spins, defines an elec-tronic shell, the termination shock, where the ambient pressure pushes back on the atom with a force equal to that jet. Though this is the *cosmological equilibrium* of the atom, it is slightly differ-ent from the analogous phenomenon in stars. Specifically, stars do not pull spacetime in and then expel it, but only *liberate* it. That means the spacetime pressure gradient in stars is a smooth (inverse square law) distribution from the surface all the way to the heliopause. By contrast, atoms exhibit a sharp distinction between *inside* and *outside* the atom. To visualize this, picture the polar jet, fired through a region (inside the atom) of very low pressure, suddenly smacking against the ambient spacetime at the limit of that low pressure region. It is like firing a garden hose at the surface of a swimming pool. The stream penetrates the surface a small distance, true, but there is also a very intense and well-defined point of collision—the termination shock. This point of collision in an atom is the electronic shell, specifically, the electron.

In view of this dynamic, it stands to reason that the pres-sure of the ambient spacetime has much to say about the equilib-rium condition of the atom. If we knew nothing about derivative axes, we might expect that the proton would spin at whatever velocity allowed it to maintain an ideal internal pressure at all times: slower when the ambient pressure is high, faster when the ambient pressure drops. By doing so, the pressure exerted on the proton's core by the jet could remain constant regardless of external conditions. If, by analogy, we want a jet engine to maintain a constant thrust, regardless of atmospheric pressure, we would have to increase the power as the altitude increases (and the air pressure decreases). This could be done in a smooth, continuous manner, because the engine does not also spin.

However, we now know that proton spin is dictated by the complex geometric requirements of an entire series of derivative axes. When an atom is spinning in accordance with one of these series (is in a particular energy state) it pulls in and evacuates spacetime at a constant rate, *independent of the external pressure*. That means the proton is always pushing either a little too hard or not quite hard enough to maintain an ideal core pressure.

We also know that only certain sets of derivative axes allow for the symmetrical absorption and evacuation of spacetime. Speed up or slow down the proton only slightly (placing it in between two accepted energy states), and spacetime will either begin to pool within the electronic shell or will be evacuated so fast that the jet will lose its power. Neither of these states represents an equilibrium condition and would deteriorate immediately. Yet because the acceptable energy states will not allow the proton to remain at its ideal internal pressure, the atom is always under a greater or lesser amount of stress (**Figure 7.4**). As the ambient pressure rises, the proton's convection increasingly stresses the core by raising its pressure beyond its equilibrium value. It finally becomes so high that the atom jumps, all at once, into the next (slower) rotational pattern, relaxing the pressure on the core. Likewise, as the ambient pressure drops, the proton core gradually decompresses until it reaches a critical point, after which it instantly leaps into the next (faster) series of approved derivative axes, pumping the pressure back up. Hence, the three contributions to the equilibrium state of an atom are:

1. The ambient pressure of spacetime (the temperature).
2. The symmetrical rate of spacetime evacuation and absorption by a series of derivative axes.

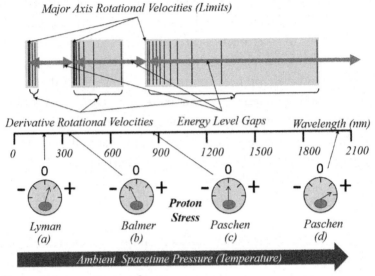

Figure 7.4:   Proton Stress

Starting from the top of the diagram, the shortest wavelength (on the left) of each series of derivative axes (energy states) is a direct measure of the proton's actual rotational velocity. The longest wavelength in each series is the rotational velocity of the nth derivative axis. Hence, the distance between the limits is the gap between energy states. Protons are stressed, one way or the other, by any ambient pressure that does not perfectly correspond to a limit. If the ambient pressure is higher than the ideal for the Lyman series (a), the proton's constant convective velocity gradually compresses its constituent partons, pushing it toward a jump to the Balmer series. If, on the other hand, the ambient pressure is lower than the ideal for the Balmer series (b), the partons gradually decompress because of the relative weakness of the proton's polar jet, pushing against the core, and leading to a jump to the Lyman series. If the pressure just happens to be perfect (c), the proton will neither compress nor decompress until the ambient pressure changes. And finally, if the ambient pressure rises dramatically (d), the proton will rapidly compress and will soon jump into the next highest (slower) energy state.

3. The internal pressure of the proton (i.e., the pressures of its constituent partons).

Condition number one varies continuously over an enormous range, from the extremes within a stellar core all the way to the intense negative pressures in an atomic nucleus. Condition two varies over a large but discontinuous range, adopting only certain discrete values. Condition three varies continuously over a small range in protons and a small but somewhat larger range in neutrons (larger, because of parton expansion during decay). Now we need to look at the behavior of an atom as it jumps between energy states.

Energy State Transitions

If the pressure on an atom is somewhat higher than the ideal for its current set of derivative axes, the nucleon(s) will gradually expand under the stress of its excessively energetic polar jet. The inflexible geometry of the axes lock the atom into a state in which the jet pushes too hard to keep the nucleon(s) stable indefinitely. Eventually, even if the ambient pressure remains constant, the atom will reach a critical point at which it must, at least temporarily, jump into the next (slower) series of axes in order to relieve the excess pressure. Still, if the original rotational pattern (energy state) was preferable, given the ambient pressure, it will quickly jump right back. The atom will do this spontaneously even if nothing else happens to it (e.g., it absorbs a *photon*).

When an atom jumps into a higher energy state, it spins more slowly, evidenced by the longer and less energetic waves emitted by warmer atoms. Therefore, an energetic atom is actually a more relaxed (more ionized) atom. Within a stellar core, protons barely move at all and neutrons are stable. Indeed, a proton, as opposed to a hydrogen atom, is under so much pressure that it simply mills around rather than spinning in a controlled way. It is completely relaxed (totally ionized).

A leap to a higher energy state is accompanied by a sudden change in the rate of spacetime absorption and evacuation— a new equilibrium condition. Specifically, the atom permits a greater quantity of spacetime to remain within the electronic shell, increasing its extrinsic mass. This sudden change means the atom must rapidly absorb spacetime from the region of space just outside of the electronic shell, and that explains how atoms absorb energy when they jump to a higher energy state. Likewise, when they fall to a lower state, they expel spacetime very rapidly to accommodate the requirements of the new, faster series of derivative axes. This expulsion manifests itself as a decrease in extrinsic mass and a shock wave that we interpret as a free electron.

Unlike in a hydrogen atom, the nucleons in multinucleonic atoms are not required to jump into different energy states all at once. Only those nucleons that are bound by an orbital configuration (series of axes) must jump in unison. Naturally, this means the energy states of such atoms are much more complex than those of hydrogen. Exactly which orbitals will jump and what effect such jumps will have on the rest of the atom varies considerably from atom to atom and, as always, only a computer simulation will allow us to piece together the whole puzzle.

Any change to one orbital will alter the pressure of the entire atom, including the neutron core. Such a change might very well prompt another orbital to jump as well. Indeed, a jump to a higher energy state by one orbital could actually cause a different orbital to jump to a lower state, in an attempt to balance the pressure in cases in which doing so gets the atom closer to an ideal value. The possibilities are virtually endless, but as long as we keep it in mind, we do not need to get bogged down in all of this complexity to understand the general principles.

Heat

Using the principles just discussed, we can understand what it means to heat or cool an object. When we heat, say, a block of iron, what we are actually doing is increasing the ambient spacetime pressure. As I have shown, atoms respond to higher ambient pressure by leaping into higher (more relaxed) energy states, absorbing spacetime from the surrounding region. It is in this way that an object is heated and is able to retain such heat. If we then allow the block to cool, the atoms on the surface, because the pressure is lowest there, will jump to lower energy states and pump out a quantity of spacetime that corresponds to the different requirements of the new series of axes. The liberated spacetime pushes down against the block as well as up against the ambient spacetime, creating a pressure gradient. As always, a pressure gradient is a gravitational field. Hence, hot objects are slightly heavier (have more extrinsic mass) than cold ones, particularly while in the process of cooling.

Outside the object, the gradually diminishing gradient radiates the heat away from the block. At the same time, spacetime liberated from deeper inside the block will tend to compress atoms closer to the surface, causing them to jump back and forth from higher to lower energy states as they alternately absorb spacetime and then liberate it. Collectively, this behavior is the *conduction* of heat through the material from regions of higher temperature to regions of lower temperature. Metals are better heat conductors than nonmetals because their valance protons are capable of adopting a greater variety of configurations, thereby accelerating the transfer of heat from high to low pressure regions. Still, even in metals, the heat associated with the non-valance proton orbitals, as well as the neutron orbitals, prevents the process from being instantaneous. By contrast, all the orbitals in nonmetals (insulators) must wait for the stress of a given set of derivative axes to become untenable before it can leap, transferring heat to an adjacent atom or to the surrounding space.

Brownian Motion

Heat has nothing to do with atomic *vibrations*, nor with the *kinetic energy* of atoms. Other than their nuclear asymmetries—which give rise to magnetic moments—atoms do not possess a physical mechanism that would allow them to vibrate or move around in proportion to their energies. Clearly, magnetic moments have nothing to do with heat, as it is just as easy to heat helium as it is to heat hydrogen, though the former does not, while the latter does, have a wobble.

The origin of this concept (what we can call the *kinetic theory of thermodynamics*) comes from the observation that tiny grains (such as dust or pollen), suspended in a gas or liquid, wiggle and dance as if the atoms were physically slamming into them. Known as *Brownian motion*, Einstein calculated the statistical relationship between the energy of the atoms (or molecules) and the movement of these dust grains. Naturally, he assumed the atoms imparted their energy to the grains by ramming into them, and from that assumption he concluded that thermodynamics is the measure of the kinetic energy (either vibratory or rectilinear) of the liquid or gas particles.

It is certainly true that atoms in motion possess kinetic energy. When they run into something they compress it, and compressed spacetime is heat. But this energy of motion is usually only a trivial fraction of a particle's total energy. Most of its energy comes from the spacetime pressure maintained inside the electronic shell. When an atom releases heat, it does so by dropping to a lower energy state, which means a faster series of derivative axes. Such a jump is accompanied by the sudden release of whatever quantity of spacetime is necessary to accommodate the new, faster, rotational velocity. It is this sudden release of spacetime—in the form of a shock wave—that pushes against any dust or pollen grains in the vicinity of such atoms. The atoms themselves need not move much at all.

This same phenomenon is responsible for keeping a balloon inflated. The current theory explains the pressure inside a balloon as the collective kinetic energy of the gas molecules physically slamming into the latex skin. As the gas is heated, the average velocity of the atoms increases and the balloon expands. However, we now know that atoms and molecules actually *slow down* when they are heated, evidenced by the longer, slower waves emitted by hotter atoms. Nor, as mentioned, do these particles possess any machinery with which to propel themselves about. Therefore, the latex of the balloon is actually pushed outwards by the collective effect of the atoms as they release spacetime as countless tiny shock waves.

I have shown that spacetime does not move unimpeded through solid objects. The latex skin of a balloon is not only solid, but is a nonmetal insulator. As a result, spacetime can only pass through the balloon by compressing the atoms in the latex molecules, forcing them to absorb spacetime from the interior of the balloon as they jump to higher (slower) energy states. They then must give up that spacetime by falling to lower (faster) energy states, expelling it outside of the balloon. It takes time for nonmetals to do this. In theory, though perhaps not in practice, rarified spacetime—with no actual gas molecules within it—could be used to inflate a balloon. Nevertheless, even in a typical gas-filled balloon, it is the spacetime, not the gas molecules that push out against the latex skin.

Light Absorption

Only now do we finally have enough information to explain the absorption of light, a phenomenon that has, over the course of the twentieth century, led to nearly all of the mind-bending weirdness of modern physics. Here is a brief review of the salient points:

1. The different series of derivative axes (the energy states) associated with an orbital permit an atom to regulate its nucleons' equilibria, but only in the discontinuous way commensurate with the three conditions of equilibrium (see above).
2. An atom absorbs or releases spacetime, increasing or decreasing its internal pressure, only in the discrete amounts corresponding to the differences between the acceptable energy states.
3. At any moment, the nucleons in an atom are stressed, to a greater or lesser degree, because they are always locked into an energy state (a convective velocity) that does not

perfectly reflect the ideal balance between the ambient pressure and the pressure their jets exert on their cores.

4. Identical atoms under identical conditions, even those in the same sample, will not behave identically, because they do not all exhibit the same degree of nucleonic stress. Some will be closer to the tipping point than others.

If a wave generated by one atom (or anything else for that matter) impinges on a distant atom, there is a possibility that the second atom will absorb the energy of that wave. We will look at the simple, classical example of a *photon* striking a detector and releasing an *electron*—the so-called *photoelectric effect*.

Entanglement

Now that we have a light-propagating medium, we can assume that the transmission of light through spacetime is exactly analogous to the transmission of sound through air. All of the paradoxes that seem to follow from accepting this simple picture have been the result of not understanding the goings-on at either end of the process. As we now have a very robust model of atoms, we can resolve all of these paradoxes.

The first thing to note about light waves is that they are generated by spinning electron orbitals. These orbitals, however complex, always have at least one plane across which they exhibit bilateral symmetry. Essentially, if the electron is moving up on one side of this plane, it (or its counterpart) is moving down on the other side (**Figure 7.5**). That means photons (if they are misconceived as particles), emitted on opposite sides of this plane of symmetry, have opposite *spins*. One will exhibit an "up" spin while its counterpart on the other side exhibits a "down" spin. Photon spin is nothing more than a record of the direction of the electron orbital that created the wave. The entanglement of photons, therefore, is a perfectly obvious and *physical* process. The strangeness of this phenomenon (the apparent ability of the two widely separated particles to remain in instantaneous com-

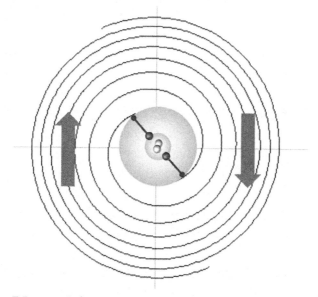

Figure 7.5:   Spin
Light waves emitted from opposite sides of an atom are created by electrons spinning in opposite directions. Hence, if the wave is mischaracter-
ized as two entangled photons, they appear to be in direct communication, regardless of their separation.

munication) is related only to the fact that we cannot actually
measure which way the electrons are spinning. The correlation
between entangled photon pairs, regardless of their separation,
is not the result of any sort of "spooky action at a distance." It is
merely an artifact of the bilaterally symmetric manner in which
they were emitted.

From the above paragraph, we now know that *spin* must
be added to the traditional wave properties of phase, amplitude,
and frequency. All four of these (yes, including phase, *gauge theory* notwithstanding) influence the manner in which an incident
wave interacts with an atom in a detector. To register a detection
event, the wave and the atom must be in phase, have the same
spin direction, and share a common frequency. The amplitude of
the wave must be sufficient to have an effect on the atom. Finally,
the nucleons in the orbital with which the wave shares these values must be close enough to their tipping points for the wave to

push them over the edge, into a new energy state. We will look at each one of these factors in turn.

Frequency

Because of the complex series of derivative axes in both the transmitting and absorbing atoms, the frequencies of both are always complex affairs, simultaneously exhibiting the whole range of values corresponding to some particular array of energy levels. Unless the emitter and the detector are both made of the same material, there is no chance the waves and the atoms will resonate in a simple one-to-one way. Instead, one or more frequencies from the emitter will resonate with one or more frequencies of the detector, and more often than not those frequencies will belong to various mid-level derivative axes (simply because there are so many more of them) rather than the nth axis that tracks the path of the primary electron.

The minimum requirement is that at least one frequency from the emitter matches at least one frequency in the detector atom. This picture is further complicated by the fact that the flexible valance protons in metals, of which experimental detectors are always constructed, can be coaxed into new orbital configurations by the waves themselves. As a result, a metal atom might not exhibit the right frequency until a wave impinges on it, forcing it into a new resonance pattern. That is why metals are much better detectors than nonmetals.

Phase

Besides sharing at least one frequency, the wave and atom must also be *in phase* in order to register a detection event. In particular, the wave must constructively reinforce or destructively interfere with the electron orbital with which it shares a frequency. If the wave and orbital reinforce one another, the wave will mimic the effect of dropping the ambient pressure around the atom. With each orbit, the nucleon fires its polar jet right into the trough of the incident wave (**Figure 7.6**), re-

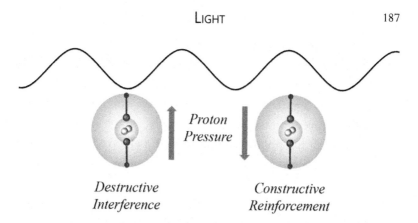

Figure 7.6:   Reinforcement-Interference
When an orbital and incident wave are in phase, the wave can either mimic the effect of increasing the ambient pressure (left), or decreasing it (right). The former pushes the orbital toward a jump to a higher (slower) energy state, while the latter pushes it toward a jump to a lower (faster) one.

ducing the pressure of that jet and lowering the pressure of the nucleon. In response, the atom may, if the amplitude of the incident wave is high enough and the nucleon is close enough to its tipping point, jump into the next (faster) energy level. When that happens, the affected nucleons rapidly pump out whatever quantity of spacetime is required in order to bring the pressure inside the electronic shell into agreement with the dynamics of the new, faster, series of derivative axes. That sudden release of spacetime is the shock wave (electron) detected by the detector. With reinforcement, the atom does not actually absorb the energy of the wave, and the wave continues past the atom. Indeed, this is the phenomenon behind the process of *laser cooling*, a technique used by scientists studying temperatures near absolute zero.

If, on the other hand, the wave interferes with the orbital, it will have the opposite effect, mimicking an increase in ambient pressure. With each orbit, the nucleons' jets will fire into the crest of the incident wave, canceling the wave and increasing the pressure on the relevant nucleons. Eventually, the orbital may reach its tipping point, stressing the nucleons and triggering a jump to a higher (slower) energy state. However, the ambient pressure may still favor the lower (faster) series and so, after a brief stay in the higher state, the atom quickly falls back to its lower state, releasing an electron. It is this phenomenon, rather than the case of constructive reinforcement, that gives the impression that an atom absorbs a photon and converts the energy of that photon into an emitted electron.

Consider that the wave is cancelled by the orbital with which it resonates, and indeed, the atom really does absorb some of this energy. The frequency of the incident wave and the energy of the freed electron are directly related; the frequency of the wave determines which orbital is affected. When that electron is emitted, it appears, for all the world, as if the entire photon was absorbed and subsequently re-emitted as an electron with an energy correlated to the frequency of that photon. However, it should now be obvious that the energy of the emitted electron comes from the atom, not from the photon. By analogy, the speed of your car is determined by how hard you push down on the accelerator, but the energy required to actually accelerate the car does not come from your foot. It comes from the engine. The photon (via its frequency) merely *determines how much* energy the electron will have. It does not *provide* that energy.

Spin

Spin is similar to phase, but whereas phase deals with the congruence of crests and troughs, spin is related to the relative angular orientation of the wave and electron orbital. While two entangled photons can be called *up* and *down*, as if there are only two possibilities, in practice, a wave or electron orbital can be oriented anywhere from zero to 720 degrees relative to one another (**Figure 7.7**). The spin value tells us whether the two are orbiting in the same plane and also whether they are orbiting in the same direction on that plane.

The plane on which the electrons orbit can be rotated through 360 degrees and the entire atom can be rotated through another 360 degrees. That is why spin values go all the way from

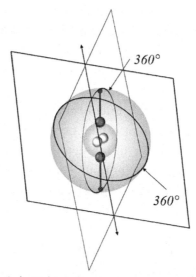

Figure 7.7:   Spin Orientation
The spin value of a wave refers to the angular orientation of the orbital
that generated it, as well as the direction of the electron within that orbital.
Since both the orbital and the whole atom can be rotated through 360°,
spin values range from zero to 720°.

zero to 720. To get back to its starting point, an orbital must
spin through 360 degrees, while the entire atom must also spin
through 360 degrees. Since waves and electron orbitals can both
be oriented anywhere within this 720-degree range, it is unlikely in any given case that the two will have the same spin. Still,
because there are so many atoms in the detector, it is almost certain, despite the low probability of spin parity in any particular
atom, that a given wave will easily find an atom with which it
shares the same angular orientation. Moreover, if the amplitude
is high enough, a wave can force (particularly in the case of a
metal) an orbital into spin parity if the two are out of sync by
only a few degrees.

You may be wondering why we would stop at 720 degrees. After all, the derivative axes of a given electron orbital
spin the poles of the previous axis over and over, presumably
multiplying the original 360 degrees dozens of times. Why, then,
should photon spin not track all the complexity of the electron

orbitals that give rise to it? The reason we stop at 720 is because when we rotate the plane of an orbital, we give rise to a separate frequency, a new spectral line. We do not simply rotate the same frequency through dozens of different orientations. Again, beyond 720 degrees of rotation, we are talking about a new derivative axis, a separate and distinct orbital period—a new wave. If spin parity depended on matching every frequency of the emitter with every frequency in the detector atoms, then it might make sense to expand the notion of spin to include all the tens of thousands of degrees through which an entire series of derivative axes passes. But because the rotation of each axis gives rise to a distinct wave, we need only consider the degrees of freedom of that wave, not all the subsequent waves derived from the rotation of the first one.

Amplitude

If a wave and atom have the same frequency, are in phase, and have the same spin, a detection event depends next on the amplitude of the wave. Briefly, the wave must be strong enough to mimic the drop or rise in ambient pressure necessary to trigger a nucleonic orbital to jump into the next energy state. Two factors are relevant: the strength of the wave itself, and the current stress level of the nucleons in question.

As we saw earlier, the discreteness of the energy states means they are never optimal; the nucleons' polar jets are always pushing a little too hard or not quite hard enough to maintain the equilibrium of their partons. This, because only certain, acceptable series of derivative axes allow the atom to both evacuate and absorb spacetime at the same rate. Consequently, all nucleons are gradually either decompressing or hyper-compressing, and each orbital (actually, each nucleon) is at a different point in this process, more or less close to jumping into a new energy state. It is this relative proximity to the tipping point, as well as the direction (either to a higher or lower state) toward which it is tipping, that determines how powerful an incident wave must be to trigger a detection event in a given time period.

Consider a wave of constant amplitude that is constructively reinforcing an orbital. If the atom with which it is resonating was, prior to the introduction of the wave, nearly at the point of jumping to a higher (slower) energy state, the wave will have to lower the atom's pressure all the way from its hypercompressed state to its decompressed state before triggering a jump to a lower (faster) energy state. By contrast, if that atom was already decompressed before the wave was introduced, it will take little to trigger the jump.

The opposite is true if the wave interferes with the orbital; it pushes a highly compressed nucleonic orbital into the next higher state quickly, but requires time to compress an already decompressed orbital. Combined with the state of the atom, then, the amplitude of the wave governs how quickly an atom is affected.

Also, it is reasonable to assume, particularly for detectors constructed of metal, that high amplitude waves are more able to influence the phase, frequency, and spin of the atoms upon which they impinge than those of low amplitude. In a sense, a powerful wave can grab hold of a metal atom and force it to march to a different drumbeat, even if the spin, phase, and frequency originally did not match up very well.

Finally, the amplitude of a wave decreases as the square of the distance from its source. Everything else being equal, atoms farther from the emitter are less likely to register a detection event than those closer to it.

The Frequency/Energy Illusion

We now return to the idea, mentioned earlier, that the energy of a freed electron does not come from the incident photon, but from its host atom. The photon merely dictates *which* orbital and therefore *how much* spacetime is released when the atom changes energy states. The energy from the photon does not transfer itself into the atom where it is subsequently trans-

formed into the released electron. The regular relationship between the frequency of the incident light and the energy of the
freed electron is due to the constant quantity of spacetime that is
pumped out of an atom when a given set of derivative axes is replaced by the next fastest set. This is the loose thread that, when
pulled, causes the whole Copenhagen interpretation of quantum
theory to unravel.

When light is emitted it is propagated as a wave in all
directions through space. Its energy, therefore, gets distributed
over an ever-increasing volume, causing it to weaken in proportion to the square of the distance from its source. However,
when the photon is detected, it seems, based on the energy of
the released electron, that all of the energy of the photon, regardless of the distance it has traveled, is focused on one particular location—it exhibits *non-locality*. If the photon has traveled
a great distance before being detected, it appears that the entire
wave, no matter how widely disbursed, somehow *knows* that a
detection event has occurred (perhaps a million light years from
the far side of the wave), and suddenly concentrates itself at that
discrete location.

This phenomenon creates the illusion (wave-particle du-
alism, non-locality) that the photon is spread probabilistically
across millions of light years *and* is in one particular place, all at
once. However, now that we know the energy of a freed electron
does not come from the photon, but from its host atom (based
on the regular relationship between two consecutive series of
derivative axes), we are no longer under any obligation to explain how a photon magically rematerializes after being spread
all over the universe. That is, we no longer must contend with
the *superposition* of particles, and the whole idea of an *uncollapsed
wave function* is meaningless. Nor is there any sense in claiming
that an *observation* is required in order to coax reality into some
discrete, measurable state; *Heisenberg's Uncertainty Principle* simply disappears.

Now, because the *frequency* of the photon dictates which

orbital will undergo a transition, it appears as if the energy of the released electron is related to the frequency of the incident photon. If we have already assumed (incorrectly) that the energy of this freed electron comes from the photon, rather than its host atom, then we must also assume that photon energy is related to frequency. Mercifully, we now know this is not correct. The energy of a light wave is, like all other waves, related to its amplitude, not its frequency. Light is always a wave, never a particle. There is no such thing as a *photon*, if by this term we mean a *particle* of light. The discreteness of a detection event is caused entirely by the relationship between energy levels in the affected atom. The freed electron gets all of its energy from the sudden expulsion by the nucleons of a precise quantity of spacetime that corresponds to the difference in internal pressure associated with two consecutive series of derivative rotational axes. The frequency of the light dictates *which* transition will take place. And, the amplitude determines how *fast* it will take place. But the atom itself determines the energy of, and imparts the energy to, the resultant shock wave (electron).

Extrapolating from the above discussion to the rest of quantum theory, we can eliminate all of the paradoxes related to superluminal communication as well as the probabilistic superposition of matter. Doing so not only restores the universe to a realistic, physical phenomenon, but it should put a decisive end to the Copenhagen interpretation of the quantum wave function. Anything that qualifies as a *detection event* is actually the measurement of a change in that which does the detecting, not a measurement of that which is supposedly being detected. In general, it is not correct to attribute the energy of a freed particle (shock wave) to an incident light wave. The probabilistic nature of such a measurement is related, in the ways discussed, to the frequency, amplitude, phase, and spin of both the emitted wave and the receiving atom, as well as to the stress on the relevant nucleons. It has nothing to do with a wave/particle in an indeterminate superposed state.

The illusory detection of such exotic entities as neutrinos, muons, gluons, quarks, and all the rest of the particle zoo, is nothing more than measurements of various and sundry goings-on within whatever is employed to make such measurements. These imaginary particles are artifacts of either a typical, run-of-the-mill spacetime wave of some kind, a confluence of waves that reinforce one another with some statistical regularity, or a spontaneous behavior of the detector atom that may or may not have anything straightforward to do with whatever might be going on outside of it. There is only one fundamental particle (the parton), and it comes in only two stable configurations (protons and neutrons). Everything else must be understood in terms of these three particles interacting with one another within normal space.

8

Chemical Bonds

Soon after I came up with the concept underlying the fundamental substance—my new conception of spacetime—I set myself the goal of explaining chemistry in terms of it. A theory of physics is only truly proven when it can form the foundations of chemistry. If the descriptions of chemical bonds I am about to give prove to be correct, then the sub-discipline of *theoretical physics* will be well on its way to completion.

Chemistry is so vast that it seems odd that we refer to it with only a single term. With the exception of physics, all of the natural sciences are either based on, or at the very least beholden to, chemistry. Indeed, physics itself is devoted to little more than explaining the forces that underlie this boundless discipline. Whether it is nuclear chemistry, geochemistry, organic chemistry, biochemistry, petro-chemistry, neurochemistry, or anything else, appending the word *chemistry* to the title says little more than, "We are dealing with this topic rigorously." Ignoring chemistry is tantamount to being unscientific.

Given the daunting scope of this discipline, I make no claim to completeness in this chapter. I am not going to run through all the various chemical bond types, and I am not going to try to extrapolate the physical properties of various compounds from theory alone. Only a computer simulation will permit anything so specific to become evident. Rather, I will examine a small number of examples in order to give a sense of how this theory is to be applied. In that respect, this is a decidedly *theoretical* presentation, and even if this theory proves wildly

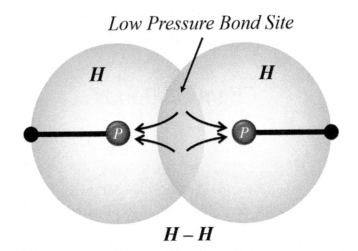

Figure 8.1:   H-H Bond

In the H-H bond, the north poles of both protons are, on average, aimed at the volume of space shared by the atoms, while the south poles propel the atoms, on average, in the direction of the bond site. Both the extent of the shared volume and the depth of the low pressure are proportionate to the strength of the bond.

successful, chemistry, as always, will remain a painstaking endeavor in need of dedicated scientists to unravel all of the details.

The H_2 Bond

The simplest chemical bond is the one that holds together two atoms of hydrogen. Now that we have a very robust model of atoms, we need do little more to understand the H-H bond than place two hydrogen atoms side by side and see what happens (**Figure 8.1**).

The first thing to notice is that the mechanisms for chemical bonds are the very same as those for nuclear bonds: the proton's south polar jet and the suction generated by its north pole. The difference in scale between chemical and nuclear bonds reflects the radical difference in stability between protons and neutrons. Nuclear bonds are very strong and very short because neutrons are incredibly demanding, in need of extremely low pressures in order to maintain their internal equilibria. By contrast, protons, which are the main players in chemical bonds, are already stable at SEP and make use of chemical bonds only for the sake of fine tuning an already workable situation. The ratios of the lengths and strengths of the chemical, H-H, bond in diatomic hydrogen (H$_2$) to the nuclear, P-N, bond in deuterium (^{2}H), reflects the dramatic difference in the urgency, if you will, between the desperate, literally existential, requirements of neutrons on the one hand, and the relatively trivial needs of protons on the other.

When two hydrogen atoms bond, their south polar jets push them, on average, in the direction of the bond site. At the same time, their north poles are aimed toward a common volume of space that was formerly part of each separate atom. The two atoms share a fraction of the volume within their electronic shells, thereby decreasing the demands of each of them by fifty percent, *with respect to that particular volume*. The sole purpose of a hydrogen atom is to evacuate spacetime from a spherical volume of space within the radius of its electronic shell in order to establish its cosmological equilibrium. By pairing up, each atom decreases its workload by half with respect to the fraction of that spherical volume that now belongs to both of them. And because protons do not have any effective nuclear angular momentum, it is not a problem that each member of the H-H molecule orbits in such a way as to, on average, orient itself in an asymmetric manner—its north pole pointed toward and south pole away from the bond site.

The force involved in a chemical bond, like the nuclear bond, is twofold. The south polar jets of all relevant protons vigorously propel them toward the bond site. At the same time, the north poles evacuate spacetime from that site, creating an attractive low-pressure region. The length of a chemical bond is related, as in nuclear bonds, to the proton's equilibrium state. As the proton's pressure rises, its convective circulation slows and the particle moves farther from the bond. As its pressure falls, its convection intensifies and it pulls itself closer to the bond.

In general, the higher the temperature the weaker the bond. To determine what sorts of bonds a given atom can form, we must exploit what we learned earlier about nuclear configurations. Correlatively, we can use known chemical bonds to determine the nuclear configurations of atoms we have not yet examined.

One more thing to note about the H_2 bond is that it is not quite accurate to say that the atoms "share electrons." Instead, the electrons are, on average, located opposite the bond. They represent the positive pressure, at the ends of the protons' polar jets, that balances the negative pressure at the bond site. They create the thrust that pushes the atoms together. As epiphenomena, electrons attempt, like the protons that create them, to remain equidistant and diametrically opposed. They are the shadows of their underlying protons, and that is true whether they are part of the same atom or belong to different atoms in the same molecule. What is shared by both atoms is not the electrons *per se*, but the *effort* of those electrons. By working together, the pair of electrons in H_2 decreases the overall energy of the system, as compared with the two separate hydrogen atoms.

Bond Energy

The energy released in an exothermic chemical reaction comes from three sources:

1. The common volume of space that corresponds to the bond site.
2. Any increase or decrease in pressure that results from altering the orbital configurations of the affected protons.
3. Any increases or decreases, relative to the original atoms, of the magnetic moment of the new molecule.

Each hydrogen atom of an H_2 molecule was, prior to bonding, evacuating a region within its own electronic shell that is, after bonding, shared by both atoms. Once bonded, half of the spacetime in this new, shared volume must be evacuated, reducing the extrinsic mass of the molecule relative to the parent atoms. The sudden release of this excess spacetime is part (typically most) of the energy of a chemical reaction.

Notice that the quantity of spacetime released is proportionate to the pressure and volume of the space occupied by the resulting bond, which is exactly what we would expect. The strength of the bond, therefore, is related to the degree of relaxation implied by the sharing of a particular volume. If two atoms share a large volume of relatively low pressure, it means they depend on each other more and are bound more tightly than two atoms that share a small volume of relatively high pressure. This relaxation manifests itself as a decrease in the combined convective vigor of both protons and, therefore, a drop in the intensity of the spacetime gradient (gravitational field) on the electronic shells. This behavior is the cause of the small but measureable *chemical mass defect.*

The second contribution to a chemical reaction's energy comes from the rearrangement of protons as the bond is formed. As I have shown, the particular series of derivative axes expressed by an orbital determines the pressure of that orbital, as well as the quantity of spacetime maintained within the electronic shell. When a chemical bond forms, the protons must reorient themselves such that they are, on average, aimed at the bond site. That modest reorientation, in turn, requires them to exhibit a significantly different orbital geometry, as well as a different series of energy states.

When an orbital changes energy states, it either absorbs spacetime (heat) from its surroundings or expels it as a shock wave (electron). This is true whether the change in energy state is the result of a jump between states in a lone atom, or a change that results from the creation of new series of energy states during a chemical reaction. Changing its entire series of energy states, after all, also implies changing from one particular state to another during the reaction. Such a jump either releases or absorbs spacetime, over and above any that is expelled from the shared bond site.

Finally, the magnetic moment, or wobble, of an atom tends to increase the energy required for it to spin. A lone hydrogen atom has a fairly substantial magnetic moment. With each rotation, its south polar jet pushes one way and then the other, and there is nothing opposite this pushing, as there is in helium, to balance it out. It takes less energy to rotate something smoothly than to rotate something that possesses angular momentum. Therefore, any net decreases in magnetic moment that are realized by combining a given group of atoms into a molecule will tend to increase the difficulty of breaking them apart. Generally, wobbly atoms, because they expend more energy to rotate, will tend to jump between energy states more readily than those that rotate more smoothly. That means, all else being equal, a chemical bond that decreases its atoms' magnetic moments requires more energy to break than it releases when it forms.

Because of these three different contributions to the energy of a chemical reaction, it is not a simple affair to determine the energy of a given chemical bond. An H_2 molecule is not simply two hydrogen atoms stuck together. When the bond forms, the protons rearrange themselves, and it is nothing more than this arrangement that determines their behavior—what they are. Hence, an H_2 molecule is, in a very real sense, qualitatively distinct from the two atoms that came together to form it. It has a different emission spectrum, apparent mass, chemical properties, and magnetic moment. It is a very different object.

Methane

The CH_4 molecule (**Figure 8.2**) illustrates, all by itself, many of the important aspects of chemical bonding. So, instead of plodding through simpler compounds first, we will jump ahead to this more complex example.

Obviously, the most interesting aspect of methane is that it contains carbon—quite possibly the single greatest invention

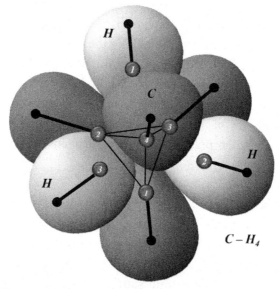

Figure 8.2:   Methane
When bonded in methane, the valance protons in carbon can mimic the diametric opposition of an octahedral or spherical valance shell. They do this by aiming themselves directly across the atom at the opposite hydrogen proton. No change in the carbon atom's geometry is required. The matching numbers indicate the pairs of bonded protons.

of the cosmos. Carbon-12 has a 6-member neutron core ($1n^2$ $2n^4$), two protons in a spherical orbital around that, and a tetrahedral valance orbital. What makes this arrangement so remarkable is that it is exceedingly stable while at the same time being incredibly flexible. This flexibility comes from the unique properties of a tetrahedral orbital. Notice that the vertices of a regular tetrahedron are equidistant when transcribed on a sphere, but they are *not* diametrically opposed. Nevertheless, the vectors of the protons taken two at a time, pushing on the core, are diametrically opposed. What this means in practice is that the protons in this shell can be thought of as focused either straight across the atom, one at a time, or along a line that corresponds to the vectors of two of them taken as a pair. Hence, carbon can make one, two, three, or four bonds, all without altering its stable tetrahedral geometry at all.

Each C-H bond allows the protons in the carbon atom to retain their tetrahedral geometry, but also permits them to point directly at the core, mimicking the diametric opposition in helium and oxygen. The bonds are similar to H-H bonds in that they involve two protons each, one from hydrogen and one from carbon. The even spacing of the hydrogen atoms is due entirely to the geometry of the carbon atom and has nothing to do with any electrostatic repulsion from the hydrogens.

Water

Oxygen sports an extremely stable octahedral valance shell and on cursory inspection seems incapable of forming any bonds at all. All of its protons are already equidistant and diametrically opposed. Nothing can be bonded to it while it is configured in its monatomic state, because all of the protons are perfectly balanced. Wherever we try to place a bond, the opposite proton will cancel it out (pump it full of spacetime). Clearly, we need something to move. As stable and balanced as oxygen is, chemical bonding is not a zero-sum proposition. The question is not, How stable (relaxed) is it now? But rather, How stable could it become? No matter how stable an atom might be, it will always benefit from sharing some volume of space with another atom—assuming it is capable of adopting a geometric configuration that permits it. Despite appearances, oxygen is very capable.

The answer comes from examining how the six protons in oxygen's valance orbital rotate (**Figure 8.3**). To maintain their octahedral configuration, they cannot all fly around in different directions. Instead, they must rotate as a group, all in the same direction. When that happens, what we discover is an easily identifiable axis of rotation connecting opposite sides of the orbital. If we bend that axis at its center, the protons fit together like the teeth in a pair of gears. Indeed, if we bend it exactly the right amount, the protons can remain nearly equidistant, though within a smaller surface area, while also generating two powerful

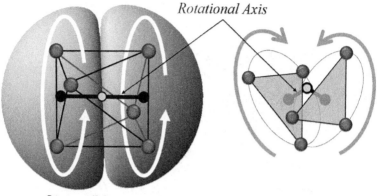

Rotational Axis

Linear (Monatomic)   Bent (Molecular)

Figure 8.3:   Oxygen Rotation
When we rotate the octahedral valance shell in oxygen, an axis becomes clearly evident. And if we bend that axis at its center, the protons fit together like the teeth in a pair of gears, reorienting themselves in such a way as to create two powerful low pressure regions suitable for chemical bonding.

low pressure regions suitable for chemical bonding. Introduce a couple of hydrogen atoms and we get water (**Figure 8.4**).

Further examining the H_2O molecule, we see that each O-H bond is created by three oxygen protons and only one from hydrogen. Each proton draws spacetime from the bond site into its north pole and ejects it in the opposite direction, toward the electronic shell. In a water molecule, the oxygen is responsible for considerably more suction and expulsion than the hydrogen, and that results in a low-pressure region on the hydrogen side and a high-pressure region on the oxygen side. Traditionally, this has been interpreted as a positive electric charge on the hydrogens and a negative charge on the oxygen. It is responsible for the hydrogen bonds of this and other polarized molecules. Unfortunately, with a 50-50 chance of getting it right, electrical charges are currently backwards. Positive charge is actually a negative spacetime pressure and vice versa. Prior to this theory, *positive* and *negative* were entirely arbitrary, functioning as nothing but opposites of one other. Now that the term *charge* has a

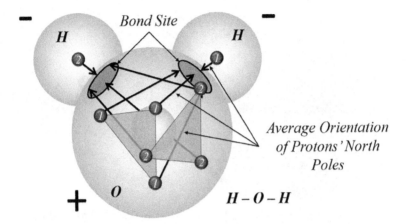

Figure 8.4:   Water Molecule
The geometry of a water molecule is governed by the manner in which oxygen's valance orbital reorients itself during chemical bonding. The strong "electrical charges" on the atoms (responsible for hydrogen bonding) are the *effects* of this geometry, not the *cause* of it.

definite meaning (related to spacetime pressure), this error will have to be corrected by switching *positive* and *negative* throughout the physical sciences.

Because spacetime resists any contrast in pressure, H_2O molecules in their liquid state tend to line up head to tail. The decompressed hydrogen atoms will preferentially pull spacetime from the high-pressure regions just beyond the electronic shells of the oxygen atoms. Similarly, the oxygen atoms will tend to push away anything with a high pressure; and in a sample of pure water, that leaves nothing but the hydrogen atoms.

In addition to its behavior toward other H_2O molecules, water also sticks, one way or another, to anything with a pressure that is either positive or negative relative to either end of the atom. If a given particle has, for example, a positive pressure, the hydrogen ends will adhere to it, encircling it by water molecules, and dissolving the particle in the solution. The hydrogen bonds are so strong—because of the 3-to-1 proton ratio in the O-H bonds—that water is often referred to as the universal solvent.

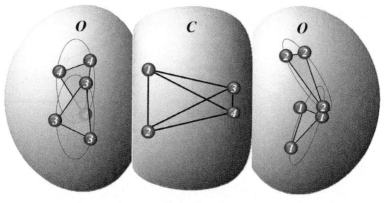

$$O = C = O$$

Figure 8.5:   Carbon Dioxide
The numbered protons in this diagram indicate each of the four features
in the two double bonds of carbon dioxide. These double bonds depend
on their relative angular orientation and, therefore, are difficult to twist.

Carbon Dioxide

The two C=O bonds in CO_2 (**Figure 8.5**) are unlike
either the C-H bonds in methane or the O-H bonds in water.
Notice that none of the orbital features in any of the three atoms
is aimed directly at the bond sites. Notice also that there is a very
clear reason the bonds in CO_2 are double bonds. Two groups of
three protons in oxygen are paired up with two groups of one
proton in carbon for each bond. That is, each bond is made up of
four distinct features, two on a side.

The strength of these bonds depends on all of their features remaining in the same planes, and that means they cannot
be twisted easily. The molecule rigidly maintains the same proton
geometry. Also, because there are oxygens on either end, evacuating and expelling spacetime at the same rate, the molecule is
nonpolar. Yet, it does not have a constant pressure throughout.
The 6 to 2 ratio of oxygen to carbon protons means the carbon
atom is decompressed (negative) relative to the oxygen atoms.

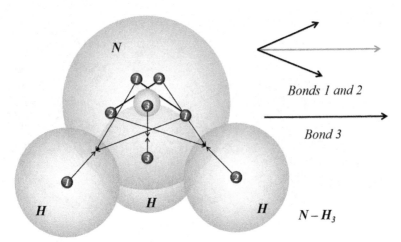

Figure 8.6:   Ammonia
Nitrogen can form three bonds of two different types. In an ammonia
molecule, bonds one and two each have two nitrogen protons, while bond
three has only one. Using vector addition, we can speculate about why
these bonds are observed to have the same length and strength, but this
is a clear case in which high-speed computer simulations would be helpful
in verifying a hypothesis.

Ammonia

Ammonia (**Figure 8.6**) is a strange molecule because
nitrogen is a strange atom. Nitrogen has three valance features:
two 2-proton orbitals, and one 1-proton orbital. Therefore, it
can form three bonds, but of two different types. At first glance,
we might expect the N-H bonds involving the 2-proton orbitals
to differ in some important way from the single-proton orbital.
But empirical observations suggest this is not the case. All three
bonds are the same strength and length. It is easy enough to
invent an explanation for this phenomenon, but this is a case in
which a computer simulation will be of particular value in test-
ing the hypothesis. If we look at the two 2-proton orbitals, we
see that they are not aimed directly at the bond site. To calculate
their strength, we must use vector addition. When we compare
those results to the strength of the 1-proton orbital, pointed directly at its bond site, it is easy to see why they might have the
same strength. Still, this is nothing but a hypothesis, very much

in need of verification.

Traditionally, according to the Valence Shell Electron Pair Repulsion (VSEPR) model, the equal length of the three bonds in NH_3 is attributed to something called *resonance*. This *ad hoc* theory states that whenever it is possible to draw equivalent, but different, Lewis diagrams for a given molecule, the actual molecule exhibits the characteristics of all such diagrams simultaneously. The theory does not explain how this could be true, or even what the term *resonance* means in this connection. What I suspect a simulation will show, in this case and others, is that chemical bonding is intimately related, often in unpredictable ways, to all of the complex factors we have been considering throughout this book. In some cases, extreme magnetic moments may play a much larger than usual role. In others, such as oxygen bonds, difficult-to-visualize geometric contortions will appear. The possibilities are endless and theory alone will never be sufficient to determine which variables have the greatest impact in a particular example.

Monovalent Bonds

There is at least one major bond type that does not follow the model I have described thus far. In all the molecules discussed above, the number and geometry of the bonds is determined by the proton configurations of the atoms; they are all *covalent* bonds. For every proton or proton feature in one atom, there is a corresponding proton or feature in the atom to which it is bonded. These protons and features realign themselves such that they are pointed, on average, toward one another. This explains how the force of the protons' polar jets can propel the atoms toward the bond site, while the protons' north poles evacuate a common volume of space and create an attractive low-pressure region. However, there is a different mechanism at work in certain other chemical bonds.

In Chapter 6, we saw that each nucleonic orbital evacuates spacetime from the region between itself and the orbital just below it. However, each orbital is completely indifferent to the geometry of that next lower orbital. The orbitals spin according to the requirements of their particular series of derivative axes. They do not line up in any way with the nucleons either above or below themselves. It makes no difference, therefore, if a spherical proton orbital is just above a tetrahedral, octahedral, or another spherical orbital. It simply adjusts itself to the ambient pressure in its immediate vicinity, regardless of how that pressure was generated. Though they are attracted to the low pressures implied by this arrangement, the protons in these orbitals do not attempt to avoid, for example, the relatively high pressures at the ends of the polar jets of the nucleons underneath them. These minor fluctuations in pressure are not strong enough to interrupt the orbital patterns dictated by their derivative axes. This is very different from most chemical bonds, which *do* line up in accordance with specific high and low pressure regions.

More accurately, they *usually* line up according to the pressure differences implied by the bonds. But in some cases, atoms can bond in much the same way that nucleons bond, by ignoring the specifics of the geometry and simply attaching themselves, in general, to the low pressure region inside another atom's electronic shell. This phenomenon is particularly apparent in certain fluorine compounds.

Lithium Fluoride

Fluorine has a single valance proton orbiting an octahedral oxygen core. When this atom forms a single bond, it does not achieve an octet of electrons. This is just one of the endless number of examples in which electron dot diagrams are misleading and inaccurate. The reason for fluorine's extreme chemical reactivity has to do with the tremendous advantage of sharing a volume of space created by a bond. The single valance proton in fluorine has a very large volume to evacuate, and so any bond it forms greatly reduces its workload.

Consider that fluorine's single valance proton must pump out all the spacetime being pumped out of the core by six protons just below it. When a fluorine atom comes across an atom with a relatively relaxed valance proton (e.g., lithium), it presses that proton into service. The lithium proton has a lot of spare capacity, whereas the fluorine proton is stretched to the limit. Though this is a covalent bond like those already discussed, the extreme vigor of the lithium-fluorine reaction points to the high reactivity of fluorine, which is especially relevant for monovalent bonds.

Xenon Fluorides

Another interesting behavior of fluorine is its ability to form compounds with some of the noble gases, including krypton, xenon, and radon. Given their usual lack of reactivity, it is unlikely that these gases benefit much from a chemical bond. Rather, the bond must be explained by taking both the noble gas and fluorine into account. That is, the fluorine gains so much by the bond that, even if the inert partner gains very little, the energy of the system—the entire molecule—is reduced in the process. If it makes sense to discuss valance orbitals for noble gases, then they each have a spherical orbital (like beryllium) with two protons. If these protons are forced to create bonds, we would expect the resulting compounds to have the same linear geometry as those in group II (Be, Mg, etc.). That is, they should form two single bonds and, indeed, xenon difluoride (XeF_2) is created by simply exposing the two gasses to sunlight.

However, it is not obvious, simply from what I have said so far, that the xenon atom has, like beryllium, actually reorganized its protons in order to create these two bonds. Notice that, if the two fluorine atoms simply attach themselves, in general, to the low pressure inside the xenon atom's electronic shell, they would exhibit the same linear geometry as they would if the xenon protons acted as two distinct features. Furthermore, the existence of XeF_4 and XeF_6 suggest the same sort of orbital filling scheme that we normally see in nucleonic orbitals. And finally, various di-, tetra-, and hexafluoride molecules are fairly common, further bolstering the case that fluorine atoms can, because of their extreme electronegativity, treat an entire atom in much the same way that a proton treats the low-pressure region generated by the nucleonic orbitals beneath it.

With this in mind, it is clear that xenon tetrafluoride is a very different phenomenon than, for example, carbon tetrafluoride. In XeF_4, the geometry is dictated by the fluorine atoms, while in CF_4, it is dictated by the underlying geometry of the carbon atom.

Another piece of evidence for the monovalent bonds in XeF_6 (**Figure 8.7**) comes from the observation that the octahedral geometry of the fluorine atoms is *distorted* by the two free electrons in xenon. Since the underlying xenon protons are not directly involved in the bonding (they are not valance protons), their electrons continue to spin across the entire surface of the electronic shell, bumping into the fluorine atoms and disrupting their arrangement.

Finally, we already know that a spherical proton orbital that is located just outside of an octahedral orbital is inviolable. Consider that if the outermost nuclear proton in cesium is incapable of penetrating that spherical orbital, then there is no chance at all that the external protons in fluorine could do so. From this we can be very confident that the noble gases have no valance protons and form molecules exclusively by means of monovalent bonds.

Aside from these rather extreme examples, there are many other similarly peculiar molecules that possess more bonds than their valance protons would seem to permit. Boron has only three valance protons, but can make four bonds. It is reasonable to assume that this extra bond is merely connected to the negative pressure region as a whole, rather than to any particular proton feature. In general, these sorts of bonds will be relatively difficult to identify or predict. Moreover, it is likely that there is

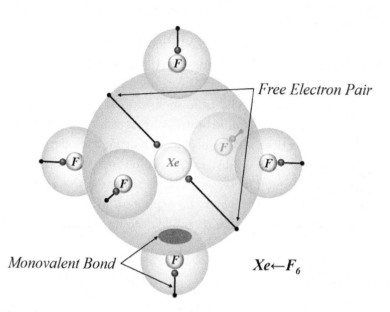

Figure 8.7: Xenon Hexafluoride

In xenon hexafluoride, the six fluorine atoms simply bond themselves, in general, to the low pressure region inside the xenon atom's electronic shell. And because xenon's outermost proton orbital is not a valance orbital (it does not reorient itself to create bonds), the associated electron pair is free to continue spinning across the entire electronic shell surface, distorting the molecule's octahedral geometry.

no sharp distinction between regular, covalent bonds, and these monovalent bonds. In some cases, for example, it is possible that a bond alters the proton configuration, but only very slightly. Indeed, it is possible that the outermost protons in xenon, when bonded into XeF_2, are *somewhat* more likely to orient themselves toward the bond site than they would when not in a molecule. If so, the Xe-F bonds are actually hybrids or borderline cases, not easily classified. Even in obviously covalent bonds, it is only the *average* location of the protons that change. And this suggests that chemical bonds are a continuum, anywhere from strongly covalent to strongly monovalent. It also means that the valance of a given atom cannot be reliably determined by reference to its highest fluoride. None of the noble gases has any intrinsic valance at all, despite their ability to form bonds.

Larger Orbitals

So far, I have only talked about nuclear orbitals containing from one to six nucleons, yet there is good evidence that there are more to consider. The lanthanide and actinide series both extend the periodic table such as to suggest the filling to two different *icosahedral* proton shells. If we locate protons on the twelve vertices of a regular icosahedron, they are diametrically opposed and equidistant. As orbitals get farther from the core and their radii increase, it stands to reason that such a fortuitous geometric fact would be exploited. Indeed, it is next to impossible to imagine that it could fail to be exploited.

9

Complexity

Typically, the principles of complexity, chaos, turbulence, and the like are not thought to apply to the atomic nucleus. In the temple of protons and neutrons, everything is perfectly ordered and governed by precise mathematical formulas—our modern day music of the spheres. But alas, it isn't so. In order to grasp the true nature of reality we must pay heed to its, literally, infinite subtleties, requiring us to delve into the extremely fine structure of its fundamental constituents to see how that structure manifests itself, often in unexpected ways, in larger scale phenomena.

First Order Systems

The main component of this model of complexity (**Figure 9.1**) is a gear. The gear is then attached to a motor that is itself attached to a battery. The battery, in turn, is linked to an energy source that recharges it. It is very similar to the configuration in a diesel-electric train locomotive. Further, there is a meter attached to the battery that indicates its charge. If the needle is in the middle, the battery has zero charge. If it is to the right or left of the middle, it has a positive or negative charge, respectively. If the battery has a positive charge, the gear rotates clockwise, if negative, counterclockwise. Remember, either a positive or negative pressure gives a positive energy value.

Also, it is not necessary that the energy source be constant or regular. It might be entirely random (though unlikely in most physical systems). It might, like the sun, provide gradually increasing and then decreasing energy during the day, and then

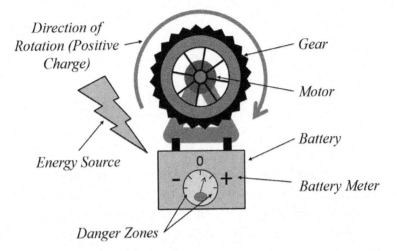

Figure 9.1:   First Order System
This relatively simple-looking, first-order system is sensitive to a surprising number of variables. Most of the labeled properties can vary independently.

none during the night. As the gear rotates in either direction, energy is drained from the battery tending to restore, or relax, the charge to zero. Moreover, it takes some span of time (the exact rate varies with the system under consideration) to convert the chemical energy in the battery into the kinetic energy of the gear. Finally, the distance of the needle from zero electric charge is directly proportionate to the force exerted by the motor on the gear. The greater (either positive or negative) the charge, the faster or more powerfully the gear rotates, just like a regular battery.

We can easily create a system like the one just described by attaching a solar panel to a battery and then attaching the battery to an electric motor. If nothing else is involved, the battery will gradually charge in the morning, ultimately receiving enough energy to overcome the inertia of the gear and start it spinning. Over the course of the morning, the gear will accelerate as the charge in the battery increases faster than its chemical energy can be converted into kinetic energy. In the afternoon, as the sun's energy wanes, the gear will begin sapping the battery faster than the Sun can charge it, causing it to gradually slow down. Then, after the Sun has set, the gear will continue spinning, into the night, until the last of the charge has been used.

The rate at which the chemical energy in the battery is converted into kinetic energy contributes to the lag between the times of most intense energy and the times of most intense spinning. Also, the mass and diameter of the gear determine how much energy is required to start it spinning and also how much energy is required to slow it to a stop. If the gear is very massive, it may not start spinning until well into the afternoon or later. And once it gets going, it might very well take the motor all night and part of the morning to finally slow it down. Moreover, the process of slowing the gear will push the battery into an increasingly negative charge, finally stopping the gear and reversing its rotational direction, spinning it counterclockwise. Just as if it were attached to a rubber band, the gear will change directions, back and forth, until it finally comes to rest. Simple as this system might appear, its exact behavior is highly sensitive to a surprising number of variables:

1. The total quantity, intensity, and delivery schedule of the energy.
2. The rate of energy conversion from the battery to the motor.
3. The capacity of the battery.
4. The power of the motor.
5. The angular momentum of the gear (related to both its mass and diameter).
6. The balance of the gear. Is it symmetrical or lopsided (i.e., does it have a "magnetic moment")?

Change any one or more of these variables and the entire system will change in ways that are very difficult to predict. Connect several of these systems together, and the possibilities are virtually endless.

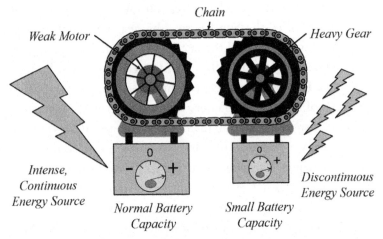

Figure 9.2:   Second Order System

The system on the left is stressed (indicated by the location of the needle on the battery meter) because its weak motor must contend with a great deal of energy. The system on the right is stressed because its heavy gear is difficult to start and stop in a manner commensurate with its discontinuous energy source. By chaining the gears together, these weaknesses are averaged, relieving some of the stress on both of them.

Second Order Systems

Since I went out of my way to call the objects rotated by these motors *gears*, it is only fitting that we now connect those gears with chains (**Figure 9.2**). We will start with two gears connected by a single chain, just like a single-speed bicycle. The first question that comes to mind is, Why would something like this ever happen? Viewed separately, the gear systems appear to do just fine by themselves. Where is the advantage in pairing up?

To answer this question, we must look again at the six variables listed above. In particular, we need to imagine a system in which one or more of them has a rather extreme value, one way or the other. For example, imagine a system with an intense, continuous energy source, but a weak motor. Or imagine a system with a small battery capacity but a large, heavy gear. Both of these systems are put under extreme stress by the unlucky contrast between the energy they are forced to process and the machinery available to them for such processing. But look what happens if we link the two systems together with a chain. All of the variables are averaged together. True, the strengths are all diminished to some extent, but the weaknesses are mitigated as well. In the linked (second order) system, the chain will remain in motion continuously because of the continuous energy source of the first gear system. This benefits both systems because the heavy gear on the one is kept in constant motion by the other (eliminating the need to overcome its inertia to start and stop it), and the weak motor on the first is aided by the angular momentum of the second. Likewise, the small battery capacity on the second is mitigated by the now constant motion of its heavy gear, obviating the jerky, start-and-stop strategy that was formerly required. Both systems benefit.

We can imagine any number of first order systems linked together in this manner, creating a second order system (**Figure 9.3**) that averages all six variables of each. Once linked, only the velocity and tension of the chain can be queried to establish the balance into which the complex system has evolved. And that makes the job of disentangling the relative contributions of which variable on which gear system virtually impossible. In any natural system that exhibits this sort of behavior, we do not have any readily available battery meters to consult. That is, it is very difficult to determine what range of charges a given first order element exhibits within the second order system. From outside, the second order system looks very harmonious and perfectly synchronized.

Consider the incredible, even beautiful, manner in which the ocean's thermohaline circulation (THC) regulates the water temperatures all over the globe in almost exactly the right way to maintain the required heat gradient between the poles and the tropics. Heat is pumped out of the tropics toward the poles, where it is subsequently radiated into space. That process occurs at almost exactly the right rate so that the earth's heat gradient does not become so depolarized or hyperpolarized that the THC itself is destroyed. Heat is pumped away from the earth at

Second-Order System

Figure 9.3:   Second Order System
A second order system is composed of any number of first order systems
connected by a single chain. I've simplified this diagram by showing the
battery meter directly on the gear.

nearly the same rate at which it is received from the sun. But it is
not done in a simple, single step. Instead, this process is accomplished by regulating the temperatures of dozens of local circulations (gyres) throughout the oceans. The THC (chain) snakes its
way around and between all of the continents, from the surface
to the ocean floor, visiting each local gyre in turn, while deriving
its own nature from exactly those same gyres (gears).

The THC is at least a second order system (probably a
higher order) that averages the variables exhibited by all of the
more or less circular gyres worldwide. Through the auspices of
the THC, the gyres are far more efficient than they would be if
they functioned independently. Correlatively, the gyres themselves are altered by their mutual association.

N^th Order Systems

Besides linking various first order systems together with
a single chain, we can also link multiple second order systems
together with additional chains. Such chains can link second or-

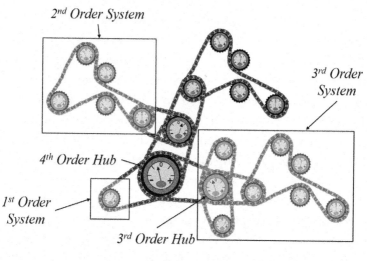

2ⁿᵈ Order System

3ʳᵈ Order System

4ᵗʰ Order Hub

1ˢᵗ Order System

3ʳᵈ Order Hub

4ᵗʰ Order System

Figure 9.4:   Fourth Order System

Any number of systems, of whatever order, can be linked together, either directly or via hubs, to create n^{th} order systems of indefinite complexity. Clearly, as the number of gears increases, the sensitivity of the overall system to any one of them diminishes. It is this disparity—between the speed and tension in the chains on the one hand, and the requirements of the individual gears on the other—that gradually causes the system to collapse.

der systems to other first order systems, to other second order systems, or indeed, to any n^{th} order system or series of systems. And these links can be multiplied indefinitely to connect as many different systems (**Figure 9.4**) of any order we choose.

Now, as we link more and more gears together, regardless of how they are linked, the chains that connect them become increasingly indifferent to the requirements of any particular gear. As an average of perhaps hundreds of gears, no particular gear has more than a trivial effect on the behavior of the overall system, which is reflected in the velocities and tensions of the chains. It is this indifference to the individual gears by the chains that can ultimately result in the collapse of the entire system.

Instability

Though this is an entirely hypothetical model, it is worth pointing out that most, if not all, natural systems that behave in this manner will not provide us with anything analogous to a battery meter with which to gauge their conditions. For example, all the local ocean currents add heat to the THC, but they do so discontinuously, connecting to and disconnecting from the THC as necessary. Local gyres deposit their heat into the THC, and the THC subsequently dumps that heat into cold regions near the poles. The contrast in temperature, the ocean's heat gradient, is manifested in the temperature differences between these local gyres and the THC at every point along its entire length. It is this gradient, ultimately derived from the temperature contrast between the tropics and the poles, that drives the whole system. If the heat gradient becomes either excessively depolarized (the ocean temperature becomes too uniform) or hyperpolarized (the contrast between poles and tropics becomes extreme) the whole system will collapse.

Still, the temperature at any particular point in the THC, or in any given gyre, fluctuates significantly over time. If heat from, for example, the colossal North Pacific Equatorial gyre, is in the process of dumping its heat, the THC will be warmer worldwide, altering the climate thousands of miles away for many decades or even centuries. This could be misinterpreted as a major and worrisome climatic shift, when in fact the increase in temperature in, say, Europe, is exactly offset by a decrease in the temperature of the North Pacific. This is especially confounding when one of the deep ocean currents gives up its heat, because there is no correlative drop in temperature by any surface feature. The surface temperature simply rises worldwide, and we have no way to identify the source of this heat, miles beneath the ocean's surface. Since we do not know when these various gigantic currents will dump their heat or what global effects they will have when they do, we can rarely say if an observed climate

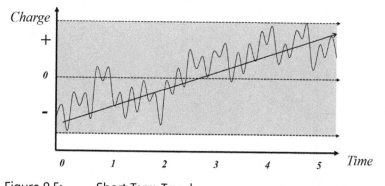

Figure 9.5:   Short Term Trend
Measuring the charge of a system (either the gradient that drives the whole thing, or of a particular gear) over any given time period will yield a trend line. Only by reference to the entire cycle, can any sense be made of such trends.

fluctuation is normal or catastrophic (**Figures 9.5 and 9.6**). Only when we know how warm the THC and the local gyres are *supposed* to be (to maintain global equilibrium) can we say if we are headed for disaster or simply witnessing a routine cycle of heat transfer. And since the North Pacific gyres—at both the surface and the floor of the ocean—do not have battery meters, their ideal temperature ranges are very difficult, if not impossible, to ascertain. Indeed, their ideal temperatures are always intimately related to the present temperatures of every other gyre on earth, and not in a simple, obvious way.

　　If we link a number of gears with a system of chains, the angular velocity of each gear will reflect the velocity of the chain, which itself reflects the average force imparted to it by the gears. If all the gears are connected to similar energy sources, motors, and batteries, such a linkage can be very stable for a long period of time, though even relatively small differences can gradually become problematic. Over any given time span, a gear will either be pushing the chain forward (if the battery is positively charged) or retarding its motion (if it is negatively charged), and the battery will either be discharging toward its equilibrium value or being charged. It will be charged in the

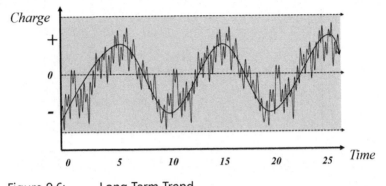

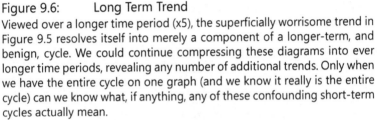

Figure 9.6:   Long Term Trend
Viewed over a longer time period (x5), the superficially worrisome trend in Figure 9.5 resolves itself into merely a component of a longer-term, and benign, cycle. We could continue compressing these diagrams into ever longer time periods, revealing any number of additional trends. Only when we have the entire cycle on one graph (and we know it really is the entire cycle) can we know what, if anything, any of these confounding short-term cycles actually mean.

positive direction if its energy source exceeds the rate at which the chain allows it to dump its energy. It will be charged in the negative direction if the chain is moving faster than the battery is being charged by its external energy source.

If we watch the battery meter of a particular gear, we can try to gauge its health by observing the point about which the needle fluctuates. If the average location of the needle, even if it moves back and forth a great deal, is right in the middle, right at the point of zero charge, then that gear is *healthy*. If, over a longer time, the needle continues to exhibit the same average location—again, no matter how wildly it moves in order to arrive at that average—we can conclude that that particular gear is not only healthy but *stable*.

The possibilities for instability are more complicated. For example, if the needle's average location, over a certain time span begins inching to the right—even if it is currently fluctuating within its equilibrium range—we might conclude that this particular battery is slowly hyperpolarizing and will eventually burn out its motor. However, the only way to be certain is to watch the meter for a very long time and determine if the slow movement to the right is not merely part of a benign long-term movement back and forth from right to left and back again. When we have many gears connected, there can be many independent fluctuations, on all different time scales, about any number of local averages. The most obvious fluctuations will coincide with the simple periodic delivery of energy to the battery, and have nothing to do with the long-term stability of the system. But any other gear, system, or combination of gears and systems can alter the tension on the chain and cause a distant gear's needle to move in seemingly inexplicable ways. Only an exhaustive analysis of the entire system over an extended period of time can begin to determine if any particular fluctuation is malignant.

Collapse

There are three different ways the system of gears we have been looking at can collapse:

1. The force exerted by a gear can exceed the tensile strength of the chain, kinking or breaking it.
2. A local gear system can self-destruct when its battery explodes under excessive charge.
3. Both one and two, above. A kink can, by undermining the delicate equilibrium, trigger an explosion, though this is not possible in all systems (e.g., obviously the oceans are not going to explode under any circumstances). If, however, the explosion is first, the system has collapsed and there is no point in searching for a secondary cause.

When a chain connects a series of gears or systems, its movement corresponds to the average forces exerted by those gears *when they were connected*. The chain has very limited flexibility with respect to any fluctuations that crop up after it is in place. As a result, the stability of the system depends a great

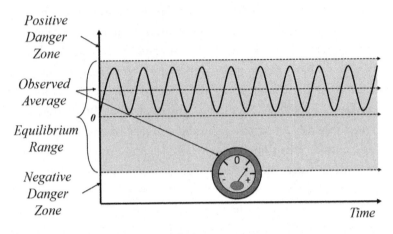

Figure 9.7:   Positive Equilibrium Average

A chain locks its gears into an equilibrium state that reflects the average of all the gears *when the chain was introduced*. It is likely, therefore, that certain of these first order components will be forced to fluctuate well above or below their zero-charge points. If the overall system is stable, such anomalies may never become apparent. This is interesting, because it means that any particular first order element of a complex system may not behave as it would in isolation. It may even appear, if the complex system is not understood, to violate the laws of physics.

deal on how representative of their true averages the motions of the gears were when the chain was introduced. Now, this does not imply that any unexpected departures from the mean will destroy the system. If a gear has a reasonably high battery capacity, its needle can fluctuate regularly about a point well to the right or left of zero charge (**Figure 9.7**), but never drift out of its equilibrium range. Such a condition might be less than ideal, but still perfectly stable.

The crux of the problem with these systems comes from the fact that the average of all the gears will most likely be slightly too fast or too slow for at least one of them. As mentioned, over any given time frame, it is difficult to distinguish benign long-term cycles from slow malignant drifts of the needle into the danger zones.

For example, the current rise in global temperature may represent a genuine drift of the system into its danger zone, or it might be a cyclical fluctuation such as the *Medieval Warm Period* or the *Little Ice Age*. But there is no way to decide this question simply by taking the earth's temperature. Only by reference to some benchmark, *a zero charge point* for the entire climatic system, can particular temperature trends, however lengthy or dramatic, have any meaning. We simply do not have any such knowledge of the ideal polarization of the earth's heat gradient. For all we know, deep ocean circulations are currently dumping their heat and cooling off in direct proportion to the surface's warming. Nor would trends lasting only decades or centuries tell us anything. As we have seen, the most dramatic and noticeable fluctuations of the system are the least relevant to its long-term stability. Such fluctuations reflect the cyclical variations in the energy sources (e.g., solar cycles or Milankovitch Cycles), not long-term instabilities in the entire system. Therefore, if the recent rise in temperature is dramatic, it almost certainly has nothing to do with the long-term stability of the THC, which is the only feature we really have to worry about.

Very Small Numbers

An unstable system ultimately collapses because the averages manifested in the chains are not precisely calibrated to the gears. In many cases, the average may only conflict with a single gear and deviate by a seemingly trivial fraction, such as $\pm 0.000000000001\%$[1]. Nevertheless, this slight deviation will cause the affected gear to slowly hyperpolarize, a phenomenon that will only become visible if we watch the battery meter for a very long time, noting its gradual drift (over and above all confounding short-term trends) in one direction or the other. In the case of the earth's oceans, the cycle lasts many thousands of years and is masked by any number of short and longer term fluctuations. As we will see in the next chapter, even longer spans of time apply to certain radioactive isotopes.

---

1   The small numbers in this section are for illustrative purposes only and do not represent actual data or estimates.

If a system is completely stable, it means that all the gears of which it is composed are able to, over an indefinitely long time frame, discharge their batteries at the same rate as they are charged (both by the chains and external energy sources). Or, from the opposite perspective, the chain must maintain the proper speed and tension to keep all the gears charging and discharging at a constant rate. Such stable systems will, like the unstable ones, exhibit long-term trends and superficially worrisome drifts toward the danger zones, and it may never be possible to observe a system long enough to confirm its stability. For example, if we had only a dozen or so ^{10}Be atoms (half-life, 1.5 million years) at our disposal, it is unlikely we would ever witness a decay event. Likewise, if we knew nothing about the regular cycles of glaciation on Earth over the past three million years, we would naturally assume the Earth's climate, though variable within its equilibrium range, is stable forever. Nothing has happened in all of recorded history to suggest a major glaciation. Only because scientists have extended our hindsight with such climate proxies as ice core samples, lakebed sediments, and rock strata analysis, among others, do we know for certain that our THC is gradually destabilizing. It is depolarizing the Earth's heat gradient and will eventually collapse. To put it another way, our interglacial THC is slightly too good at what it does. It pumps heat from the tropics to the poles just a bit too fast to maintain, permanently, the temperature gradient that drives the whole system. At some time over the next few millennia, the THC will become too warm to accept heat from at least one of the major gyres. As these circulations, one after the other, fail to connect to the THC, it will lose its source of energy and grind to a halt, plunging us into the next glacial period.

The lesson to take from this discussion is that the collapse of an unstable system is the result of either a slight (e.g., ±0.000000001%) inefficiency or hyperefficiency in the chain that connects the gears. Or, from the gears' perspective, collapse is caused by one or more gears gradually drifting into one of its danger zones (becoming depolarized or hyperpolarized), retarding or accelerating the chain, and causing it to kink or break. Looking at the oceans, we can focus on either the THC itself (the chain), or on the local gyres that drive it (the gears). The interglacial THC is hyperefficient, pumping heat from the tropics to the poles too quickly, thereby depolarizing the earth's heat gradient. Or, from the local perspective, at least one of the circulations receives just a tiny bit *less* energy from the Sun than the THC takes from it. This causes the local circulation to gradually depolarize in the negative direction, retarding the motion of the THC. Both of these perspectives describe the same unstable system.

Rise and Fall of the Thermohaline Circulation

Even if everything I have been presenting here is dead wrong, we can still say with almost absolute certainty that we are headed inexorably for another glaciation. We know this simply because glacial periods have beset the globe like clockwork, roughly every 100,000 years (lately) and 40,000 years (earlier), for the past three million years. Still, the evidence suggests very strongly that the theory of complexity I have been developing here can explain this phenomenon.

Our interglacial THC is doomed to collapse some time in the next few thousand years, and it could happen at any time; we do not know enough about the system to predict the timing of the next transition. Unfortunately, its collapse will be heralded by unprecedented global warming, including significant melting near (especially) the north pole, but the south pole as well. I say unfortunately, because people love to panic, and we are currently in a relatively warm period that may or may not mean a thing. The earth will warm because the THC, according to this theory, is depolarizing the earth's heat gradient, pumping heat from the tropics faster than it can be radiated into space at the poles.

It stands to reason that the tipping point will come when

this process has reached its most extreme state, when the poles and tropics come as close to the same temperature as they ever get. It is worth pointing out that none of this has anything to do with *greenhouse gases* in general, or carbon dioxide in particular. As the THC warms, it becomes increasingly less attractive to the local gyres; the transfer of heat occurs most robustly when the contrast in temperature is greatest. As the contrast diminishes, the local circulations are left to fend for themselves. Eventually, the contrast becomes so tiny that the gyres no longer dump their heat into the THC at all and, obviously, that means the THC grinds to a halt. When this happens, all hell breaks loose.

Ice Age

Hell may be an understatement. Nothing has ever happened to mankind that even begins to compare to the nightmare that will ensue when the THC bids us farewell. Without a THC, the ocean's heat transfer system is all but destroyed. Yes, there are still the gyres, but instead of dumping their heat into a global conveyor belt, they must transfer it from gear to gear along their edges. As there is little contrast in temperature between adjacent circulations, this method is horribly inefficient, requiring an extremely long time to transfer heat from the tropics to the poles. As a result, absent the THC, the tropics bake while the poles freeze, leading to a very unpleasant environment.

For the most part, extreme weather is not caused by a generally warming climate. It is caused by the collision of air masses with radically different temperatures and pressures. If you doubt this, talk to someone in Kansas or Oklahoma. Tornado Alley is a consequence of this phenomenon. With the disappearance of the THC, the large northern land masses (as well as high altitudes worldwide) will be rapidly covered in snow and ice, dramatically raising the albedo of earth's surface, and creating a feedback loop: an increasing albedo reflects more solar heat, which leads to more snow, which leads to increased albedo, repeat. The ice pack and glaciers start thickening, while sea level and global average temperature start dropping. Very soon, there is a radical difference in temperature between the poles and the tropics, and that is a formula for some serious weather.

Evidence from previous (Wisconsonian) glaciations suggests that the ice pack in North America will extend all the way south to Ohio. As cold, dry air races southward off of the ice pack—where Canada used to be—it will meet up with, and be overridden by, the superheated, moist air billowing up from the tropics. Currently, air masses of greatly different temperatures rarely collide because they originate so far apart; they moderate before meeting. But remember, the tropics, despite a lower average global temperature, will no longer be able to efficiently move their extreme heat, and will be at least as hot or hotter than they are now. Arctic cold will extend much farther south. These two air masses will collide right on top of what is now the southern United States. Future climatologists might very well name this and similar locales, *kill zones*, the miserable ice age counterparts to our delightful temperate regions. It is very hard to picture anything remotely resembling modern civilization existing in such a place. Imagine cold fronts with 80° to 100° temperature gradients sweeping across the landscape year round. Normal weather would consist of an endless barrage of EF5 tornados, torrential downpours, and epic blizzards. Organized agriculture will be nearly impossible and every structure will have to be built of reinforced concrete, no more than twenty feet tall, and anchored to solid bedrock. It is almost certainly no coincidence that man's agricultural revolution occurred just *after* the last glaciation. Hurricane season may well be similarly awe-inspiring. If people still live here, life will amount to little more than tracking the weather and fighting for survival.

In addition, the earth's climatological regions will both shift in latitude and be compressed, changing the long-term weather patterns everywhere. Jungles will extend north and south into regions that are now deserts (e.g., the Sahara was a forest during the last glaciation). The earth's breadbaskets in the northern hemisphere will, as I just said, become virtually uninhabitable. And many of the intermediate zones, such as tundra, taiga, temperate forests, etc, will exist only in small pockets around the globe. For the most part, there will be arctic, tropical, and the kill zones where these two meet, and little else. To make matters even worse, the new arable land will require centuries to be transformed from its current state into suitable farmland. Hearty grasses will need to take root first and start the agonizingly slow process of creating top soil. Nothing can be done to speed this process, making agriculture, particularly during the transition period, very difficult.

Finally, there will be some interesting geological changes that will not be helpful. As the ice packs thicken, they will compress the earth's crust, pushing it down into the mantle near the poles. At the same time, sea levels will drop worldwide as the ocean is converted into polar ice. This sudden shift of mass to the poles will trigger an *angular momentum crisis* for the entire planet. To resolve it, the Earth must either begin spinning faster, relocate mass toward the equator, or both. The law of angular momentum conservation is not negotiable. Most likely, the Earth will bulge near the tropics as the mantle is squeezed down under the poles. The bulge should be particularly pronounced under the continental shelves, which will (as the oceans evaporate) suddenly be relieved of the water pressure above them. No coastal city on earth will remain near the water. This bizarre process will also have the effect of raising the average elevation of all land masses not covered with ice, and especially those that were recently covered with water. Greater elevation results in colder, dryer conditions—just the opposite of what will be needed. Exactly what this upheaval might mean for volcanism and tectonic activity, I can only guess, but it will not be good. Shuffling that much mass around under the earth's crust—generating tremendous heat—will almost certainly result in increased activity on the surface as well. For example, it is easy to imagine the Yellowstone caldera licking its chops in anticipation.

Over the following several thousand years or so, a new, ice-age THC will slowly develop. It develops slowly, because the interglacial period leaves the oceans depolarized, and the THC is driven by a contrast in temperature between the tropics and poles. It will take a long time to repolarize the oceans and start the next THC. It may or may not have the same general shape as the current one, but however it forms, it will be significantly less robust than the one we have now. It will still be the dominate feature, no question, but the ocean will have considerably less to do with the climate than it does now, simply because it will be so much smaller. Much more solar radiation than today will strike either land or ice, rather than water. Therefore, any THC that forms will be less of a factor, and that means anything the THC does will take much longer to do; any tiny instabilities will require much longer to manifest themselves and collapse the system. That is why the glacial periods are much longer than the interglacial ones. Nevertheless, we know from the geologic record that the glacial THC will, like its interglacial counterpart, eventually disappear. The difference is that it will collapse for the opposite reason—because it is slightly *inefficient*.

The Younger Dryas

The glacial THC, like the interglacial THC, defines a unique equilibrium condition. The overall solar energy is reduced by the ice, the oceans are smaller, and the average global temperature is lower. As a result, maintaining a constant quantity of heat on Earth is a completely different proposition and requires a different solution. Over the next 70,000 years (assuming it takes 10,000 years or so for it to form), the glacial THC will slowly cause a hyperpolarization rather than depolarization of the ocean's heat gradient. The poles will warm, but the tropics will warm even faster. What matters is that the *contrast* in temperature increases, even though both get warmer. Eventually, one or more of the gyres will become so energetically attached to the THC that the chain is kinked and begins to wobble.

A kink, in this context, refers to an excessively warm segment of the current—not an actual, physical bend. As more kinks are introduced, the THC will wobble even more until it finally flies apart in a chaotic display of turbulence. This process is currently understood by chaos theory as *period doubling*.

Just as with the interglacial period, the glacial period will experience its greatest warmth just before it collapses. And when the glacial THC collapses (just as it appeared the ice age was about to end), the heat pump is destroyed and the earth freezes again. But in this instance, the heat gradient is in the exact opposite condition (hyperpolarized) than it is at the end of the interglacial period (depolarized). As a result, there is a tremendous amount of potential energy in the oceans, contained in this radical contrast in temperatures between the tropics and poles.

As the local circulations continue to spin, they quickly generate a new and very powerful THC (the one we have now), and heat is rapidly pumped from the tropics to the poles, putting a quick end to the refreeze, the latest of which is known as the *Younger Dryas*. This brief (~1,300-year) reglaciation at the end of the last major glacial period resulted from the collapse of the glacial THC. The rapid thaw was caused by the formation of the interglacial THC, the great power of which was derived from the dramatic hyperpolarization of the ocean's heat gradient, which itself developed slowly over the interminable glacial period. What we see, then, is that any THC is better than none, and the earth freezes whenever a THC (glacial or interglacial) collapses. However, the polarization of the Earth's heat gradient at the time of the collapse determines how quickly the thaw will occur. When the interglacial THC collapses, the oceans are left with very little potential energy with which to create a new THC. Hence, there is plenty of time for the ice pack to take over and much time is required to repolarize the ocean. On the other hand, when the glacial THC collapses, the oceans have tremendous potential energy because they have been, over the previous millennia, hyperpolarized by the slightly inefficient THC. Therefore, the thaw happens rapidly, evidenced in the geologic record by the brevity of our most recent Younger Dryas.

Preventing the Next Ice Age

Making predictions is a hazardous occupation, but unless man becomes vastly more adaptable than he is now, I would estimate a 90% drop in the human population within the two centuries following the collapse of the current THC. Between mass migration, voluntary childlessness, wars over land and resources, widespread civil chaos, starvation, and disease, 90% strikes me as a fairly conservative estimate. Even if there were someplace to put everyone, there will not be anything to feed them. In desperation, every edible thing on the planet will be hunted, fished, or harvested to extinction, greatly complicating any effort to sustain life in the long run. If nuclear weapons play a role, the population collapse will be significantly worse, perhaps even total. In brief, the term *horrific* will be utterly redefined by the next ice age and, by comparison, nothing else on the horizon is even worth worrying about. If this scenario were not so grim, I would never suggest anything as radical as what follows. It is a long shot to say the least. Still, it costs me nothing to write it down, and I will be long gone before it becomes an issue. Maybe a great leader of the future will be able to make use of it.

According to the theory I have been advancing, the interglacial THC is slowly depolarizing the earth's heat gradient. Historically, the only way to repolarize it has been to suffer through an ~80,000-year-long ice age, followed by a 1,300-year-long Younger Dryas-type refreeze. Only after all of that do we finally get to enjoy fifteen or twenty thousand years of nice weather. In a sense, our whole civilization is built on the punctuation marks in between long tales of woe. The only solution is to artificially repolarize the heat gradient ourselves, before nature steps in to do it for us. Sounds impossible, I know. The THC moves a truly monumental quantity of heat. How could anything manmade possibly make a dent in something so enormous?

There is one aspect of the theory that makes such an un-likely venture worth the effort. The hyperefficiency of the THC is very small, on the order of 0.00000001%. Its collapse is not the result of a huge imbalance, but rather of a tiny imbalance that compounds over thousands of years. The THC is *almost* perfect. Therefore, we do not have to compete with it head on, moving trillions of megawatts from one place to another. All we have to do is alter its efficiency from 100.00000001% to 99.999999%, a change of only 0.00000002%. Still a daunting task, true, but no longer obviously impossible. Nor does it matter how long it takes. Since the THC has not yet collapsed, all we have to do is get it working in the opposite way soon, slowly repolarizing the oceans rather than depolarizing them. It will take thousands of years to restore the gradient to an ideal value (whatever that might be), and that is just fine—as long as things get moving in the right direction. Now, the only way to do this is to remove some of its heat and pump it into the atmosphere, where it can then radiate easily into space. What we would be doing, in ef-fect, is transforming the THC from a slightly *hyperefficient* into a slightly *inefficient* heat transfer mechanism.

To remove heat from the THC, we will need to drape gigantic hydrostatic nets, hundreds of miles across, right into the path of the current itself. They can be anchored on the surface to huge oil platforms and to the ocean floor with giant bolts driven into the bedrock. These nets will be fitted with millions of small turbines that resist the flow of the water, converting its kinetic energy into electricity, which can easily be rerouted into the atmosphere. The mesh will have to be large enough to permit the largest of sea creatures to swim through unimpeded. Otherwise, they will require constant repair, to say nothing of what a tighter mesh would do to the whale population. Quite likely hundreds, even thousands, of these contraptions will have to be deployed worldwide to alter the THC by even the tiny per-centage required. On the up-side, the electricity generated in the process can be used to power coastal cities or anything else, just so long as the heat does not end up back in the oceans. The aim is to eventually get the heat into the air and out into space. The resulting rise in air temperature, if it is even detectable, is completely irrelevant. The ocean, not the atmosphere, drives the climate.

The entire system of nets will require constant monitoring, and it will be centuries, at least, before we even know for sure if it is working. The climatic canary in the coal mine, as always, will be the arctic. If enough heat is removed from the THC to have any effect, it will manifest itself first as an increase in the arctic ice coverage. Unfortunately, it will not be time to pop the champagne corks just because the arctic gets colder. The arctic will almost certainly go through at least a few more natural cooling cycles (Little Ice Ages) before the next major glaciation, regardless of what we do.

The only way to really gauge our success will be to painstakingly measure, over many decades, the local contrasts in temperatures between the THC and all of the various local gyres, including the ones in the deep ocean, all over the world. If, gradually, the data suggest that this contrast is, on average, increasing slightly, we can at least hope that we are on the right track. But we can never let down our guard. We must also take care not to overdo it and accidentally hyperpolarize the oceans (though it would be a great sign if we ever had the power to do that). That will cause a THC collapse and subsequent ice age as well. As climate science improves, things will get easier, but this massive project will have to become a permanent part of human civilization to have any chance of success.

10

Radioactive Decay

This chapter comes at the end of the book, because we will need to bring to bear everything we have learned up to this point on the question of radioactive decay. As always, only a computer simulation will permit us to actually witness the decay process in a particular nuclide. There are simply too many variables in play to do this sort of thing with pencil and paper. That is not a weakness of the theory, just a nod to the extreme complexity and subtlety of nature. As with chemical bonds, I make no claim to completeness here. Instead, I will focus on one particular decay event to give a sense of how to apply the theory. I will describe in general the several mechanisms involved in the process, and try to paint an abstract picture of what the computer will someday show us in detail. And because everything we have been discussing up to this point is required in order to paint that picture, this topic also serves as a review of the entire theory.

Hard as it might be to believe, the model of complexity from the previous chapter, the same one that applies to the Earth's climate, is also the one that describes the stabilities and instabilities of all the nuclides. As you can probably guess by now, *W* and *Z bosons* are, like all other quantum phantoms, artifacts of various detection events, related more to the detector particles than to anything that is presumed to have triggered changes in them. They do not exist and have nothing to do with the *weak nuclear force*, which is itself not really a force at all, but rather a mechanical phenomenon that issues from the nearly inscrutable behaviors of complex nucleonic systems.

The strangest aspect, at least to my mind, of radioactive decay are the unfathomably long half-lives of some of the nuclides. For example, selenium-82, which is considered stable, for all intents and purposes, actually has a half-life of 1.08 x 10^{20} years, nearly eight billion times greater than the age of the universe! And there are any number of other nuclides with half-lives in the hundreds of billions of years. When we consider how rapidly the nucleons in an atom move, it is nothing short of astonishing that an imbalance of any kind would require such an incredibly long time span to manifest itself. One could be excused for assuming that if there were something out of kilter in a system that evolves so quickly, it would show itself in very short order, and in many cases it does. But in many other cases, these systems can persevere for eons before finally giving up the ghost, and they can do it for no apparent reason. Ten billion years without a hitch, and then poof, gone in an instant, with no discernable external cause whatsoever. In order for a slight imbalance to build up slowly over billions of years, an atom must be able to register changes with virtually infinite precision. Ask yourself, what is the difference between a selenium-82 atom now, and that same atom five minutes from now? Certainly not very much, but somehow the atom must change to reflect this infinitesimal creep toward decay. To explain a phenomenon as subtle as this one, without invoking all of the mysterious nonsense of quantum theory, is going to require some fairly nuanced reasoning. We will, therefore, build the system methodically from the bottom up, taking as much time as needed to get all the details right.

Back to Basics

Everything in the universe is composed of spacetime, and that spacetime manifests itself in a very limited number of ways. The overwhelming majority of the universe's volume is occupied by spacetime slightly above its equilibrium pressure (~2.7 on the Kelvin scale). The rest is concentrated in either high-pressure gravitational and magnetic fields (typically in or about various stellar phenomena), or in matter composed of partons (i.e., protons and neutrons). All other apparent configurations of matter, such as the phantoms of quantum theory (the particle zoo), are illusions created by mistakenly attributing the complex internal behaviors of "detector" particles to otherwise unobservable causative agents. Likewise, the detritus created by high-energy particle accelerators falls into only a handful of categories. They are:

1. Unstable configurations of partons: A collision between two protons, neutrons, or multinucleonic atoms can result in shattered nucleons. These bits and pieces are composed of unstable associations of partons (more or fewer than in a stable nucleon) that decay rapidly, typically in a manner analogous to that of neutrons. Since these ephemeral particles can exhibit any conceivable mass and decay rate (remember the confusion between intrinsic and extrinsic mass), the "right ones" can easily be misconstrued as experimental verification of some prediction of the standard model. In fact, they are all merely variations on a theme.

2. Beta radiation: This is simply a shock wave, and the observed energy can be generated in any number of ways: when the particles in an accelerator initially collide; when partons decompress; and when stable or rapidly decaying particles jump between energy states.

3. Protons and neutrons: When large atoms are slammed together, some of the debris will be nothing but run-of-the-mill nucleons.

4. Gamma rays: As mentioned above, whenever an unstable but reasonably well organized association of partons is created, it will decay in much the same way as a neutron. Gamma rays are generated by any such energetic rotation.

5. Spacetime: If enough partons decompress at the same time, the resulting spacetime itself might be detectable.

If so, it would behave as a perfect, frictionless fluid or plasma, rather like an intense magnetic field but with no particular orientation.

The most recent target of high-energy physicists has been something called the *Higgs boson*. It is the hypothesized force particle associated with the *Higgs field*, and it is meant to explain why objects have mass. Inasmuch as this hypothesis is based on quantum theory, it is fundamentally flawed for all the reasons we have discussed in previous chapters. Neither is such a theory necessary, as I have already explained why objects have mass. Finally, nothing that comes out of a particle accelerator can credibly be touted as proof for the existence of this or any other quantum entity. Particles of any physically possible mass and decay rate can, with enough energy, be created, and yet they are all nothing but various unstable configurations of partons. Even if the Higgs boson really did exist, it could not be verified by creating a particle with the right mass in an atom smasher.

The Nuclide Chart

If we can now agree that we have very little to work with, we can move on to the challenge of explaining, in physical terms, the truly bewildering array of atoms that make up the material universe. A superficial perusal of the chart of nuclides (**Figure 10.1**[1]) reveals a few interesting facts that dovetail nicely with the theory of complexity described in the previous chapter. First, the overwhelming majority of known nuclides are unstable. As we can extrapolate from the previous chapter, it would be an incredible coincidence if the THC just happened to move heat at exactly the same rate that all of the local gyres receive it from the sun, as well as the same rate at which it radiates back into space. Mathematically, instability should be the norm, and indeed stable atoms are found only on a narrow strip

---

1   Background image courtesy of the National Nuclear Data Center, Chart of Nuclides Database. http://www.nndc.bnl.gov

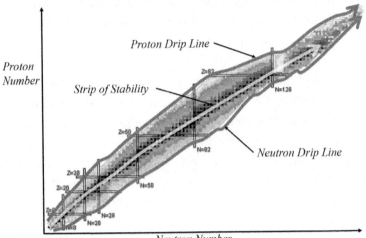

Figure 10.1:   Nuclide Chart
The chart of nuclides reveals a narrow strip of stability in the middle of a sea of unstable species. As expected, instability, on average, increases in proportion to the distance of a nuclide from the ideal ratio of protons to neutrons.

right in between proton-rich and neutron-rich species. Second, the entire range of half-lives, from nanoseconds to tera-years, is represented. Nothing is left out. This makes sense, because the dynamics of complex systems permit any degree of variation between the averages manifested in the chains and the equilibrium requirements of the individual gears. Finally, on average, half-lives decline in proportion to the distance of a nuclide from the strip of stability. Modest deviations from these trends are expected because of the unique properties inherent to particular orbital geometries (i.e., magic numbers). At first glance, then, we seem to be on the right track.

Nucleonic Variability

One of the things we have learned from our consideration of atoms is that nucleons are always either being compressed or decompressed. This happens because each series of derivative axes (energy states) locks its nucleons into a convective velocity that is never perfectly calibrated to the ambient spacetime pres-

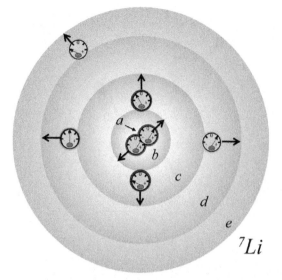

Figure 10.2:   Lithium 7

In a lithium-7 atom, there are five distinct pressure zones. The inner neutron core (a) has two neutrons aimed at a single point in space at the very center of the atom, generating as intense a negative pressure region as is found anywhere in the universe. A second zone (b) also highly negative is located between the inner and outer neutrons. A third zone (c), less intense but still negative, exists between the neutrons and the inner, spherical proton orbital. A fourth zone (d) is located between the inner and outer protons, and a fifth (e) between the valance proton and the outermost electronic shell. Each of the four orbitals affects and is affected by the pressures just above and below itself. When the average battery meter reading reaches a positive or negative danger zone, the entire orbital jumps into a new energy state, restoring its own equilibrium and altering the pressure on adjacent orbitals.

sure. An energy state, recall, evacuates and absorbs spacetime at a constant rate, regardless of the external pressure. As a result, the nucleons' polar jets are either somewhat too energetic, increasing the core pressure, or somewhat too weak, decreasing the core pressure. To compensate, orbitals jump back and forth between adjacent energy states in order to restore equilibrium to their constituent nucleons. This dynamic applies to both neutrons and protons. Moreover, a jump by one orbital will change the pressure of the entire atom (**Figure 10.2**), prompting jumps (one way or the other) in other orbitals. Those jumps, in turn,

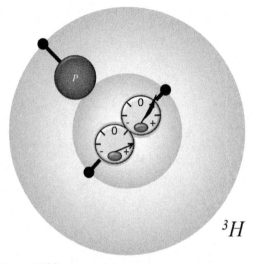

^3H

Figure 10.3:   Tritium
Once the neutrons in tritium are locked into their orbital, any changes in pressure that result from jumping between energy states affects both of them equally. Hence, any differences (notice their battery meters) that existed when they were captured to form an atom will remain until the atom decays.

can prompt still more jumps by other orbitals, etc. In atoms with many orbitals, these jumps and counter-jumps can become very involved, but they also give atoms many different options, as they allow many different combinations of energy states in all the various orbitals. The lesson to take from this is that protons and neutrons are not all identical, even within the same atom or orbital. Yes, every proton has the same number of partons, but not every proton has the same compression. This compression value, its proximity to a tipping point, has a great deal to do with that particle's behavior. Specifically, it represents the location of the needle on the particle's battery meter.

When protons and neutrons are slammed together in various nucleosynthetic events, each one of them is in some particular and random energy state and/or state of decay. Their battery meters have a particular reading, somewhere within their equilibrium ranges. If the resulting atom is anything more complex than deuterium, those readings dictate the initial conditions

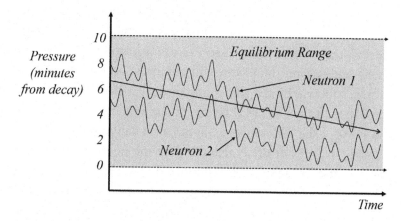

Figure 10.4:   Tritium Decay
The pressure fluctuations within tritium's neutrons are symmetrical, but because their absolute pressures are different, their paths cannot be superimposed. Moreover, it is clearly the neutron that was closest to decay when the atom formed (neutron 2) that will ultimately trigger the decay of the entire atom.

for that particular atom (**Figure 10.3**). Consider that neutrons have roughly ten minutes from the time they are expelled from a star's neutron core (or from a decaying atom) to find a stable home in an atom. As we have seen, a neutron decays over time by gradually puffing up like a marshmallow as its polar jet exerts more force on its core than the particle as a whole can counteract. Exactly when within that ten-minute window a neutron finds an atom is completely random, the result of countless protons and neutrons frantically bouncing around in a chaotic explosion. Therefore, any complex atom (more complex than deuterium) will invariably contain neutrons in differing states of decay that vary randomly over the entire ten-minute process.

Once locked into a specific neutron orbital, these randomly varying neutrons can only be recompressed at the constant rate commensurate with that entire orbital (**Figure 10.4**). They are chained together and cannot be recompressed individually. Any force exerted by the proton shells on the neutron core applies equally to all the neutrons in a particular orbital. Likewise, any changes in the energy state of a neutron orbital affects all the neutrons in that orbital in the same way, regardless of their individual pressures. Imagine tossing several balloons, all inflated to different pressures, into a piston chamber. Lowering and raising the piston will compress and decompress all of the balloons by the same amount, regardless of their initial pressures. It does not play favorites, and will put far more stress on some of the balloons than on others. Likewise, the randomly varying degrees of decay exhibited by the neutrons when they were captured can never be eliminated.

Take, for example, the two neutrons in tritium. If, at capture, one was eight minutes from complete decay while the other was only five minutes away from oblivion, that three-minute difference will remain until the atom as a whole decays. The chain (the orbital) that links them reflects the average of the two neutrons *at the moment the chain was introduced*. Also, it is clearly the neutron that is closest to decay that will ultimately trigger the collapse, as well as determine when that collapse will occur. In a sense, an unstable (neutron-rich) nuclide merely slows the process of neutron decay by decreasing the ambient pressure (slowing the local clock). If the nuclide is stable, that clock comes to a stop.

Protons vary in a similar way, though clearly not with respect to their proximity to decay. Earlier we saw that protons jump between energy states because no particular set of derivative axes perfectly corresponds to the ideal rate of compression and decompression of their constituent partons. Every orbital generates either too much or too little core pressure, causing the proton to gradually hyper-compress or decompress until it finally jumps to an adjacent series of axes, relieving the growing disequilibrium. Like a neutron, a proton enters into an atom at some particular state of compression or decompression, and that state determines how close it is to its tipping point or danger zone—how close it is to jumping into an adjacent energy state.

However, when several protons of differing compressions enter the same protonic orbital, a jump will serve some of the protons more than others. Protons are also like balloons in a piston chamber. A jump is an all-or-nothing proposition and must reflect the average state of all the relevant protons. Consequently, multinucleonic orbitals place more stress on protons than do simple hydrogen atoms. The tipping point must be reached by a preponderance of the protons in an orbital, even if that means a particular proton is pushed to its limit.

It is typically assumed that radioactive decay is a quantum event, because it is impossible to predict exactly when a given atom—or which atom in a radioactive sample—will decay. In fact, the probabilities in radioactive decay are, like those in electromagnetic phenomena, the result of ignorance about the internal states of the atoms. There is nothing intrinsically probabilistic about the phenomena themselves. A radioactive sample exhibits a half-life (rather than simply decaying all at once) because every one of the nucleons in every one of the atoms entered into its specific orbital at some random energy state and/or state of decay (with some particular battery reading). It is random simply because nucleosynthesis is a messy, chaotic affair, not because of any superposition of quantum states inherent to the particles themselves.

By analogy, if we select a large, random sample of human beings, and count how many are still alive at the end of each year, the group will show the same half-life behavior as a radioactive sample. This behavior is the result of the fact that the members of the set are selected at random, and yet all exhibit nearly the same behavior looked at over their entire lives. If the ages and medical histories of the subjects are not known (if they are treated as identical), it will seem that their deaths are intrinsically probabilistic. But if we know anything about the individuals, their deaths begin to make sense.

Applying the theory of complexity from the previous chapter, we can see that each nucleon is a gear, its battery in some randomly selected state of polarization. An atomic orbital (protonic or neutronic) is a second-order system of gears that locks them into one particular geometric arrangement. Collectively, all the proton orbitals are one third-order system, and the neutron orbitals, taken together, are another third-order system. The entire atom is a fourth-order system. The second-order chains connecting the gears are the discrete energy states dictated by the inflexible geometries of certain sets of derivative axes. The third-order chains connecting these orbitals to one another come from the fact that any jump in one orbital alters, in a very specific way, the pressure of the entire atom, prompting other orbitals to jump accordingly. Finally, the fourth-order chains, connecting the entire proton system to the entire neutron system, comes from the balance that must be struck between the pressure in the core and the internal pressures of the individual nucleons. The protons can only sustain an internal pressure that does not undermine their own equilibria. Both the protons and neutrons must jump between states in such a way that the core pressure is kept low, but not so low that the protons grind to a halt, losing their ability to pump spacetime out of the atom. This fourth-order system can almost be regarded as adversarial or dialectical; the neutrons want more than the protons are willing to provide, while the protons simply want a low-pressure region, and could not care less that neutron stability is among the consequences. In a sense, the neutrons must court the protons' affections, but without being too demanding.

Destabilization

As with the Earth's climate, the world economy or, for that matter, any other system that behaves according to this model of complexity, we can look at the system from two different perspectives. We can focus either on the individual gears (local) or the entire system (global). If the system is unstable, the energy gradient that drives the entire phenomenon will gradually depolarize (as the oceans are doing now) or hyperpolarize (as the oceans did toward the end of the last glaciation). On the local scale, some particular gear will eventually find itself charged into its positive or negative danger zone, causing it to either explode or kink the chain by either pushing it forward too hard or retarding its forward motion. In an atom, the pressure contrast that drives the system is derived from the negative pressure in the neutron core and the positive pressure generated by the protons as they push against the electronic shell. For an atom to be stable, this gradient must be maintained at a constant average value. It can fluctuate over time, but must ultimately return to its equilibrium point before it pushes any of its gears into their danger zones.

Though any particular real atom is too complex to examine without a computer, I have decided to use my best guess as to the goings-on in carbon-14 (**Figure 10.5**) as our example. A grain of salt, therefore, is advised. Based on the nuclear model from previous chapters, the carbon-14 atom has a 2-neutron orbital at its center, surrounded by an octahedral 6-neutron orbital, followed by a spherical 2-proton orbital, and finally a tetrahedral 4-proton valance orbital.

According to the current theory, ^{14}C undergoes beta decay to become ^{14}N. Unfortunately, this decay route entails transforming a neutron into a proton through the release of an electron (beta particle). As we have seen over and over, neutrons have less intrinsic mass than protons, and electrons are not discrete particles of matter. Therefore, protons, despite the mountains of evidence in support of this idea, cannot be among the decay products of neutrons. If ^{14}C becomes ^{14}N, it can only do so by destroying a neutron completely and then commandeering a proton from somewhere else during its nuclear reorganization. We might express this as:

$$^{14}C - 1n + 1p \rightarrow {}^{14}N + \beta^+ \text{ (electrons, remember, are actually positive pressure phenomena)}$$

The beta radiation (shock wave) is caused by the decompression of the decaying neutron's partons. The proton can come

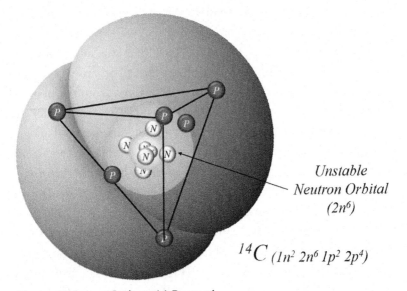

Figure 10.5:   Carbon 14 Decay 1

Carbon-14 decays, as I will show, because its $2n^6$ orbital is unstable. Collectively, all four orbitals gradually allow these six neutrons to expand slightly faster than they are recompressed. Eventually, one of them (the one closest to decay when the atom formed) explodes, destroying the atom. In a sense, a carbon-14 atom merely slows the decay clock of these six neutrons.

from anywhere in the immediate vicinity, and since protons are not in short supply, there is nothing especially irksome about introducing one simply because we need it. Also, we will soon see how a decaying atom is exactly the sort of phenomenon that attracts free protons.

There are four distinct orbitals (two each of protons and neutrons) in a ^{14}C atom. At any given moment, these orbitals are in energy states that simultaneously reflect the ambient pressure, as well as the average internal pressure of the nucleons that comprise them. The ambient pressure, in this context, must be understood as the pressure exerted on a particular orbital, not on the atom as a whole. Although, clearly, the external pressure affects the entire atom simply because it affects the valance orbital, and the valance orbital affects the rest of the atom. Still, viewed locally, the energy state of an orbital is dictated by the local ambient pressure and the internal pressures of those particular nucleons. Also, every nucleon was captured by the atom at a random compression value, more or less close to one or the other of its danger zones. To get the ball rolling, we will assume that the average battery meter readings of the valance orbital protons are approaching their positively hyperpolarized danger zone.

Since all the protons in this orbital have different compression values, the tipping point that triggers a jump to the next slowest set of derivative axes is a composite of all four protons in that orbital. It is like a secondary battery meter (a second-order hub) that averages all four by reading the velocity and tension on the chain (orbital) that locks them together. It is, therefore, only when this second-order meter dictates a jump that the orbital changes energy states, and this is the case even if one or another of the protons is much closer to its danger zone that it would ever permit if it were by itself (say, in a hydrogen or fluorine atom). When the valance orbital jumps, it jumps into a slower series of derivative axes, which we interpret as a jump to a higher energy state. When positively hyperpolarized, the convective velocity of the protons must decrease in order to relieve the pressure on their cores. This decrease in velocity causes a sudden increase in the spacetime pressure within that orbital, as the protons are no longer evacuating it as vigorously. The atom absorbs heat.

When the pressure inside the valance orbital increases, the ambient pressure on the spherical proton orbital must also increase. This is where things start to get interesting. The energy state of the spherical orbital, just like the tetrahedral orbital, represents the best solution to the problem of balancing the orbital's internal pressure against the local ambient pressure. But the ambient pressure itself tells us nothing about whether that solution is gradually polarizing the orbital in the positive or negative direction. That is, just because the needle on the valance orbital's meter was drifting right, it doesn't follow that the spherical orbital's needle was also drifting right. The series of axes associated with different orbitals are related to the geometries and diameters of those orbitals and have nothing to do with one another. They represent unique solutions to unique problems. The relationships between orbitals, as I have argued, is a new third order system, and it evolves according to different dynamics. As a result, the effect of a jump in one orbital on another orbital is literally, *complex*. Let's consider all of the possibilities.

If the needle on the composite battery meter for the spherical orbital was moving to the left when the valance orbital jumped, the increase in pressure might start the needle moving back to the right, or it might just slow its movement to the left. If, on the other hand, the needle was moving to the right, the increase in pressure could only do one thing: accelerate its rightward movement. Therefore, exactly what, if anything, happens depends on which way and how fast the needle on the spherical orbital moves after the valance orbital jumps. It also depends on where the needle was on the meter (indicating how far it is from a danger zone) when the jump occurred. So, the spherical orbital might not jump at all, or it might jump to either a higher or lower energy state. But though it can do any of the same three things it always can, it does them more or less rapidly as a result of the behavior of the valance orbital. For the sake of argument, let's assume the spherical orbital also becomes polarized in the positive direction and jumps to a higher (slower) energy state.

When we talk about the pressure inside an orbital (the ambient pressure), we are talking about the pressure between it and the orbitals just above and below itself. When the valance orbital jumps, the pressure inside of the spherical orbital doesn't change at all unless it also jumps. If it does, it changes the pressure only between itself and the next one down. This is because each series of derivative axes is indifferent to the pressure external to it. The nucleons of which the orbital is comprised, and not the dynamics of the orbital itself, are forced to deal (by compressing or decompressing) with any disparities between their pressures and the ambient pressure. In the case of the spherical proton orbital in ^{14}C, the next lowest orbital is the outermost neutron orbital. When the spherical proton orbital slows down, the pressure between it and the spherical neutron orbital increases. This happens because, at a slower convective velocity, spacetime is being evacuated from that region more slowly and, therefore, the quantity of spacetime there is greater. The atom absorbs more heat. This increase in pressure pushes down against the neutron core, just as the increase in pressure under the valance orbital pushed down against the spherical orbital. However, neutrons and protons are not the same, and similar changes in pressure have different effects on them.

Now, the pressure anywhere in any atom is relatively (compared with outside the atom) low, and it drops incrementally as we move toward the core from the valance orbital. Between the innermost proton orbital and outermost neutron orbital, that pressure crosses a threshold; it goes from *absolutely* positive to *absolutely* negative: it drops below the equilibrium pressure of spacetime (SEP). As we have seen, the pressure in the neutron core must be negative in order to pull the particles together from the inside, much as a stellar core pushes them together from the outside. So, when the pressure inside the innermost proton orbital *increases*, it means the same thing as saying the negative pressure *decreases*. Anywhere outside of this zone, increases in pressure are also increases in energy and mass. However, in negative pressure regions, increases in pressure are decreases in energy and mass.

Something I have noted about neutrons is that their convective velocity increases whenever the ambient pressure either falls from its maximum in a stellar core, or rises from its minimum in an atomic nucleus. Neutrons become increasingly frantic as the force implied by either an extremely high or extremely low pressure is diminished as it approaches SEP from either direction. Consequently, an increase in the ambient pressure on a neutronic orbital has the opposite effect that it has on a protonic orbital. It tends to push them toward a faster series of derivative axes, rather than a slower one. This is critical, because it allows the neutrons to compensate for and balance the actions of the protons. When the protons slow down, causing the overall nuclear pressure to increase, the neutrons speed up, causing the pressure to go back down. The back and forth between the protons and neutrons is the essence of nuclear equilibrium, captured in the fourth order system that unites these two third order systems.

Globally, there is a slight disparity in ^{14}C between the rate at which the pressure is increased and the rate at which it is decreased. Specifically, we know that the pressure in the core gradually rises, because atomic neutrons only become unstable when the pressure is too high. On the local level (the level of nucleons) at least one neutron is eventually stressed to the breaking point, because it cannot receive enough energy from the system. When this happens, the neutron decays and the atom explodes.

Decay

If this theory is ultimately accepted, one of the biggest changes to physics will be the recognition that protons have greater intrinsic mass than neutrons and, therefore, cannot be among the products of neutron decay. When a neutron decays, there is only one possibility. It spins frantically, creating gamma rays, and then gives up all of its partons, generating a shock wave that we call beta radiation. This fact creates a major accounting problem for nuclear decay. When ^{14}C (P-6, N-8) decays into ^{14}N (P-7, N-7) we end up with the same number of nucleons, but not the same number of each type. It certainly looks as if a neutron has been converted into a proton and has released its excess mass as energy in the form of beta radiation. But if this is incorrect, and the neutron completely decays, we suddenly have the unenviable task of identifying where the extra proton came from. To solve this mystery, we will examine a decay event and see if the answer presents itself.

Over and above the particular decay routes of any specific nuclide, there are two main categories of radioactive species: *neutron-rich* and *proton-rich*. In the overwhelming majority of proton-rich species, the decay route involves simply casting off one or more protons; no particles actually decay in this process. The atom merely reconfigures itself into a more balanced ratio of protons to neutrons. The trigger for such a decay event is the same as it is in a neutron-rich nuclide, except it is a proton rather than a neutron that reaches its danger zone. Since protons do not spontaneously decay, they simply leave the atom when the conditions become unsuitable. Neutron-rich species are more interesting because neutrons do not have the option to leave their atoms on such good terms. Neutrons depend on their atoms for their very existence. Moreover, neutrons are located in the center of the atomic nucleus, so when they decay, the entire atom is affected.

Carbon-14 is a neutron-rich nuclide, and decays when a neutron reaches its positively charged danger zone. It has eight neutrons in two orbitals, and it makes a big difference which one decays. When a neutron decays, it rapidly gives up its partons to the surrounding space, and those partons decompress as rapidly as they can. Essentially, neutrons decay by exploding. It is the same force (decompressing partons) that powers a star. Exactly where in an atom that explosion occurs determines how the rest of the nucleons are affected and how, or if, the atom can reorganize itself. The most devastating possibility for any atom is that a neutron in the innermost orbital decays, effectively blasting the entire atom apart and forcing it to completely reorganize itself from the disconnected nucleons, as well as any available protons that might be in the vicinity. Carbon-14 does not appear to decay in this manner, inasmuch as it is not blasted into two or more smaller atoms. Instead, it is more likely that the troublesome neutron comes from the octahedral orbital outside the spherical core.

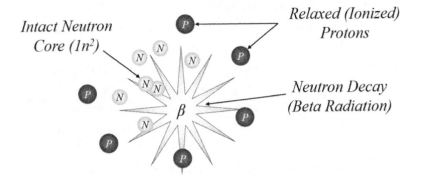

Intact Neutron Core ($1n^2$)

Relaxed (Ionized) Protons

Neutron Decay (Beta Radiation)

Figure 10.6:   Carbon 14 Decay 2

When one of the *$2n^6$* neutrons undergoes beta decay, it fills the atom with high pressure spacetime, ionizing everything except for the inner, spherical neutron core.

Whenever a neutron decays, it has a profound effect on the entire atom, but that effect is greatest on the orbitals outside of the one to which it belongs. Hence, in ^{14}C, if I am right that one of the neutrons in the octahedral orbital decays (**Figure 10.6**), the most affected orbitals will be the spherical and tetrahedral proton orbitals—and, of course, the outer neutron orbital, which is completely destroyed. By contrast, the spherical neutron orbital is only modestly affected, and that means the inner core of the atom is not destroyed in this process. When the neutron decays, it completely fills the core of the atom with high-pressure spacetime—exactly the opposite of what the atom needs. The instant this occurs, the two neutrons in the core begin spinning wildly in an effort to evacuate the excess pressure. This action pushes the high-pressure spacetime away from the core, while simultaneously creating a deep low-pressure region right around the core itself (**Figure 10.7**). The resulting pressure gradient is fantastically attractive to both protons and neutrons. Consider that if the low-pressure zone generated by a single neutron is enough to attract a proton (to form deuterium), imagine what happens when two neutrons are working together. The five surviving neutrons from the octahedral orbital are pulled violently back toward the core, spontane-

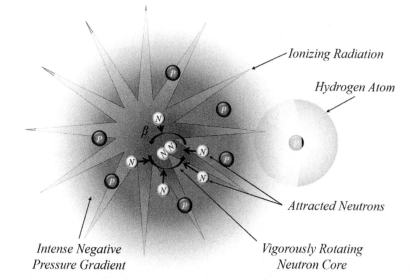

Ionizing Radiation

Hydrogen Atom

Attracted Neutrons

Intense Negative Pressure Gradient

Vigorously Rotating Neutron Core

Figure 10.7:   Carbon 14 Decay 3

To restore a low pressure environment, the $1n^2$ orbital rotates wildly, evacuating spacetime and generating an irresistibly attractive low pressure zone for the five remaining neutrons from the destroyed $2n^6$ orbital. Meanwhile, the beta radiation ionizes any nearby protons, regardless of what atom they currently belong to.

ously reorganizing themselves into the neutron configuration of ^{14}N, further deepening the low-pressure zone around the core (**Figure 10.8**).

The six protons from both orbitals are, for a split second at least, essentially free to do whatever makes the most sense under the circumstances. They are completely ionized and no longer part of any orbital configuration. However, only one thing makes any sense. With seven neutrons spinning like crazy in their immediate neighborhood—generating what amounts to one of the most intense pressure gradients anywhere in the universe—there is no question that the protons will instantly propel themselves into this low pressure zone and configure their orbital geometries accordingly. This is also where it becomes clear where an additional proton might come from. As the spacetime from the decayed neutron is energetically propelled away from the

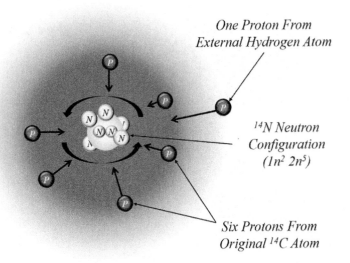

One Proton From
External Hydrogen Atom

^{14}N Neutron
Configuration
($1n^2\ 2n^5$)

Six Protons From
Original ^{14}C Atom

Figure 10.8:   Carbon 14 Decay 4

The five remaining neutrons spontaneously organize themselves into a $2n^5$ orbital, resulting in the neutron configuration of nitrogen-14. The six original carbon-14 protons, plus an ionized proton from a nearby atom, are pulled toward the incredibly powerful negative pressure zone generated by the neutron core.

atom in the form of beta radiation (shock wave), it will bump any nearby protons (whether or not they belong to a multinucleonic atom or are alone) into a much higher (more ionized) energy state, temporarily reducing or eliminating their need for whatever atomic arrangement they currently enjoy (**Figure 10.9**). Moreover, this relaxation occurs at the very same moment that the seven neutrons are busily generating an extraordinarily attractive low-pressure zone in the immediate vicinity of exactly those same protons that have just been ionized.

It is not unreasonable to assume that any such proton would find this low-pressure region more attractive than anything else in its vicinity, and would join the newly minted ^{14}N atom. Finally, because the protons from the decayed ^{14}C atom are temporarily knocked out of their orbitals, there is little or no

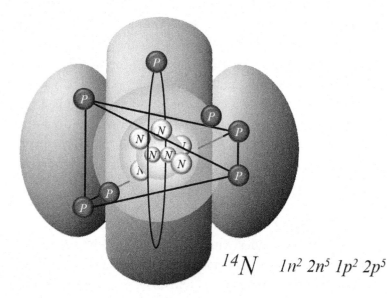

$^{14}N \quad 1n^2\ 2n^5\ 1p^2\ 2p^5$

Figure 10.9:   Carbon 14 Decay 5

Because protons possess more intrinsic mass than neutrons, it is impossible that the seventh proton in the nuclear reorganization came from the original carbon-14 atom. This decay route only makes sense if a neutron is completely destroyed (creating a beta shock wave) and an external proton is commandeered from somewhere in the immediate vicinity.

electrostatic repulsion (i.e., the electronic shell is destroyed for a brief moment) for any candidate proton to overcome in order to join the new ^{14}N atom. In brief, the conditions are perfect in the reorganizing atom to attract an external proton.

The preceding theory makes another very specific prediction that might be empirically testable. If a ^{14}C atom were to decay in *total isolation* from other baryonic matter, it would have no choice but to become ^{13}C rather than ^{14}N. That this has never been observed may be because I am wrong about all of this, but it may instead be because ^{14}C is never found naturally in a rarified and isolated state. Setting up such an experiment, accounting for every particle, will be exceedingly difficult, but if successful, it would provide powerful evidence for this theory in general, and for this new model of radioactive decay in particular. This same experiment could also be performed on any other nuclide, the decay of which seems to imply the transformation of a neutron into a proton. If successful, the daughter atom of a totally isolated parent will be missing a proton. An isotope of radon might be a good candidate, as it is a gas and easily kept in a monatomic state. Even so, these atoms must be kept in a near-perfect vacuum, away from one another, as well as away from the walls of whatever vessel is used to hold them. Finally, the process of examining the daughter atoms must not inadvertently supply the protons we are trying to prove are not there.

Multiple Decay Routes

Heavier nuclides with many orbitals often have several distinct decay routes, releasing different radiation patterns and resulting in different daughter atoms. The theory I am developing here makes sense of this curious phenomenon. Two principles are especially relevant. First, as mentioned above, every nucleon is trapped in its orbital, when its atom forms, at a random energy state. Every nucleon is more or less close to its danger zone. Second, all of the various orbitals in a nuclide are pushed toward their tipping point at some particular rate that is unique to that orbital in that atom. The same orbital in two different nuclides is not subject to the same dynamics, and therefore, can be the primary source of decay in one and a model of stability in another. Because of the complex relationships between orbitals, the whole atom must be taken into account. What this means is that, especially in very complex atoms, more than one orbital can be the source of the neutron (or proton) that ultimately causes the atom to decay. If there are two neutron orbitals, both of which are pushed toward their danger zones at roughly the same rate, we must look at the states of the individual neutrons to determine which of the two will ultimately decide the fate of the atom.

We know the following is not true, but we will assume for the moment that both of the neutron orbitals in ^{14}C can con-

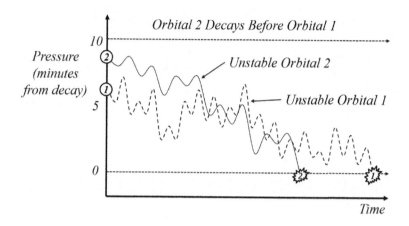

Figure 10.10:   Multiple Decay Routes 1
Neutron orbital 1 in this hypothetical example is inherently more stable than orbital 2, indicated by its slower descent toward decay. In this first case, the average neutron battery meter of orbital 1 starts (when the atom forms) closer to decay (to its danger zone) than orbital 2, but because it decays more slowly it is ultimately orbital 2 that causes the entire atom to undergo radioactive decay.

tain the neutron that eventually decays. Clearly, the decay route I discussed above would not happen if the exploding neutron came from the spherical $1n^2$ orbital rather than the outer, octahedral $2n^6$ shell. Were the core itself blown apart, we would expect all seven surviving neutrons to be blasted away in all different directions, most likely capturing protons to form two or more simpler atoms, perhaps three helium nuclei (alpha particles). As illustrated in **Figures 10.10 and 10.11**, exactly what happens in an atom where several possibilities really do exist, depends on which neutron orbital was closest to decay when the atom formed (calculated from the average battery meter reading of all neutrons that comprise the orbital), and also on the rate at which a particular orbital pushes its neutrons toward their danger zones. Combined, these two factors explain why a nuclide can decay in several different ways, and also why these different routes occur with specific probabilities. The precise location, within a nuclide's orbital geometry, of the neutron decay,

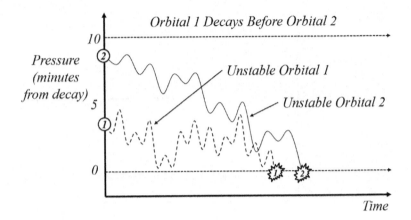

Figure 10.11:   Multiple Decay Routes 2
In this second case, the average neutron battery meter of orbital one starts
much closer to its danger zone than in the first example. Consequently,
even though both orbitals behave exactly as above, orbital 1 causes the
atom to decay, yielding different decay products and daughter atoms.

determines which nucleons are affected, what sort of energy is
released, as well as the dynamics of their nuclear reorganization.

11

Cosmology

In this book I have presented a radical new theory of physics, based on the fundamental substance of reality: a physical three-dimensional version of spacetime. Over the course of that presentation, I have touched upon many of the unsolved problems in physics (and chemistry), but often only implicitly or superficially. This final chapter provides me with an opportunity to address a few of these puzzles in more detail, further demonstrating the value of the theory, as well as showing how it applies in areas not addressed elsewhere.

Cosmic Inflation

Problem: Why is the distant universe so homogeneous when the Big Bang theory seems to predict larger measurable anisotropies of the night sky than those observed?

In the section in Chapter 4 entitled Cosmic Expansion (Dark Energy), I argued that this is a very simple problem, though only when armed with the theory described here. The reason this question is interesting to cosmologists is that quantum theory predicts energy fluctuations at the time of the Big Bang that should have manifested themselves on the macroscopic scale in a far less uniform (more anisotropic) distribution of matter and energy in the universe. One way to explain the unexpected isotropy that we observe is to propose that the universe expanded so rapidly during its first few moments that any fluctuations in energy density were, in effect, stretched uniformly across the entire cosmos, smoothing out the lumps as it were. It is further supposed that the pictures provided by the Wilkinson Microwave Anisotropy Probe (WMAP) of the microwave background radiation are snapshots, writ large, of early quantum fluctuations that are now greatly expanded and projected across the entire cosmos. If, the argument goes, the Big Bang had unfolded at a subluminal velocity (rather than at a hugely superluminal, inflationary velocity), the cosmos would be far lumpier, less isotropic, than it actually is.

It is true that the large-scale isotropy and small-scale anisotropy of the cosmos are interesting problems that need explanations. It is also true that the cosmos did indeed undergo inflationary (superluminal) expansion immediately following the Big Bang. However, quantum theory is not part of the equation and any apparent consequences of quantum energy fluctuations must be explained in other ways.

My theory predicts that the Big Bang was perfectly uniform, the result of an extraordinarily dense sphere of undifferentiated spacetime that had collapsed out of infinite nothingness over the course of eternity. At the end of its collapse, this massive sphere reached a maximum pressure, the point in cosmic evolution at which the universe was closest to its extreme infinite pole.[1] Spacetime was able to exhibit this extreme behavior only because it dramatically *ripped* away from the rest of the void and was catapulted down into a tiny volume, well above its equilibrium pressure. The kinetic energy of its collapse overcame its inherent resistance to compression—the resistance provided by its finite pole.

Two interesting questions that I cannot answer are: 1) How dense was the cosmos just before the Big Bang? and 2)

---

1   Though the Big Bang may appear to be the point at which the cosmos is closest to its *finite* pole (because it is compressed into a discrete mass of definite size), it is actually the *infinite* pole that forces space to collapse. Hence, the greatest extent of the collapse corresponds to the dominance of the infinite pole. This is so because any two points, considered from an infinite distance, become the same point (converge), as described in Chapter 1.

How big was the spacetime sphere? If we could find answers to *both* of these questions, they would tell us how much matter is in the universe and, by extension, how big the *visible* universe is by comparison to the *entire* universe: One percent? Five percent? Eighty percent? Since we cannot see beyond the edge of the visible universe, these answers will depend on extrapolating the behavior of spacetime from the first principle itself, specifically, discovering the precise dynamics that govern the collapse of the void. The target of this investigation will be the tipping point at which the pull of the collapse exceeds the resistance of the void to stretching—the ripping point—thereby defining the total quantity of spacetime that constitutes a universe. If it turns out that this tipping point is a variable rather than a constant, then the two questions may not be answerable, but even that conclusion would be enormously interesting.

Because this theory naturally results in a perfectly uniform spacetime mass preceding the Big Bang, it is not the *isotropy* but the *anisotropy* of the cosmos that is at issue. That is, at first blush, it appears that the Big Bang was entirely symmetrical at all scales and should have simply expanded rapidly back into the void, leaving behind the same nothingness whence it came. However, as explained in Chapter 2, there are two interesting components of the expansion that enabled the Big Bang to create the matter upon which our physical universe is based.

First, because the Big Bang expanded into the void, rather than normal space (i.e., spacetime at the vacuum pressure), its expansive acceleration was derived entirely from its internal resistance to compression (its finite pole) and not retarded at all by any countervailing resistance to expansion from space[time] outside of the sphere. Consequently, the expansion was hugely superluminal (inflationary), unconstrained by the customary cosmic speed limit of c, which only applies within spacetime, not within the void.

Second, this preposterously high inflationary velocity resulted in a very rapid decrease in the internal pressure of the sphere, thereby relieving the resistance to compression exerted by spacetime's finite pole. Nevertheless, the expansive acceleration, though it decreased as the pressure decreased, remained positive because the void beyond the sphere's surface continued to provide zero resistance. As a result, the inflationary velocity of the entire cosmos—from almost immediately after the Bang—dramatically exceeded the requirement of the finite pole to reduce its extreme pressure. In effect, the finite pole quickly relaxed as the sphere expanded, but the inflationary velocity did not decrease in response. Indeed, it continued to increase, though at a decreasing rate. This huge disparity between accelerating inflation on the cosmic scale and spacetime relaxation (decompression) on the local scale resulted in the formation of spacetime granules, the building blocks of protons and neutrons.

These granules of spacetime (what I have called *partons*) introduced two important asymmetries that are germane to this discussion of cosmic anisotropy. First, partons are themselves internally asymmetrical. They are spacetime gradients, defined by the inverse square law, dense in the center and less dense on their surfaces. The second asymmetry has two causes: the rapidly dropping pressure along the partons' surfaces, which are in direct physical contact; and the rapidly inflating cosmic sphere that is attempting to pull the partons away from one another. At a critical point after the Big Bang, the pressure on the surfaces of the partons dropped all the way to, and then well below, the equilibrium pressure of spacetime (SEP or cosmological constant). Then, immediately after that threshold was exceeded, when the infinite pole began to exert itself along the surfaces of the partons, the cosmic sphere of spacetime came to a dead stop. It fractured into a very complex network of filaments that foreshadowed the current filamentous architecture of the cosmos, as well as the broad outlines of the microwave radiation detected by the WMAP telescope. This network of partonic filaments is the second important asymmetry caused by the Big Bang.

The homogeneity of the universe is only indirectly relat

ed to the Big Bang and has much more to do with the cosmological constant than anything else. Even if the Big Bang had been far lumpier (due to something akin to quantum energy fluctuations) than it was, the equilibrium pressure of spacetime would have long since overwhelmed those anisotropies. The cosmological constant, as its name suggests, exerts its influence everywhere in the same way, never changes, and creates the illusion that the cosmogenic event (e.g., the Big Bang) was curiously symmetrical. The cosmos is flat and uniform not because of a symmetrical event or any communication between disparate locations, but because of its eternal ontological nature.

Cosmological Constant Problem

Problem: Why does the zero-point energy of the vacuum not cause a large cosmological constant? What cancels it out?

This problem with quantum theory is much more significant than its inclusion in this chapter suggests. All of the other questions here—even the ill-formed ones that are not, strictly speaking, answerable as stated—at least point to phenomena that can be explained in some fashion or other. By contrast, the enormous variance between the vacuum energy predicted by quantum theory and the value actually observed is decisive evidence of the failure, not only of quantum theory in particular, but of the whole notion of *fields* in general. Reflect for a moment on the first ten chapters of this book and you will note that not a single explanation of any phenomenon required the introduction of an energy field[2]: no electromagnetic field, no gravitational field, no quantum fields for nuclear forces, etc.

Fields are only necessary in the absence of three-dimensional physical spacetime, the core concept of this theory. In essence, quantum fields are an intricate amalgam of mathematical

---

2   My occasional colloquial use of *gravitational field* ought not to be confused with the specific predictions associated with field theory. I could just as accurately have referred to them as *regions*. Never was there any implication that the field itself existed as a definite entity over and above the substances and objects within it.

media (an entirely abstract substrate) that are meant to replace the simple physical medium of spacetime. And the huge variance between the actual pressure of the vacuum and the value predicted by the formulae highlights the complete invalidity of the theory. This fact should not be looked upon as the "Cosmological Constant Problem," but rather as the "Quantum Field Theory is Hopelessly Wrong Observation."

Extra Dimensions

Problem: Does nature have more than four spacetime dimensions?

Nature possesses exactly four spacetime dimensions. This problem addresses one of the central theses of String Theory, which is regarded as a highly promising candidate for the Grand Unified Theory of Everything by a substantial fraction of the physics world. This, despite the fact that even its most ardent advocates admit there will probably never be a single iota of empirical evidence to support it.

String Theory is motivated by one unshakable assumption: that the cosmos operates according to one mathematical expression or, at least, one simple set of mutually compatible expressions. It is believed that the difficulties physicists have had reconciling equations that, individually, seem to apply to only one or another isolated domain will eventually be overcome. It will then become obvious that all of these incompatible equations are actually seamless elements of one overarching mathematical theory of everything. Implicit in this assumption is a very extreme version of physical reductionism: all of the complexity of the physical universe is somehow nascent within its most fundamental constituents (e.g., strings).

Operating from this assumption, string theorists have built a mathematical model that incorporates all of the expressions that they believe are indispensable for a complete unified theory. I do not claim to understand the mathematical details, but it is not difficult to discern what String Theory is at its heart. Consider what would happen if we attempted to shoehorn ten intrinsically incompatible mathematical equations—regardless of what those equations describe—into a single expression or system. How might we do it?

The easiest way would be to introduce an independent degree of freedom for each of the equations. That way we could sidestep the difficult work of actually making them compatible in the real world, and simply plot their incompatibilities into new unseen dimensions. Of course, reality does not appear to have any such extra degrees of freedom, so maybe this is not such a great idea after all. But if we start from our unshakable assumption, articulated above, then reality must bend to our mathematical will. To demonstrate the gratuitous nature of String Theory, we can use the same basic idea to "explain" the fundamental principle that governs a major international airport.

We start by meticulously observing the comings and goings of each of the important elements, documenting their behaviors, and crafting mathematical expressions for each of them. Among the elements are the pilots and flight attendants, baggage, baggage handlers, maintenance and security personnel, passengers, ticket agents, airplanes, fuel supplies, etc. All of these elements will exhibit statistically predictable and vaguely similar behaviors because they are all part of the same overarching phenomenon (the airport). Yet because they are not all scheduled by the same management team and do not address themselves to precisely the same issues, the several equations that describe their behaviors will not exactly coincide. If we were to attempt to reconcile all of these equations, we would find that, though it seems like they should be, they are not compatible. However, if we were to simply add another dimension for each one of them, and conjecture that these dimensions are not readily visible (perhaps hidden in a bunker deep beneath the tarmac), then we would have a fully developed String Theory of the Airport.

The absurdity of this *reductio ad absurdum* example issues

from the notion that all of the complexity that drives all of the elements comprising an airport must somehow be unified and shoehorned (reduced) into a single substance. Instead, as with the universe, the complexity of the airport arises piecemeal through the increasingly complex configurations of intrinsically simple constituents.

Ultra-High-Energy Cosmic Ray

Problem: Why is it that some cosmic rays appear to possess energies that are impossibly high (the so-called OMG particle), given that there are no sufficiently energetic cosmic ray sources near the Earth?

It is currently understood that cosmic rays are, for the most part, protons. A proton is a convective circulation of partons. It propels itself forward like a miniature jet engine. Typically, this propulsion is restricted to the extremely small spaces within the nuclei of atoms. Or, when alone, the propulsion causes it to spin in place to create a hydrogen atom. To understand a cosmic ray, we need to speculate about what might cause a proton to propel itself forward along a more or less linear path rather than merely spinning in place.

The first important consideration is that a proton (or something very like it) need not derive its energy from it source. That is, we do not need to explain how a cosmic ray got its energy in the first place, nor how it managed to traverse millions of light years without gradually losing it. A proton is not like EM radiation nor is it like an inanimate object, subject to the drag of space debris. A cosmic ray is self-propelled and for that reason its energy is intrinsic to the particle itself rather than derivative of its source. This single observation solves many of the problems related to ultra-high-energy cosmic rays.

The other part of the equation has to do with how a proton can propel itself in a straight line rather than simply spin. As I have discussed at length throughout this book, the convective circulation of a proton or neutron results in zero net angular momentum. That is great for atoms, but would seem to exclude any kind of controlled linear flight path for a lone proton. That being the case, it is unlikely that a cosmic ray is an *intact* proton. And, indeed, this picture changes significantly if we consider a hadronic particle that is neither a proton nor a neutron, but is instead something in between the two, specifically, a proton that has been slightly damaged in a naturally occurring high-energy collision.

We know from the data gathered from high-energy particle accelerators that proton-proton collisions can yield any physically possible combination of partons. In highly energetic head-on collisions, for example, the debris is usually nothing but a shower of very small particles that barely resemble their parent protons. However, in an oblique or grazing collision, the damage to the protons can be far less significant, leaving them damaged but still more or less intact—still suitable for convective circulation. It is this latter case that is interesting with respect to cosmic rays.

When a proton is converted into a neutron on a star's neutrogenic shell, a specific number of partons is removed in order to bring the particle into equilibrium with the extremely high ambient pressure of the shell. The resulting neutron is stable within the star's core, but very unstable at the vacuum pressure, and its instability is a direct consequence of its missing partons. As the constituent partons of a free neutron circulate in normal space, the pressure generated by the jet in the core is too intense to be balanced by the surface tension generated by the partons farther from the core. The frantic circulation that results from this instability also increases the intensity of the neutron's polar jet, pushing against the core, puffing it up and hastening the particle's decay. This is the general picture that emerges of a particle that has fewer partons than a proton—fewer than is required to maintain equilibrium. Our question then becomes: What would happen to a particle with *almost* enough partons to maintain equilibrium—more than a neutron but fewer than a proton?

For the sake of argument, let's assume that a proton loses 5 percent of its partons on a neutrogenic shell to become a neutron. What would happen if a proton lost only 0.5 percent of its partons in, for example, an oblique high-energy collision associated with a supernova or some other cataclysmic event?[3] By theory, such a particle would be unstable in the void, since only a proton has exactly the right number of partons to create a stable equilibrium indefinitely. Yet we know from the example provided by neutrons that there are conditions within normal space (composed of spacetime rather than nothingness) that provide opportunities for stability that do not exist in the void. Specifically, the high pressure in a stellar core and the negative pressure in an atomic nucleus both exert enough force to keep a neutron compressed. The example provided by a neutron, therefore, suggests the possibility that a cosmic ray is a slightly damaged proton and that its linear trajectory is actually an equilibrium strategy.

The neutron teaches us that there are two ways an unstable particle can persevere: it either finds a very high-pressure region to push down on its surface (stellar core), or it finds an extreme negative pressure region to pull in against its core (atomic nucleus). Since cosmic rays appear to be simple lone particles, we can safely rule out the negative pressure (antimatter) strategy, which is only possible within the relatively complex environment of an atom. That leaves only the high-pressure option.

Figure 11.1 illustrates the phenomenon that is beginning to emerge from this discussion. The relevant issue here is the pressure at the *bow shock* at the leading edge of a particle moving at a high relativistic velocity. We know from the *Lorentz Factor*, that the mass/energy of an object increases very rapidly

---

3   These numbers are for illustrative purposes only and could easily be off by an order of magnitude (e.g., 0.5% and 0.05% rather than 5% and 0.5%). Research will be needed to determine exactly how many partons must be removed to transform a proton into a neutron or cosmic ray.

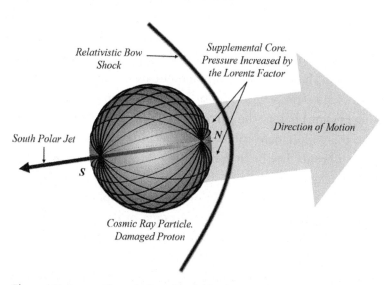

Figure 11.1: Cosmic Ray Particle

The spacetime pressure between the leading edge of the cosmic ray (damaged proton) and the spacetime bow shock increases according to the Lorentz Factor–relatively small differences in velocity result in large differences in pressure. This increased pressure is the mass/energy dilation associated with the particle's relativistic velocity. The high pressure is located just outside of the proton's north pole, enabling it to supplement the efforts of the core to recompress the partons circulating around the proton's surface.

(and without bound) as that object approaches the speed of light (**Figure 11.1**). What this means is that a cosmic ray (damaged proton) can increase the pressure at its bow shock to arbitrarily high levels in direct proportion to its velocity, which is itself directly proportionate to its convective vigor. The convective vigor, in turn, is governed by the degree of instability of the cosmic ray, which is caused by the degree of damage it has suffered. If the cosmic ray is a proton with only minimal damage, the convection will be relatively slow and the pressure and velocity will be relatively low (though still close to c). A more damaged proton, because it is less stable, will exhibit a faster rate of convection and higher pressure and velocity.

Note that the relativistic bow shock is located just outside the mouth of the cosmic ray's north pole. This is the location at which partons with the greatest decompression are pulled back into the particle's core to be recompressed. Hence, this is the ideal location for the high-pressure zone. In effect, the bow shock functions as a supplement to the core, starting the process of recompression (or at least preventing any further decompression) before the partons even get off the surface. Moreover, this supplement can be very precisely calibrated according to the Lorentz Factor by modulating the convective velocity of the particle.

In addition to explaining the general phenomenon, this hypothesis also explains the wide range of cosmic ray energies that are observed, as well as their statistical distribution. The instability of a cosmic ray is related to the degree of damage suffered by its parent proton. That instability, in turn, is responsible for both its convective intensity and resultant velocity. And because the Lorenz Factor allows for increases in mass/energy without bound, as an object approaches the speed of light, we should expect a huge array of cosmic ray energies, including the rare OMG particles that have been detected. Indeed, if we superimpose the Lorentz Factor curve onto the cosmic ray flux that has been observed, we see that they both exhibit nearly the same hyperbolic shape.

Segments *a* and *b* in **figure 11.2** represent equal linear distances along the curve and correspond to different ranges of cosmic ray energies (along the horizontal axis). The equal length of the segments reflects the random degree of damage that might be suffered by a proton, anywhere within the overall range of the cosmic ray phenomenon. Outside of this range, the damage to the proton can be assumed to be too severe (bringing it too close to a neutron) to permit it to act as a cosmic ray. These equal segments (*a* and *b*) assume that, during a natural high-energy collision, any degree of proton damage is equally likely. *P* and *P'* show that the probability of finding a ray decreases as the energy increases, because *a* is on a flatter and *b* on a steeper part of the curve. To the right of *b*, the graph becomes even steeper and the

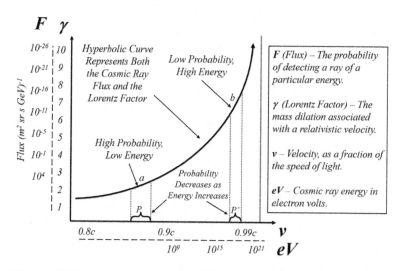

Figure 11.2: Superimposition of Cosmic Ray Flux and the Lorentz Factor

Here, cosmic ray flux is superimposed onto the Lorentz Factor. Simple linear variations in the amount of damage to a proton (a & b) yield exponential differences in cosmic ray energies. Since the damage from high-energy collisions is random and linear, while the Lorentz Factor increases hyperbolically (without bound), high-energy cosmic rays are exponentially less common than lower-energy rays.

probability becomes even lower, approaching zero as the curve approaches its asymptote (as the velocity approaches the speed of light).

Finally, this hypothesis explains the existence of extremely high-energy cosmic rays (OMG particles). Since the Lorentz Factor increases without bound as the cosmic ray approaches the speed of light, we can infer that OMG particles are protons that have suffered the maximum amount of damage that is consistent with the cosmic ray equilibrium strategy described in this section. Any additional damage would result in a particle that cannot move fast enough to benefit from mass dilation at its bow shock, and therefore would undergo decay in much the same manner as a standard neutron. There is an upper limit on cosmic ray energy because the force, proportionate to the Lorentz Factor, required to accelerate into a relativistic bow shock eventually exceeds the force responsible for parton circulation within the damaged proton. As the pressure of the spacetime at the bow shock increases, it becomes increasingly resistant to any additional compression. And because it can increase without bound, it can exceed the force a proton is capable of exerting.

Coronal Heating Problem

Problem: Why is the Sun's corona (atmosphere layer) so much hotter than the Sun's surface?

Coronal heating is a fascinating phenomenon that refers to the extreme difference in temperature between the sun's surface (~5800 K) and its corona (1–3 million K), located anywhere from a few dozen to a hundred or so kilometers *above* the surface. The obvious challenge here is to explain how a region outside of the Sun can be so much hotter than the Sun itself. Theoretically, radiative heating would require the surface to be hotter than the corona because heat transported by electromagnetic radiation dissipates according to the inverse square law. There is no generally understood mechanism that violates this thermodynamic principle, and certainly not to such an extreme degree. According to the theory in this book, temperature is defined as the pressure of spacetime. Therefore, it would appear that the pressure of the sun's surface is, for some strange reason, considerably lower than the pressure of the corona, some distance away. The question, then, must focus on the mechanism that is driving up the pressure of the corona.

Posed in this way, the answer is fairly straightforward: The corona is actually a termination shock of the solar wind, marking a radius at which it slams into the relatively slow-moving spacetime immediately beyond the sun's surface. Though simple in principle, the specifics of this phenomenon are greatly complicated by the sun's rotation, which tends to stretch, twist, and compress the wind toward the poles and equator in the manner described in Chapter 4. However, this added complexity does not fundamentally alter the theory behind the phenomenon.

Given the extreme heat of the corona, the solar wind, upon exiting the sun's surface, must be moving at a relativistic velocity, far greater than its merely supersonic velocity out beyond the corona. Under any of the current physical theories, it would not be possible to entertain such a notion, because a spacetime flow of that intensity—exceeding even the high escape velocity of the sun—would sweep up solar matter from the upper mantle at a prodigious rate and quickly transport our star piecemeal out into space leaving nothing behind. So, if the corona is a relativistic termination shock, there must be a component of this phenomenon that prevents the Sun from tearing itself apart.

As always, when a spacetime flow pushes against the cosmos (in the form of the vacuum pressure), the cosmos pushes back with an equal and opposite force. As described in Chapter 4, black holes are prevented from exploding like miniature big bangs by the steady resistance of spacetime at its equilibrium pressure way out at the black hole's termination shock. If we assume for a moment that the solar wind exits the Sun with a relativistic velocity, we can then also assume that the ambient spacetime immediately surrounding the Sun pushes back against it with an extraordinary counterforce. This collision is responsible for the extreme high temperature of the corona. When the solar wind hits the coronal termination shock, it creates something akin to an atom's electronic shell. The pressure on that shell pushes up against the cosmos (in the form of the slower, supersonic solar wind), but also pushes back down against the surface, holding the Sun together and preventing the sun's mantle matter from being swept out into deep space.

Besides explaining the coronal heating problem, this hypothesis has some other interesting consequences. It implies that there are at least four—and possibly five—important gravitational zones inside and outside the sun.

1. The **neutrogenic shell**, which transforms protons into neutrons, liberates spacetime and creates the innermost gravitational gradient, the one that holds the sun's mantle in place and compresses the core, stabilizing its neutrons.

2. The **coronal shell**, which, by decelerating the relativistic flow of spacetime, achieves a very high temperature and pressure. This means, surprisingly, that the gravitational force of the sun, measured anywhere between the corona and the traditional termination shock, issues from the corona and not directly from the neutrogenic shell or anything else inside the star.

3. The traditional **termination shock**, described in Chapter 4, which is located approximately 70–90 astronomical units from the sun, and is gravitationally implicated in the distribution of matter in the Kuiper Belt.

4. An extremely distant and hypothetical **final termination shock**, that would be gravitationally implicated in some way with the distribution of matter in the Oort Cloud.

5. The very indirect and tiny effect of the sun's liberated spacetime, spun off the disk of the Milky Way, on the **cosmological equilibrium of the entire galaxy.**

We have seen repeatedly how difficult it is to extrapolate the mass of a stellar object directly from its gravitational force. For example, neutron stars appear to become denser as they become smaller because their gravitational fields issue from their surfaces and the ratio of surface area to volume increases as a neutron star shrinks. Indeed, in view of this theory, it now appears that typical atomic matter is actually anomalous, the only known configuration of matter that does not generate its gravitational field primarily on its surface, but throughout its entire extent. That means it is not possible to accurately compare the masses of, for example, the Earth and Sun by simply comparing their relative gravitational field strengths. Because the sun's gravitational field is generated in large part by the extreme force that results from the liberation of spacetime from protons, and *not* directly from the total number of hadrons of which the Sun is composed, the mass of the Sun (measured in hadrons rather than kilograms) is actually far *lower* than is currently believed. The Earth's gravitational energy comes from the physical/mechanical convection of its innumerable protons and neutrons, whereas the sun's gravitational energy comes primarily from the transformation of mass into energy (high-pressure spacetime) through neutrogenesis. The latter process is far more energetic, per unit of mass. That is, it has a far higher gravitational energy-to-mass ratio than nucleonic convection. However, this higher gravitational energy should not be attributed to a greater quantity of matter, but rather to the completely different manner in which that energy is generated. Therefore, the Sun has considerably less intrinsic mass than it appears to have when its ratio of mass to gravity is assumed to be identical to Earth's (or any other sample of standard non-stellar atomic matter).

In Chapter 2, I discussed the relationship between the cosmological constant and the pressure responsible for uniform neutron creation on the neutrogenic shell. Briefly, the vacuum exerts itself at the termination shock, pushing back against the solar wind. Because this counterforce is based on the equilibrium pressure of spacetime (the cosmological constant), the outward force of all neutrogenic shells in all stars must exert the same pressure per unit of surface area. The pressure on this shell is responsible for causing a very specific number of partons to migrate out of a proton, resulting in perfectly uniform neutrons everywhere in the universe. However, it would now appear that the termination shock way out in the Kuiper Belt is only *indirectly* responsible, while the coronal termination shock is *directly* responsible for the pressure on the neutrogenic shell. We might even speculate that the Oort Cloud termination shock (if it exists) also plays a role, being more directly in contact with the true interstellar vacuum pressure. In fact, all of this may be true, and it certainly adds complexity to the theory. But ultimately it does not change anything; it is still the cosmological constant that drives the whole system. The pressure with which any of these termination shocks pushes back against the solar wind that creates it is dictated by the pressure between itself and the next farthest one out. Ultimately, this daisy chain of termination shocks is still dictated by the vacuum pressure of interstellar space, and the uniformity of both neutrogenic shells and the neutrons created thereon is still dictated by the cosmological constant, just not in a simple one-step process.

The Lithium Problem

Problem: Why is there a discrepancy between the amount of lithium-7 predicted to be produced in Big Bang nucleosynthesis and the amount observed in very old stars?

The theory of Big Bang nucleosynthesis (BBN) is ultimately motivated by only one observation: the cosmic abundance of helium is too high to be explained by the current theory of stellar nucleosynthesis. The other substantive prediction of BBN is that there should be a somewhat higher abundance of lithium than can be accounted for by stellar nucleosynthesis alone. The troubling absence of that extra lithium compromises the theory's credibility and leaves only the abundance of helium to support it. If, therefore, another source can be found for all of this helium, then there would be no need for BBN. In fact, if such a source could be identified, then BBN would be ruled out because it would, paired with the new source, result in too much helium—more than is observed. Throughout this book, I have presented the various elements of a new theory of nucleosynthesis that collectively solve the lithium problem. I present all of them here in one discussion to help strengthen the case for this rather radical hypothesis.

There are four relevant considerations:

1. The equilibrium conditions during the Big Bang were extremely precise and suitable only for the creation of protons, not neutrons. No helium or lithium was created.

2. Nuclear fusion is not a natural phenomenon because the energy associated with the strong nuclear force is derived from negative pressure spacetime (antimatter).

3. There is no obvious upper limit on the mass of a star because a star's gravitational force is not focused on the very center of the star, but instead issues from a neutrogenic shell that marks the boundary between the core and mantle.

4. The pressure on the neutrogenic shells of all stars is the same, driven by the vacuum pressure at the star's termination shock.

Though there are many important consequences of these hypotheses, the one that bears most directly on the current discussion is the absence of any upper limit on the mass of a star. If the gravitational energy of a star is not focused on the star's center, but is instead distributed evenly across the entire surface of a large shell located some distance from the center, then it is no longer impossible to imagine supermassive stars (on the same scale as supermassive black holes), millions or even billions of solar masses. In view of the inverse relationship between stellar life span and mass, the cosmic epoch of such stars would have been very brief, but also very spectacular.

In the very early universe, the density of hydrogen was orders of magnitude greater than it is today; there was considerably more of it and it occupied a much smaller cosmic volume. This brief period of extremely high hydrogen density provided a window of opportunity for the creation of what I have named *galactic stars*. This species of stellar object is prohibited by the currently accepted theory because its gravitational force would seem to overwhelm any counterbalancing force from nuclear fusion in the core. It could not establish a stable hydrostatic equilibrium and would collapse directly into a supermassive black hole without first going through a main sequence stage of stellar evolution. The absence of this stage means that no nucleosynthesis would occur, so this type of phenomenon could not (according to current theory) be responsible for the large amount of helium in the cosmos. Hence, all that is necessary to replace BBN is to provide an alternative explanation for these objects that allows them to enjoy, however briefly, a main sequence life.

By way of multiple scenarios, I have shown how the cosmological constant manifests itself through the auspices of a termination shock. Whenever a flow of spacetime is generated, it eventually slams into the ambient spacetime at or near its equilibrium pressure, resulting in a termination shock that pushes back against that flow with an equal and opposite force. This occurs at least twice (corona and Kuiper termination shocks) and possibly three times (Oort termination shock) in the heliosphere. The electronic shells of all atoms are generated by the termination shocks of their nucleons' polar jets. The gravitational rings around spiral galaxies (currently explained by dark matter) are actually gigantic termination shocks created as spacetime is accelerated off the edge of the rotating disk where it subsequently runs up against the intergalactic medium. It also has been observed that there are termination shocks within the relativistic jets of black holes. Termination shock is a ubiquitous natural phenomenon in a universe composed of the substance (spacetime) I have been describing.

The central insight with respect to stars in general, and galactic stars in particular, is that the termination shock of the solar wind (most directly at the corona and indirectly at the edge of the heliosphere) is governed by the cosmological constant in the form of the vacuum pressure. Spacetime at the vacuum pressure, pushing back against the solar wind, places an upper limit on the rate at which that solar wind can be created—the rate at which mass can be converted into energy in the star—and expelled. Hence, the process of nucleosynthesis is not governed primarily by the size, gravity, pressure, or rate of nuclear fusion in the star's core. Instead, a shell of maximum pressure forms inside the star, but some considerable distance from the core, and that shell is the site of neutron creation. This neutrogenic shell is related to the cosmological constant according to the inverse square law, and because the cosmological constant is a constant, the pressure per unit of surface area of all neutrogenic shells is identical.

This shell generates a high but uniform pressure throughout the star's core. This uniformity means there is no spacetime pressure gradient, and therefore no gravitational field in the core; however big and massive the star might become, it does not generate an ever more intense gravitational force that would tend to immediately collapse it into a black hole. Instead, large stars have stronger gravitational fields than small ones because their shells have larger diameters and greater surface areas, but all stars have the same pressure per unit of shell surface area.

Collectively, this means that supermassive galactic stars are no longer theoretical impossibilities, and that is a game changer with respect to the cosmic abundance of helium. Instead of Big Bang nucleosynthesis, we have gamma ray burst nucleosynthesis, a process I described in detail in Chapter 3. This path would lead to huge quantities of helium, through a combination of the direct nucleosynthesis of helium, as well as the subsequent alpha decay of a vast reservoir of unstable neutron-rich isotopes. And finally, this hypothesis does not predict a higher than observed cosmic abundance of lithium.

Nuclear Forces

Problem: What is the nature of the nuclear force that binds protons and neutrons into stable nuclei and rare isotopes?

There are two different nuclear forces: the force that holds partons together within protons and neutrons (hadronic force), and the force that holds protons and neutrons together within atomic nuclei (nuclear force). Other than the general fact that all forces are ultimately grounded in the equilibrium pressure of spacetime (the cosmological constant), it is a mistake to think of the two nuclear forces as part of the same phenomenon (i.e., the gluonic attraction between quarks).

Hadronic Force

The partons that comprise hadrons are in a state of dynamic equilibrium, and there are several factors involved. The partons themselves, understood in isolation from their host particles, want nothing more than to explode according to $E=mc^2$. Within a hadron they exert a very powerful expansive force on adjacent partons, and by extension, on the particle as a whole. At the same time, each parton resists excessive separation from adjacent partons because of the inherent resistance of spacetime to decompression below its equilibrium pressure. This can be illustrated by looking closely at the relationships between adjacent partons (**Figure 11.3**).

The first thing to note is that a parton is basically a miniature black hole. It is made of nothing but high-pressure spacetime and it exhibits a pressure gradient. What is perhaps most interesting about both partons and black holes is the curious manner in which they sustain their shapes according to the inverse square law, dense in the center and progressively less dense toward their surfaces. As explosive as they are, it might seem that either object would expand as quickly as possible into whatever space is available, not unlike an ideal gas. A black hole, as we have seen, is virtually indistinguishable from the Big Bang, and yet it endures rather than immediately exploding. The reason for this peculiarity, what amounts to a frozen explosion, is the steady resistance provided by the ambient spacetime at the vacuum pressure way out at the black hole's termination shock. Objects made of high-pressure spacetime, located within normal space, do not act like a gas and fill the available space uniformly because, unlike a gas, spacetime has an equilibrium pressure. By

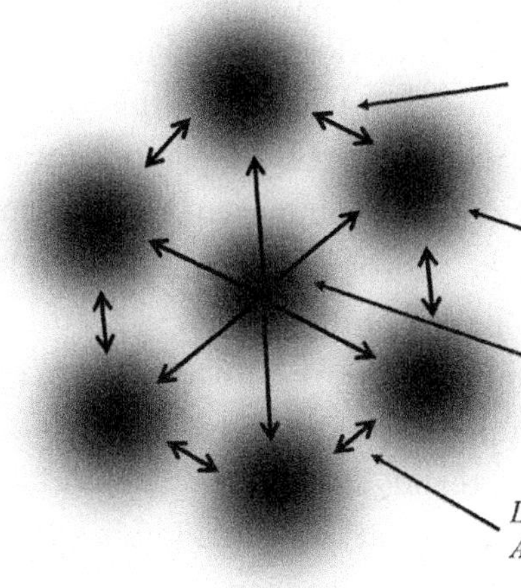

Spactime Plasma Rather than
Sharp Boundaries

Inverse Square Law Spacetime
Gradient

Extremely High (Big Bang)
Spacetime Pressure. Expansive
Force. Miniature Black Hole.

Low Spacetime Pressure.
Attractive Force. Strong "Skin"

Figure 11.3:   Hadronic Force

This highly simplified diagram illustrates the forces at play between partons within a hadron that give rise to its dynamic equilibrium. The partons
out away from the core are pushed apart, away from each other, by the explosive pressure generated in the core. The resulting stress along the surface, as the spacetime is stretched, tightens and strengthens the hadron's
skin, much as the skin of a balloon exerts more force as it is stretched. That
negative pressure force, the surface tension, allows the core pressure to
rise sufficiently to recompress the partons as they are circulated through
it. The tight skin and high-pressure core, combined with the high-speed
convection, results in an impenetrable virtual wall that maintains the equilibrium of the overall hadron.

contrast, gas particles simply want to get as far away from one
another as physically possible; they fill the volume available to
them.

The picture with partons is similar, but slightly different.
Unlike black holes, partons are not slowly evaporating. They do
not have anything analogous to solar wind that slams up against
the ambient spacetime to create a termination shock. Instead,
partons bump up against other partons along their surfaces.
There is no empty space out beyond this surface, as there is for
stellar objects, into which a parton's spacetime can dissipate. If
a black hole's outer extent were an impenetrable wall rather
than a termination shock, it is reasonable to assume that it, like a
parton, would cease to decay and instead hold its shape and mass
indefinitely.

The inability of a parton to either explode or even decay is the result of its convective circulation, its dynamic equilibrium, within a hadron. As discussed in Chapter 2, this circulation is driven by the contrast in pressure between partons located at different points in their host particles. In general, partons are compressed in and around the hadron's core and allowed to decompress as they circulate away from the core. As partons with a greater compression attempt to move into regions occupied by partons with lower compressions, those lower-compression partons are circulated back through the hadron's core and recompressed, completing the circuit and maintaining the hadron's overall equilibrium. Because a hadron is circulating near the speed of light, the positive core energy and negative surface energy are hugely augmented by the Lorentz Factor associated with their respective pressures.

Looking at this phenomenon from an intuitive, common sense perspective, the hadron turns itself inside out and in so doing creates the equivalent of an impenetrable wall for all of its constituent partons. The partons explode against this wall, in the hadron's core, instead of out beyond the surface of the particle. At the same time, the resistance of the partons, collectively, to being separated along their surfaces produces what amounts to a very strong skin for the hadron, a kind of surface tension. This skin can withstand the extreme pressure in the hadron's core, enabling the particle to recompress the partons that were recently decompressing on the surface. The strong negative pressure surface tension on the skin balances the high positive pressure in the core, resulting in the dynamic equilibrium that defines a hadron. The instability of a neutron, outside of either a stellar or atomic core, is the result of a disequilibrium between the high-pressure core and the negative pressure skin. Specifically, the skin, the surface tension, is not strong enough to hold the particle together—to balance the high-pressure core —without help from either protons or a stellar core.

This equilibrium condition is highly sensitive to the ambient pressure, outside of the hadron, because the pressure in the core is affected by the intensity of the hadron's polar jet, which is itself affected by the pressure of the spacetime it encounters upon leaving the hadron's south pole. In the void, unlike in normal space, a proton would quickly find its ideal convection rate and circulate at exactly that rate forever. In the many complex ways described throughout this book, the demands of hadrons, coupled with the ambient pressure, are critical components of all nuclear and chemical behaviors.

Nuclear Forces

The force that holds nucleons together is only indirectly related to the hadronic force described above. There is no analog in my theory to the all-purpose gluonic force that exerts itself strongly between quarks within hadrons, and then weakly between hadrons within nuclei. Instead, the nuclear force is a consequence of an equilibrium relationship established between neutrons and protons, and it exists only because neutrons are unstable at the vacuum pressure. As with the hadronic force, the nuclear force is a dynamic equilibrium and it has several components.

That atomic nuclei can exist at all is a direct consequence of the fact that the energy possessed by spacetime is proportionate to the *absolute value* of the Lorentz Factor associated with its pressure—negative pressure possesses positive energy. This is a hugely important observation because most of the cosmos is composed of positive pressure spacetime, and energy is usually conceived as resulting from that positive pressure. Negative pressure spacetime, by contrast, is rare and its associated mass/energy roughly corresponds to the current concept of antimatter. If this negative pressure energy did not exist, if spacetime did not have an equilibrium pressure, then there would be no way to stabilize neutrons outside of a stellar core.

The first places negative pressures of any consequence were created (within our cosmic epoch—in the time since the

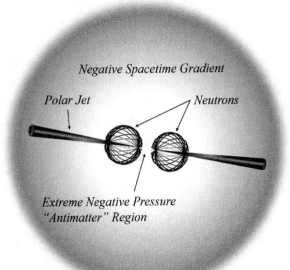

Figure 11.4:   Dineutron
Neutrons, even in the absence of protons, can increase their stability by forming various neutronium particles. By way of such cooperation, neutrons can combine their resources to create the deepest possible negative pressure region at the core of the particle. Neutronium can be expected to exist briefly within the neutron cloud of a supernova—constituting the first step of nucleosynthesis—and possibly also within the neutron cores of main sequence stars and neutron stars. One could also refer to the briefly exposed neutron cores of atoms undergoing radioactive decay as neutronium.

Big Bang) were in the spaces between neutrons that had recently been expelled from an exploding galactic star. Having been violently torn from the neutron core of their host star, neutrons were scattered through space, separated from the stabilizing pressure of the star, but not yet protected by protons within atoms. During that brief period, these unstable particles came together to create the neutron cores (what could also be called *neutronium*) of their eventual host atoms. **Figure 11.4** represents the relevant forces and geometry.

When neutrons are expelled from either a star or their host atom, they spin wildly in a desperate attempt to keep their partons compressed in the core faster than they decompress on the surface. This spin generates gamma radiation and x-rays, because the intensity of the neutron's polar jet and the velocity of its rotation are both directly related to the vigor of the particle's convection, and are responsible for the amplitude and frequency, respectively, of the emitted wave. The frantic convection also generates an extreme negative pressure region around the north pole of the neutron; spacetime is evacuated from that region as it is pulled into the particle's core. The spacetime in this region is very attractive to other neutrons (and protons) because it pulls back against the north pole of any particle that attempts to pull it into its core. This attraction is one of the two components of the nuclear force.

The other component is the south polar jet. Once neutrons are locked together by their mutual attraction to the negative pressure region that they collectively create, their south polar jets propel them directly toward that very same region. Together, these two components comprise the strong nuclear force.

An area that would benefit from further research is this theory's prediction that the strong nuclear force exerted by neutrons is considerably stronger than it is between protons. This is so because of the more vigorous convective circulation of neutrons—a consequence of their instability—and the resulting depth of the negative pressure they create.

Entropy (Arrow of Time)

Problem: Why did the universe have such low entropy in the past, resulting in the distinction between past and future and the second law of thermodynamics?

The theory described in this book implies a very specific cosmological cycle that incorporates everything from the origin of matter out of infinite nothingness, through the collapse of space into the Big Bang, through the evolution and ultimate de-

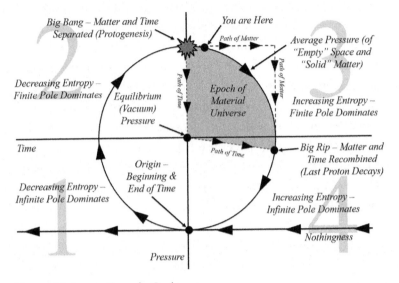

Figure 11.5: Cosmic Cycle

God's eye view. The fundamental principle of the cosmos is the tension between the paradoxical poles of nothingness. Infinity and finitude are equal, opposite, and logically contradictory, making the whole cosmic cycle into an epic struggle for equilibrium.

mise of our familiar reality, and finally back to the nothingness whence it came.

Figure 11.5 shows the evolution of the universe from the most comprehensive perspective possible, a *God's eye view*. Because it is a giant cycle, technically it does not matter where we begin. Nevertheless, we have certain expectations about what constitutes a satisfying cosmogenic narrative, so it is best to start in the lower left quadrant.

Quadrant 1

The origin of the cosmos is, at its core, not a *thinkable* phenomenon. It is based on a logical-geometric paradox that is intrinsic to the nature of infinite nothingness (**Figure 11.6**). Our brains are not capable of apprehending, in any truly meaningful way, either infinity or a logical paradox. The best we can hope for is to simply accept, however painfully, that the void is indeed best characterized as infinite nothingness, and that

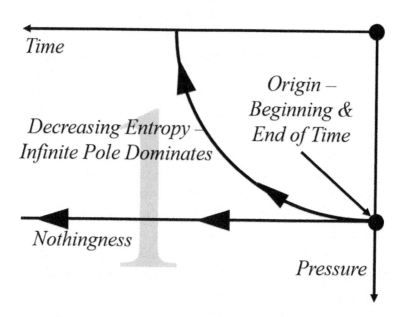

Figure 11.6:   Cosmic Cycle Quadrant 1
The simplest definition of *rational* is: follows necessarily. Since the first principle does not follow, but comes first, it cannot be rational. Indeed, the origin of matter is necessarily irrational and incomprehensible, mediated by the paradoxical characteristics of infinite nothingness.

our observation of the cosmological constant (primarily as the vacuum pressure and/or the acceleration of cosmic expansion) inescapably suggests an ontological tension within the most basic stuff of existence. Thankfully, it is not necessary to form a rational notion in our minds of how such a bizarre event could possibly unfold or what it would look like. Indeed, though I am the originator of this idea, I have no better intuitive sense of it than you do. Chapter 1 of this book—the chapter that will no doubt cause the most headaches—is nothing more or less than an uncompromising application of Occam's razor. Once we accept the unpalatable fact that the universe emerged from infinite nothingness and that there is in fact a cosmological constant, then the theory presented here is simply the most parsimonious explanation possible. It starts from the fewest assumptions (it explicitly assumes *nothing*) and has the fewest moving parts.

Its incomprehensibility is, perhaps, unfortunate, but not entirely unexpected, given that logic requires a *premise* in order to be "rational" and nothingness does not meet that requirement.

Though incomprehensible, we can nonetheless speculate that the origin is characterized by a gradual increase in the density of spacetime as the infinite pole of nothingness pulls together points that, from a finite perspective, appear to have a discrete separation. Prior to the commencement of this paradoxical process, there is very little we can say about the void, except perhaps that it exhibits three spatial dimensions. However, once space begins to collapse, it makes sense to start describing it, not simply as empty space (the void), but as *spacetime*, a substance manifested by the tension of its paradoxical internal coherence. At first, the pressure of spacetime would be extremely negative, still dominated by its infinite pole, far below the equilibrium pressure that is approximated by the vacuum.

As we have seen, negative pressure spacetime is roughly equivalent to the traditional concept of antimatter. Though I hope to have successfully demonstrated that there are no actual *particles* of antimatter, the concept is still very important in our cosmic epoch because of the role intense negative pressure plays in stabilizing neutrons within the cores of atomic nuclei. It is with respect to stabilizing neutrons that we get out first hint at the relationship between antimatter, entropy, and the arrow of time. In unstable nuclides, the decay clock of at least some of the neutrons is not stopped as it is in stable species, but merely slowed to a greater or lesser degree. In stable species, the clock is stopped (if not forever, then at least for a very long time). Negative pressure spacetime, by pulling rather than pushing, acts in its own small way against the general expansion (entropy) of the universe during the current cosmic epoch.

Immediately after the origin of the cosmos, negative pressure dominated on a much larger scale than that of an atomic nucleus. That cosmic epoch was the exact opposite of the one we are in now. Instead of high-pressure expansion, it was marked

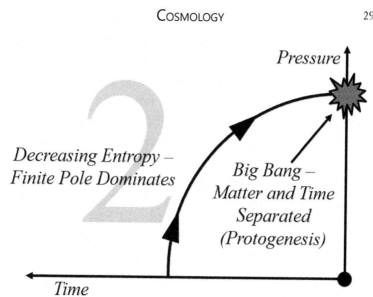

Figure 11.7:   Cosmic Cycle Quadrant 2
In quadrant 2 the signs of entropy and spacetime diverge—spacetime becomes positive while entropy remains negative all the way to the Big Bang.

by negative pressure contraction. Both entropy and time moved
in the opposite direction, as indicated by the arrow of time (the
circle) in Figure 11.6.

Quadrant 2

The transition from the lower left quadrant to the upper left quadrant (**Figure 11.7**) occurs when the pressure of
the collapsing cosmos reaches, and soon thereafter exceeds, its
equilibrium pressure (SEP). Up until this moment, the cosmos
was exhibiting an accelerating collapse, just as our current epoch is exhibiting an accelerating expansion. And, just as we are
currently building up a tremendous reservoir of expansive momentum—enough to ensure a Big Rip in the very distant future—the accelerating collapse built up a comparable reservoir
of contractive momentum—enough to crush space all the way
down into the spacetime sphere that we know as the Big Bang.
Perhaps the most interesting aspect of the transition from quadrant 1 to quadrant 2 is that the sign of spacetime and the direction of entropy diverge.

In quadrant 1, both the pressure of spacetime and value of entropy are negative; the collapse causes the pressure to rise and the cosmos to become increasingly orderly, more compact. In quadrant 2, the pressure of spacetime switches sign and becomes increasingly positive, yet because of the momentum of the collapse, entropy continues to decrease all the way to the Big Bang. What this means is that entropy is not tied directly to the dominant pole of spacetime and is, therefore, not a fundamental aspect of the cosmos. In quadrant 1, the infinite pole dominates and is responsible for the accelerating collapse, while in quadrant 2 the finite pole dominates and causes the collapse to decelerate until it stops just before the Big Bang. The arrow of time changes direction with the changing polarity of spacetime, while entropy remains negative throughout the transition from quadrant 1 to quadrant 2. Overall, the arrow of time points forward (to the right) in quadrants 2 and 3 (our current epoch), and backward in quadrants 1 and 4. Meanwhile, entropy is negative in quadrants 1 and 2, and positive in quadrants 3 and 4. Entropy and the arrow of time do not match. So, what are we to make of the concept of entropy?

In the broadest possible terms, entropy could be defined as the inverse of the average pressure of the cosmos. At the transition from quadrant 4 to quadrant 1, the universe has reached its minimum pressure (absolute nothingness) and maximum entropy (minimum orderliness). At the transition from quadrant 2 to quadrant 3 the universe reaches its maximum pressure (the Big Bang) and minimum entropy (maximum orderliness). It is not at all clear, however, that this overarching cosmic fact has much or anything to do with the other more discrete uses of the concept. For example, in quadrant 2, cosmic entropy is decreasing, and yet during most of that epoch (because time is moving forward) matter would behave more or less as it does today. Heat would disperse and equalize throughout an object; gas particles would quickly achieve a uniform distribution within a closed vessel; and statistical observations about flipped coins and

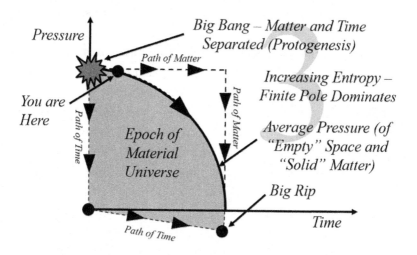

Figure 11.8: Cosmic Cycle Quadrant 3

Quadrant 3, our cosmic epoch, is unique. Matter and time become separated through the mechanism of protogenesis, resulting in a virtually constant rate of change within most of the material universe.

shuffled cards would be the same as today. All of these events would unfold predictably, despite the fact that cosmic entropy was steadily decreasing at that time. Stripped of this correlation between local, closed systems that strive for thermodynamic equilibrium, on the one hand, and the overall evolution of time and the cosmos, on the other, entropy ceases to be a particularly interesting or foundational concept. On the cosmic scale, entropy is—driven by the more basic laws that govern the polarity of spacetime—merely a derivative artifact of whichever direction (collapse or expansion) the universe happens to be moving. On the local scale, using the term *entropy* is a misnomer; it mistakenly conflates a general cosmic phenomenon with discrete local ones. These familiar phenomena are better understood in the more pedestrian terms of thermodynamics and statistics.

Quadrant 3

The transition from the upper left quadrant to upper right quadrant (**Figure 11.8**) is the most spectacular of the four and is headlined by the Big Bang, the event that is traditionally associated with the birth of the cosmos. The most fascinating aspect of quadrant 3, our current cosmic epoch, is that it is the only one of the four in which time passes at a constant rate. In quadrants 1, 2, and 4 there is no stable vacuum pressure as there is in our epoch. Instead, the collapse (quadrants 1 and 2) or expansion (quadrant 4) results in an ever-changing average spacetime pressure and, therefore, more or less extreme relativistic time dilation effects. In quadrants 1 and 4, time flows backward, slowly in some parts, but very rapidly near the origin. In quadrant 2, time flows forward, but at a slower and slower rate as it approaches the Big Bang.

I have represented the cosmic cycle as a simple circle with congruent quadrants, suggesting that each epoch is of roughly equal duration. That is very unlikely to be the case. Instead, quadrants 1 and 4—the epochs of infinite nothingness and eternity—are almost certainly vastly larger than quadrants 2 and 3. Nevertheless, if we permit ourselves a bit of teleological wish fulfillment, the whole cycle appears to exist solely to bring about the phenomena of our current epoch, the other three being devoid of complex matter. The Big Bang is the key to our universe of plenty.

Figure 11.8 shows that the Big Bang resulted in the separation of matter and time through the mechanism of protogenesis. Typically (quadrants 1, 2, and 4), spacetime (matter) and time move in lockstep; the higher the spacetime pressure (the greater the density of matter) the slower time moves. Positive pressure means forward flowing time, while negative pressure results in backward flowing time. Quadrant 3 is different. Protogenesis locks the majority of spacetime into extremely dense but stable particles that do not immediately decompress in accordance with the finite pole. Instead, the equilibrium state achieved by a precise number of partons (in a proton) allows the average pressure of spacetime (outside of protons and neutrons) to remain very nearly constant (the vacuum pressure) for an extremely long period (13.7 billion years and counting). Relativistic time dilation still occurs, of course—the pressure is not the same everywhere in the universe—but only at high speeds and in and around extreme phenomena such as stars and atomic nuclei. The overwhelming majority of the cosmos exhibits the same conditions across both space and time, and will continue to do so until the transition into quadrant 4, when the Big Rip kicks off. Time flows at a constant positive rate throughout quadrant 3, and this separation of matter and time provides the necessary vantage point to understand exactly what time really is.

What we typically refer to as matter is largely exhausted by protons, neutrons, and black holes. Black holes are an interesting case, because they exhibit simultaneously the high pressure of a proton, but also the undifferentiated uniformity of spacetime in its more usual state (e.g., the vacuum). If protons were physically impossible, quadrant 3 (our epoch) would look like nothing more than a backward replay of quadrant 2, a featureless expanse of decompressing spacetime, beginning at a point of maximum density and becoming increasingly nebulous over time. There would be no complex matter, and obviously, no life or any of the other interesting phenomena with which we are familiar.

At one level, time refers to the pressure of spacetime, specifically the manner in which spacetime pressure affects the rate at which phenomena unfold within it. It is widely believed, for example, that within a singularity (no such thing), where spacetime supposedly exhibits infinite pressure (it doesn't), time comes to a standstill. I said above that time changes in lockstep with the spacetime pressure in quadrants 1, 2, and 4—running faster and slower, forward or backward at various points—but that is only true in an abstract, theoretical sense. In fact, there are no atomic objects in those three quadrants, nothing that changes against the spacetime background. If there is nothing to change, it makes little sense to discuss the *rate* of change. We can say with a high degree of confidence what would happen to an atomic object if it were placed at some specific point in one of these three quadrants, but only by reference to comparable scenarios within our own epoch. But that still does not seem to get at the essence of time itself.

There is one brief period that contained what was simultaneously the most revelatory and the most disconcerting event with respect to time: the existence of protons immediately following the Big Bang, but before the infusion of empty space with spacetime—before the complete decompression of the leftover partons that did not find homes within protons. For a brief period, protons existed in the void between the parton filaments. They achieved a convective equilibrium and, presumably, settled into a constant convection rate. But relative to what? The fact that protons can and did exist, however briefly, in the void, is supremely strange by reference to our usual understanding of time. The existence of matter in the void, outside of spacetime, has never been considered, but because it can and actually did occur, we have the uncanny opportunity to separate the concept of *change* from the properties of spacetime wherein that change typically occurs.

Perhaps the first and most important thing to note is that a proton is, intrinsically, a dynamic equilibrium. That is, it cannot be conceived as something that does not change; its movement is an integral part of what it is. In that respect, it would appear necessary that time passes, even in the void, assuming we want to retain *change* as an indispensable component of time. This is strange because objects in relative motion within the void do not exhibit any relativistic effects and are not constrained by the speed of light. Hence, two protons could (and likely did) pass by one another in the void at superluminal velocities, yet without either of them suffering any time or mass dilation. They were, though in relative motion, moving through the same non-relativistic, absolute reference frame. During those brief moments, Newtonian physics took precedence over the Einsteinian variant.

It must be kept in mind that the void is not the same

thing as spacetime at its equilibrium pressure. It makes sense to refer to SEP as *zero* on, for example, the Kelvin scale. That is, if spacetime has neither a positive nor a negative pressure—is at equilibrium—it could be said that it is at zero (using either temperature or pressure units). However, this equilibrium pressure is vastly higher than the absolute nothingness of the void, which, on the scale of spacetime pressure, would have an infinite negative value, not a value of zero. Yet clearly the void does not behave as infinitely negative spacetime, since such a pressure would instantly tear a proton apart. For better or worse, the need to invoke the notion of infinity here places us back within the paradox discussed in Chapter 1, at the heart of ontology. Specifically, there is a categorical and irrational difference between spacetime—of any pressure—and the void. Moreover, there is no possibility of finding a rational, comprehensible tipping point or threshold where the nothingness of the void, as it collapses, suddenly starts behaving as the somethingness of spacetime. Any such threshold is mediated by infinity and eternity and is, therefore, fundamentally incomprehensible.

Yet here we are, forced to contemplate the existence of matter as we understand it (protons) against the fundamentally irrational background of the void. More to the point, we are forced to make sense of the juxtaposition of two incommensurable realities, each on an opposite side of the infinity paradox. Thankfully, there is another example of this juxtaposition we can use as a reference point: the overall expansion of the cosmos.

The most compelling and direct evidence we have for the presence and characteristics of the void is the current superluminal expansion of our universe. The most distant galaxies exhibit a red shift that corresponds to a velocity of recession well in excess of c, demonstrating beyond any reasonable doubt that the leading edge of the cosmos, whatever and wherever that might be, is encroaching on the void faster than the speed of light. The second most compelling argument comes from the strong circumstantial evidence for cosmic inflation during the first few moments after the Big Bang. Both of these related phenomena imply the juxtaposition of spacetime and the void, as well as the fact that the void allows superluminal, nonrelativistic velocities.

All of this points to the fact that events occur both within spacetime and within the void, and those events transpire differently. In general, events within spacetime unfold according to Einstein, while events within the void unfold according to Newton. This is unnerving because we have been trained to accept that Einstein's universe is a more accurate depiction of reality—an improvement—and that it has completely supplanted Newton's version. It would now appear that Relativity Theory is actually the special-purpose theory, correct only within the rare (relative to the infinite vastness of the void) pockets of spacetime that constitute universes. Here are some of the things we can say about reality in the void:

- Only protons (or the universe as a whole) can exist in the void. Neutrons and complex atoms would immediately decay.
- Because light is composed of spacetime waves, light does not exist in the void. In any case, nucleons do not emit south polar jets (of spacetime) in the void, so there is no source of energy for light waves in the first place.
- Despite the absence of spacetime and light, it is still possible to define fundamental units of both time and space:
  - » Time – the duration of a single circulation of a convective cell within a proton can define the basic unit of time.
  - » Length – the diameter of a proton can define the basic unit of distance.
- There is no maximum velocity.
- Objects move against an absolute reference frame and exhibit no relative time or mass dilation. There is no need to apply Lorentz Transformations to Newtonian formulae in order to get the right answers.

If, then, we treat the Newtonian and Einsteinian worlds as competing theories of physics, it would appear that we are stuck with two different and incompatible realities that, at least at some times and places, exist right alongside of one another. Indeed, immediately following protogenesis, as the leftover partons (those that did not find homes in stable protons) decompressed and filled space with spacetime, the newly minted protons actually migrated from Newtonian reality into Einsteinian reality. That, I submit, is not a tenable way to characterize the universe. Instead, both of these realities must find an appropriate expression in an overarching theory of physics—without either claiming any sort of priority over the other.

It is telling that this discussion has forced us to define the ultimate background against which events unfold. In addition to the Newtonian (void) and Einsteinian (spacetime) variants, there is also the quantum mechanical (fields) version. As described above, however, the last of these has far bigger problems than the other two; until its predicted value bears at least some vague resemblance to reality, it is not worth considering here. With respect to the first two, it is perhaps valuable to simply state the obvious and see if that sheds some light on the subject. The following statements follow from the theory in this book:

- The void is true nothingness, not a contrived or mathematical version of nothingness (e.g., empty quantum field or spacetime field).
- Spacetime is related to the void through the auspices of infinity. Specifically, spacetime is an infinite compression or collapse of nothingness according to $x = 0 \cdot \infty$.
- Objects made of spacetime exist within the void, within nothingness, evidenced by the inflationary expansion of the Big Bang, as well as the current superluminal velocity of recession of distant galaxies.

In essence, therefore, spacetime—in all of its various incarnations, from the vacuum to partons—is not the ultimate background. Instead, the void is the background and spacetime is the substance that exists within the void. Only when we treat spacetime as the fundamental *background*, as opposed to the fundamental *substance*, do we find ourselves wrestling with conflicting definitions of reality. By analogy, objects behave differently within the Earth's atmosphere than they do in the vacuum, just as they behave differently within the vacuum than they do in the void. However, in the former case, we understand that the atmosphere is a *thing* that needs to be accounted for, whereas in the latter case we are ambivalent, sometimes treating the vacuum as a thing and other times treating it as the ultimate ontological background of reality. Hereafter, it must always be treated as a thing.

Treating spacetime as a thing, we can better characterize the relationship between spacetime and time. Specifically, the denser spacetime becomes, the slower events unfold. High spacetime density can be caused by a gravitational gradient or by the compression associated with high velocity. This definition of time enables us to define an absolute reference frame, independent of velocity and gravity. Absolute time can be defined either as the rate at which events unfold within spacetime at its equilibrium pressure (the cosmological constant), or the rate at which events unfold in the void. In effect, the term *relativity* is a misnomer. Considering two objects (within the universe of spacetime, not within the void), the one with the highest velocity or within the stronger gradient will have the slower clock. Their *relative* motion is beside the point. For example, the clocks of astronauts move slower than their earthbound counterparts because the astronauts are moving more rapidly through spacetime than the Earth's surface.

Quadrant 4

The transition from quadrant 3 to quadrant 4 in **figure 11.9** occurs when all of the main sources of decompressing spacetime (primarily black holes by that time) have been exhausted.

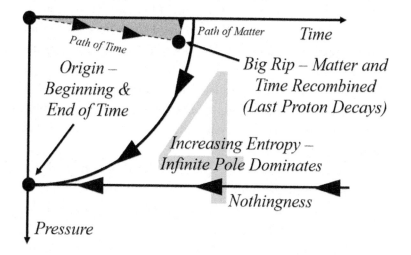

Figure 11.9: Cosmic Cycle Quadrant 4

In quadrant 4 the spacetime pressure becomes increasingly negative, resulting in the accelerated decay of all complex atomic matter. Then, after untold eons of expansion, spacetime succumbs to the infinite paradox and is restored to a state of absolute nothingness.

By then, the universe will have achieved a truly phenomenal size and velocity of expansion, the consequence of untold eons of positive pressure spacetime (Dark Energy) pushing the outer limits of the cosmos ever faster into the void. The moment the last black hole disappears, this rapid expansion will no longer be abetted by the release of additional new spacetime, filling the cosmic volume. Spacetime will first drop below the vacuum pressure, then soon thereafter below its equilibrium pressure (SEP). Dark Energy will reverse sign, becoming negative, now a force of contraction rather than expansion.

However, though spacetime will reverse sign and cause a general deceleration in cosmic expansion, there will be far too much momentum built up by then to stop it—ever. Over time, as the spacetime pressure drops to ever more intense negative values, any remaining complex matter will become increasingly unstable and be gradually torn apart. In this Big Rip, molecules will decay first, followed, in order, by less stable and finally more stable atoms. As neutrons are liberated from their host atoms, they will decay and rapidly add their mass to the huge expanding spacetime sphere, leaving only lone protons behind. Protons will eventually decay as well, although I cannot say exactly how. Protons can straddle the transition from spacetime to void, across the infinity paradox, so it is unclear what their ultimate undoing will be. A computer simulation could probably shed some light on this subject.

Over the course of the eternal expansion in quadrant 4, spacetime eventually undergoes a transition related to its internal and paradoxical polarity. Looked at from an inflexibly logical perspective, the eternal expansion of our cosmos ought to result in an infinitely negative spacetime pressure—the pressure we would assign to the void on, for example, the Kelvin scale. Clearly that is not what actually happens. The void is not a logically limiting case of spacetime; it is ontologically distinct, categorically different, and logically incompatible. Apparently, as the cosmos expands, it reaches some indeterminate minimum negative pressure, and then, by virtue of the infinite paradox, denatures in some strange way and transitions into pure nothing rather than into infinitely negative something. Just as the collapse of nothing into something ($x = 0 \cdot \infty$) thoroughly defies human comprehension, the reverse, the transition from something into nothing ($x / \infty = 0$), is also beyond rational thought.

Acknowledgements

Several years ago my wife, Jill, gave me the greatest gift anyone could ever hope to receive—Freedom. In the old-fashioned spirit of scientific patronage, she let me quit my job and devote myself fulltime to a life of the mind. Despite understanding little or nothing of what I was doing, she extended her unflagging support and, what is infinitely more important, her trust, with only my vague assurances and her faith to keep her going. Without her, this book would not exist. I look forward to spending the rest of my life justifying her inexplicable belief in me, and rewarding her with all the love and affection my undeserving heart can muster.

Others whom I would like to thank for their talent and support in this work are:

- Will Troxell, reviewer. While we received comments and reviews from several people while working on the first edition, a special thanks to Will Troxell for his continued support and input through this process.
- Kelly Kagamas Tomkies, editor. Kelly was a tremendous asset to the revision of this book. Her attention to detail and ability to enforce continuity have greatly improved the final product, allowing the reader to stay focused on the science.
- Paula Ryan, cover artist. Paula's creative eye combined the elements of space, time and infinity into a captivating and meaningful cover image.

Glossary of Scientific Terms

absolute value: A nonnegative number equal in numerical value to a given real number

accretion disk: A disk of usually gaseous matter surrounding a massive celestial object (as a black hole) in which the matter gradually spirals in toward and accretes onto the object as a result of gravitational attraction

angular momentum: A vector quantity that is a measure of the rotational momentum of a rotating body or system, that is equal in classical physics to the product of the angular velocity of the body or system and its moment of inertia with respect to the rotation axis, and that is directed along the rotation axis.

antimatter: Negative pressure spacetime, as in the neutron core of an atomic nucleus. Spacetime stretched to values below the Spacetime Equilibrium Pressure (SEP).

atomic matter: Mass composed of hadrons, understood as distinct from other, less organized, configurations of spacetime

beta radiation: A high pressure spacetime shock wave that mimics some of the properties of a high pressure atomic electron.

Big Bang: The super-luminal cosmogenic expansion that followed the collapse of nothingness—out of the void over the course of eternity—into a uniform spacetime sphere of maximum density.

Big Bang nucleosynthesis: A theory of nucleosynthesis, premised on the Standard Model of Particle Physics, designed to account for the high cosmic abundance of helium. Superseded in this theory by gamma ray burst nucleosynthesis.

binding energy: The energy required to break up a molecule, atom, or atomic nucleus completely into its constituent particles.

black hole: A hyper-compressed region of spacetime resulting from the compression of a star's neutron core during a supernova or gamma ray burst.

Brownian motion: A random movement of microscopic particles suspended in liquids or gases resulting from the impact of spacetime shock waves emitted from adjacent atoms during energy state transitions.

cardinality (size): The number of elements in a given mathematical set

centripetal force: A force that pulls an object moving in a circular path toward the center of its path

Cepheid: Any of a class of variable stars whose very regular light variations are related directly to their intrinsic luminosities and whose apparent luminosities are used to estimate distances in astronomy

chemical mass defect: The difference in mass between a molecule (weighed together) and its constituent atoms (weighed separately). It results from a quantity of spacetime being expelled from the bond site of a molecule during a reaction.

corona: A very high-pressure termination shock of the solar wind, moving at relativistic velocity, located a few miles above the solar surface.

cosmic abundances: The relative proportions of chemical elements in the universe

cosmic expansion: The ongoing and accelerating increase in cosmic volume, driven by the decompression of spacetime, primarily in stellar phenomena (e.g., stars, black holes). Currently explained by dark energy.

cosmic ray: A slightly damaged proton that maintains its stability by accelerating into a relativistic bow shock

cosmological constant: The equilibrium pressure of spacetime. Slightly lower, on the Kelvin scale, than the 2.7K value of the vacuum.

cosmological equilibrium: A relatively stable system in which a high-pressure, expansive phenomenon is restrained and balanced by the resistance of the ambient spacetime to compression above its equilibrium pressure.

covalent bond: A chemical bond formed between atoms in which both atoms pull spacetime from their shared bond site

dark matter: A hypothetical variety of matter that is thought to be responsible for the large gravitational fields that govern galactic rotation.

derivative axis: Related to nuclear spin, a secondary, tertiary, etc. rotation that results, ultimately, from the pressure generated by a hadron's south polar jet. The complex array of derivative axes in an atom are the consequence of hadrons' having zero net angular momentum and, therefore, the ability to rotate such as to equalize the pressure inside of their electronic shells.

derivative electron: A bump on an atom's electronic shell, the termination shock, that corresponds to a derivative axis.

detection event: Any experimentally observable transition between atomic energy states that is reasonably attributable to incident energy rather than to a spontaneous behavior of the atom

dialectic: This book borrows the Hegelian understanding of this term. Put simply, it refers to an ongoing relationship between opposites that yields a synthetic unity that is categorically distinct in some manner from its constituents.

E=mc²: Einstein's famous equation relating energy and mass. In this book it also functions as the factor (c^2) by which partons (m) must be decompressed in order to achieve the equilibrium pressure of spacetime or the cosmological constant.

electron: A high pressure spacetime bump, caused by a nucleon's south polar jet, on an electronic shell. Results from the termination shock with the ambient spacetime and defines an atom's (or orbital's) cosmological equilibrium.

electronic shell: A high-pressure termination shock defined by the collision between a nucleon's south polar jet and the ambient spacetime

emergent order: Contrary to scientific reductionism, the organized behavior of a complex entity that cannot be fully (mathematically) characterized by reference to its simple constituents.

endothermic: Characterized by or formed with absorption of heat

energy: The absolute value of the Lorentz Factor associated with the pressure of spacetime

energy state: Any of several series of derivative axes, exhibited by a nucleonic orbital, that creates an identifiable array of light frequencies.

eternity: An irrationally long span of time; an infinite degree of temporal freedom

event horizon: Most likely, the innermost termination shock, analogous to the sun's corona, of a black hole.

ex nihilo: From nothing

extrinsic mass: Any spacetime pressure generated by an object that is not an integral part of the object

frame dragging: In Relativity Theory, the wholesale movement of a region of spacetime, along with its occupants, against the background of absolute nothingness. Opposed to the movement of an object through spacetime, resulting in time and mass dilation.

free electron: A longitudinal spacetime shock wave that mimics, in some respects, the high pressure bump on an atom's electronic shell. May result from beta decay or energy state transitions.

galactic star: Super-massive stars created primarily in the very early universe during the period of high hydrogen density. No upper mass limit.

gamma ray burst (GRB): The supernova of a galactic star responsible for the nucleosynthesis of most of the complex atoms in the universe

gauge theory: Any of several theories in physics that explain the transmission of a fundamental force between two interacting particles by the exchange of an elementary particle

gravitational event horizon: The radius at which the spacetime pressure gradient generated by an object becomes equal to the vacuum (or ambient) pressure

gravitational lensing: The bending and focusing of light and especially the formation of multiple images of a more distant object by a celestial object acting as a gravitational lens

gravitational time dilation: The slowing of atomic movement within a high-pressure spacetime region

heliopause: The outermost radius at which a star has any direct gravitation influence

heliosheath: The region of turbulent spacetime between a star's termination shock and heliopause

heliosphere: the region in space influenced by the sun

hydrostatic equilibrium: The balance achieved in a main sequence star between the upward pressure exerted by the neutrogenic shell and downward gravitational pressure exerted by the mantle

hyperefficient: Describes a complex system that discharges its energy slightly faster than it receives it from an external source(s)

infinitesimal: An irrational concept that captures the meaning of "zero" in the equations: $x/\infty = 0$ and $0 \cdot \infty = x$

infinity: A paradoxical concept that refers to an unbounded set of discrete elements

intrinsic mass: The spacetime of which an object is comprised. Excludes any external pressure generated by its behavior.

ionization: The process of adding energy (increasing the spacetime pressure) and slowing an atomic proton sufficiently to prevent it from generating an electron.

kinetic theory of thermodynamics: The theory, inspired in large part by Einstein's observation of Brownian motion, that heat is the product of atomic movement.

Lorentz Factor: The factor (1-10) by which time, length, and relativistic mass change for an object while that object is moving; also applies to any other instance of spacetime compression or decompression.

luminiferous aether: Traditionally, this has referred to the ineffable medium thought to be the transmitter of electromagnetic energy. In the theory described in this book, three-dimensional spacetime improves on and replaces the luminiferous aether.

main sequence star: Any stellar object with a stable neutrogenic shell

mass defect: The difference between the mass of an object's nuclear (or chemical) constituents weighed individually and within an atom (or molecule).

mass dilation: Related to extrinsic mass, any spacetime pressure generated by an object's motion.

matter: Anything composed of spacetime

monovalent bonds: A chemical bond in which one of the atoms does not contribute a valance proton

neutrogenic shell: One of the two poles, along with the termination shock, that generates a star's cosmological equilibrium. Site of neutron creation and the star's primary gravitational gradient.

neutron: A hadron whose number of partons reflects the equilibrium conditions on a star's neutrogenic shell

neutronium: An unstable but organized association of neutrons, often destined to become the neutron cores of stable atoms during nucleosynthesis.

neutron core: The neutrons within an atom's inner nucleus

neutron star: A dense stellar object that consists of closely packed neutrons and that results from the removal of a star's mantle during a supernova

nothingness: Four infinite degrees of freedom: three spatial and one temporal.

nuclear fusion: The hypothesis that simple atoms are combined into more complex atoms under high pressures, such as those in a stellar core, while releasing energy associated with binding energy.

nuclear magnetic moment: A measure of the wobble associated with nucleonic orbitals composed of odd numbers of nucleons

nuclear mass dilation: The extrinsic mass resulting from extreme velocity of, especially, a spinning neutron.

nucleosynthesis: The creation of complex atoms. Occurs when a star leaves the main sequence and its proton mantle is mixed, in various ways, with its neutron core.

ontology: The study of the fundamental nature of reality and existence

Oort cloud: A spherical shell of cometary bodies which is believed to surround the sun far beyond the orbit of Pluto. Possibly associated with the outermost termination shock of the sun.

particle: Any association of partons

parton: Created during the Big Bang, a subnucleonic spacetime gradient. Sole constituent of all atomic matter.

phase: Refers to the relative frequency congruence of an incident light wave and receiving atom

photon: A quantum of light. Hypothesized to exist because of the discreteness of photoelectric detection events.

physical spacetime: The actual material manifestation of the tension between the infinite and finite poles of nothingness. Opposed to the purely mathematical (abstract) two-dimensional analog used in Relativity Theory.

polar jets: The intense, focused spacetime flow created by the vigorous convection of a nucleon. Via its termination shock, responsible for electrons and electronic shells.

positivism: Contrasted with realism, a philosophical position holding that knowledge consists in describing phenomena (usually mathematically) without regard to any underlying physical (noumenal) reality.

protogenesis: The creation of protons from partons immediately following the Big Bang

proton: A convective circulation of partons in which the total pressure of the particle exactly balances the pressure of each constituent parton. This balance is achieved in the void, and does not reflect any additional pressure that would otherwise be introduced by the proton's polar jet.

proton spin: The complex pattern, driven by its vigorous convection, of derivative axes that characterize a proton's rotational dynamics.

protostellar: A hypothetical flat, circular cloud of gas and dust in space believed to develop into a star.

pulsars: A rapidly rotating neutron star. Pulses are created by the repeated snapping of intense magnetic arcs, analogous to the sun's 11 and 22 year cycles.

quasar: The consumption, by a newly created supermassive black hole, of the remaining neutron core of its parent galactic star.

realism: Contrasted with positivism, a philosophical position holding that knowledge ultimately consists in accurately describing the objects (noumena) that underlie all observable phenomena.

red giant: A star, off the main sequence, in which the neutrogenic shell is alternately disappearing and reforming in a series of rapid but relatively weak implosions. This weakens the gravitational gradient of the star and causes a huge increase in stellar volume and decrease in average surface temperature.

solar wind: The spacetime flow, created by the release of spacetime from neutrogenesis, emanating from a star. The flow is responsible for the termination shocks at the corona, Kuiper belt, and possibly the Oort cloud.

spacetime: The physical manifestation of the paradoxical tension between the finite and infinite poles of absolute nothingness. This dialectical relationship exhibits a perfect continuum and an equilibrium pressure (the cosmological constant).

spacetime continuum: Refers to the non-existence of either a minimum distance (e.g., Planck distance) or minimum quantum of mass/energy.

spacetime equilibrium pressure (SEP): See cosmological constant

string theory: Contrasted with the notion of emergent order, an extremely complex effort to reduce all physical phenomena to a single set of consistent mathematical expressions.

substance: See spacetime

sunspot: The location on a star's surface at which the negative pole of a magnetic arc re-enters the star

supernova: The spectacular explosion of a large star that occurs when its neutrogenic shell disappears, having converted all available protons into neutrons.

superposition: The idea in quantum theory that a single entity can exist simultaneously as both a wave, distributed in space, and as a discrete particle.

superstable: Refers to the extraordinary stability of a proton. The result of the fact that protons are stable within, and reflect the equilibrium conditions of, the void, yet have access to spacetime at SEP to become even more stable.

termination shock: A ubiquitous phenomenon in a universe dominated by the physical substance of spacetime. Occurs wherever a relatively fast flow of spacetime slams into a stationary or slow region. This collision drives up the pressure at the termination shock, raising the temperature and pressure, and causing a pressure gradient (gravitational field).

The Kuiper Belt: A band of small celestial bodies beyond the orbit of Neptune from which many short-period comets are believed to originate

The Younger Dryas: A brief ~1300-year glaciation immediately following the most recent stadial of the Quaternary period.

thermohaline circulation: The dominant worldwide ocean current that regulates the temperatures of all local gyres. It is the manifestation of the complex dynamics driven by the temperature gradient between the tropics and poles.

variable star: A star, off the main sequence, whose brightness changes usually in more or less regular periods. A consequence of repeated, sub-nova, collapses of the mantle onto the neutron core.

void: Any location that is not best characterized by spacetime. Location in which Newtonian equations do not require Lorentz transformations at any velocity to be accurate. See nothingness.

white dwarf: A small neutron star cloaked in a thick blanket of dense atomic matter.

Wilkinson Microwave Anisotropy Probe (WMAP): A spacecraft that measured small variations in the cosmic microwave background (CMB)

x-shaped galaxy: A galaxy in which two central supermassive black holes of similar mass are present. The black holes orient themselves such that their equatorial planes are at roughly 45 degrees relative to one another, thereby defining two galactic planes that make an X-shape.

Selected Bibliography

The path I followed to the theory described in this book was so circuitous and unconventional that a bibliography may be incapable of doing much more than complicating the matter. Typically, one might hope to be able to recreate, in more or less rough outline, the trajectory of the author's development by piecing together the volumes listed in this section. Whether that is possible in this instance I can only guess. The selections provided below are not a complete list of sources but did, at least to my mind, contribute something of significance to the evolution of myself and my thesis.

Physics and Cosmology

Al-Khalili, Jim. *Quantum: A Guide for the Perplexed*. Italy: Weidenfeld & Nicolson. 2003.

Arnett, David. *Supernovae and Nucleosynthesis: An Investigation of the History of Matter, From the Big Bang to the Present*. USA: Princeton University Press. 1996.

Bohm, David and F. David Peat. *Science, Order, and Creativity: A Dramatic New Look at the Creative Roots of Science and Life*. USA: Bantam Books. 1987.

Borrow, John D. *The Infinite Book: A Short Guide to the Boundless, Timeless and Endless*. USA: Vintage Books. 2005.

Close, Frank and Michael Marten and Christine Sutton. *The Particle Odyssey: A Journey to the Heart of Matter*. Italy: Oxford University Press. 2002.

Davies, Paul. *Superforce: The Search for a Grand Unified Theory of Nature*. USA: Simon & Schuster, Inc. 1984.

Einstein, Albert. *Relativity: The Special and the General Theory, A Clear Explanation that Anyone Can Understand*. USA: Estate of Albert Einstein. 1961.

Fay and McMurry. *Chemistry: Fourth Edition*. USA: Pearson Education, Inc, 2004.

Ferreira, Pedro G. *The State of the Universe: A Primer in Modern Cosmology*. Great Britain: Weidenfeld & Nicolson. 2006.

Ferris, Timothy. *The Whole Shebang: A State-of-the-Universe(s) Report*. USA: Simon & Schuster Paperbacks. 1997.

Feynman, Richard P. *QED. The Strange Theory of Light and Matter*. United Kingdom: Princeton University Press. 1985.

Ford, Kenneth W. *Quantum Physics: The Quantum World For Everyone*. USA: President and Fellows of Harvard College. 2004.

Fraser, Gordon. *The New Physics for the twenty-first century*. USA: Cambridge University Press. 2006.

Freeman, Ken and Geoff McNamara. *In Search of Dark Matter*. Germany: Praxis Publishing, Ltd. 2006.

Greene, Brian. *The Elegant Universe: Superstrings, Hidden Dimensions, and the Quest for the Ultimate Theory*. USA: First Vintage Books Edition. 2000.

———. *The Fabric of the Cosmos, Space, Time, and the Textures of Reality*. USA: First Vintage Books Edition. 2005.

Isaacson, Walter. *Einstein: His Life and Universe*. USA: Simon & Schuster. 2007.

Jeans, Sir James. *Physics and Philosophy*. USA: Dover Publications, Inc. 1981

Katz, Jonathan I. *The Biggest Bangs: The Mystery of Gamma-Ray Bursts, The Most Violent Explosions in the Universe*. USA: Oxford University Press, Inc. 2002.

Kirshner, Robert P. *the Extravagant Universe: exploding stars dark energy and the accelerating cosmos*. United Kingdom: Princeton University Press. 2002.

Lindley, David. *Uncertainty: Einstein, Heisenberg, Bohr, and the Struggle for the Soul of Science*. USA: DOUBLEDAY. 2007.

Martin, B.R. *Nuclear and Particle Physics: an Introduction*. England: John Wiley

& Sons, Ltd. 2006.

Pan, Xing-Wang, Da Hsuan Feng and Michel Valliéres, Eds. *Contemporary Nuclear Shell Models: proceedings of an international workshop held in Philadelphia, PA.* Germany: Springer-Verlag Berlin Heidelberg. 1997.

Peat, F. David. *The Philosopher's Stone: Chaos, Synchronicity, and the Hidden Order of the World.* USA: Bantam Books. 1991.

Penrose, Roger. *The Emperor's New Mind: Concerning Computers, Minds, and the Laws of Physics.* USA: Oxford University Press. 1989.

Prialnik, Dina. *An Introduction to the Theory of Stellar Structure and Evolution.* USA: Cambridge University Press. 2000.

Root-Bernstein and Robert Scott. *Discovering: Inventing and Solving Problems at the Frontiers of Scientific Knowledge.* USA: First Harvard University Press. 1991.

Russell, Bertrand. *The ABC of Relativity: Fourth Revised Edition.* USA: George Allen and Unwin, Ltd. 1985.

Schlegel, Eric M. *The Restless Universe: Understanding X-ray Astronomy in the Age of Chandra and Newton.* USA: Oxford University Press. 2002.

Schumm, Bruce A. *Deep Down Things: The Breathtaking Beauty of Particle Physics.* USA: Johns Hopkins University Press. 2004.

Smolen, Lee. *The Trouble with Physics: The Rise of String Theory, the Fall of a Science, and What Comes Next.* USA: Houghton Mifflin Company. 2006

————. *Three Roads to Quantum Gravity.* USA: Basic Books. 2001.

Vilenkin, Alex. *Many Worlds in One: The Search for Other Universes.* USA: Hill and Wang, A division of Farrar, Straus and Giroux. 2006.

Watson, Andrew. *The Quantum Quark.* United Kingdom: Cambridge University Press. 2004.

Wilczek, Frank and Betsy Devine. *Longing for the Harmonies: Themes and Variations from Modern Physics.* USA: W. W. Norton & Company, Inc. 1987.

Philosophy and Neuroscience

Bergson, Henri. *Matter and Memory.* Trans. N.M. Paul and W. S. Palmer.

USA: Zone Books, Urzone, Inc. 1988.

Calvin, William H. *The Ascent of Mind: Ice Age Climates and the Evolution of Intelligence*. USA: Bantam Books. 1990.

Camus, Albert. *The Myth of Sisyphus & Other Essays. 1st American Edition*. USA: Alfred A. Knopf, Inc. 1955.

Churchland, Patricia S. and Terrence J. Sejnowski. *The Computational Brain*. USA: Massachusetts Institute of Technology. 1992.

Churchland, Patricia Smith. *Neurophilosophy: Toward a Unified Science of the Mind/Brain*. USA: The Massachusetts Institute of Technology. 1986.

Crevier, Daniel. *AI: The Tumultuous History of the Search for Artificial Intelligence*. USA: Basic Books. 1993.

Damasio, Antonio R. *Descartes' Error: Emotion, Reason, and the Human Brain*. USA: G.P. Putnam's Sons. 1994.

Dennett, Daniel C. *Consciousness Explained*. USA: Little, Brown & Company Limited. 1991.

Derrida, Jacques. *Limited Inc*. USA: Northwestern University Press. 1988.

————. *Of Grammatology*. Trans. Gayatri Chakravorty Spivak. USA: The Johns Hopkins University Press. 1997.

Descartes, René. *Meditations on First Philosophy: With selections from the Objections and Replies*. Trans. John Cottingham. Australia: Press Syndicate of the University of Cambridge. 1986.

Deutsch, Georg and Sally P. Springer. *Left Brain, Right Brain, Third Edition*. USA: W. H. Freeman and Company. 1989.

Dilman, Sid and Sarah Winans Newman. *Manter and Gatz's Essentials of Clinical Neuroanatomy and Neurophysiology, Edition 8*. USA: F.A. Davis Company. 1992.

Dostoyevsky, Fyodor. *Notes from Underground, White Nights, The Dream of a Ridiculous Man, and selections from The House of the Dead*. Trans. Andrew R. MacAndrew. USA: NAL Penguin Inc. 1961.

Edelman, Gerald M. *Neural Darwinism: The Theory of Neuronal Group Selection*. USA: Basic Books, Inc. 1987.

Gleick, James. *Chaos: Making a New Science*. England: Penguin Books. 1987.

Hamilton, Edith and Huntington Cairns, Eds. *Plato: Collected Dialogues.* USA: Princeton University Press. 1961.

Hegel, G.W.F. *Hegel's Phenomenology of Spirit* Trans. A.V. Miller. USA: Oxford University Press. 1977.

Heidegger, Martin. *Nietzsche:Volumes Three and Four.* Ed. David Farrell Krell. USA: HarperCollins Publishers. 1991.

————. *BasicWritings: Nine Key Essays plus the Introduction to Being and Time.* Ed. David Farrell Krell. USA: Harper & Row, Publishers, Inc. 1977.

————. *Being and Time: A Translation of Sein Und Zeit.* Trans John Macquarrie and Edward Robinson. USA: Harper & Row, Publishers, Incorporated. 1962.

————. *Nietzsche: Volumes One and Two. Trans.* David Farrell Krell. USA: HarperCollins Publishers. 1991.

————. *The Question Concerning Technology and Other Essays.* Trans. William Lovitt. USA: Harper & Row, Publishers, Inc. 1977.

————. *What is Called Thinking?* Trans. J. Glenn Gray. USA: Harper & Row, Publishers, Inc. 1968.

Hofstadter, Douglas R. *Gödel, Escher, Bach: An Eternal Golden Braid.* USA: Basic Books, Inc. 1979. Vintage Books Edition. 1989.

Hooper, Judith and Dick Teresi. *The 3-Pound Universe: Revolutionary Discoveries About the Brain — From the Chemistry of the Mind to the New Frontiers of the Soul.* USA: Jeremy P. Tarcher, Inc. 1986.

Horkheimer, Max. *Eclipse of Reason.* USA. Oxford University Press. 1947.

Humphrey, Nicholas. *A History of the Mind: Evolution and the Birth of Consciousness.* USA: Simon & Schuster. 1992.

Husserl, Edmund. *Ideas, General Introduction to Pure Phenomenology.* USA: First Collier Books Edition. 1962.

Kant, Immanuel. *Critique of Pure Reason.* Trans. Norman Kemp Smith, Unabridged Edition. USA: Macmillan & Co., Ltd. 1965.

Kaufmann, Walter, Ed. and trans. *The Portable Nietzsche.* USA: Penguin Group, Viking Penguin Inc. 1982.

————. and trans. *BasicWritings of Nietzsche: Modern Library.* USA: Random House, Inc. 1968.

Kierkegaard, Søren. *Fear and Trembling.* England: Penguin Group. 1985.

Klawans, Harold L., M.D. *Toscanini's Fumble and other Tales of Clinical Neurology.* USA: Contemporary Books, Inc. 1988.

Kolb, Bryan and Ian Q. Whishaw. *Fundamentals of Human Neuropsychology: Third Edition.* USA: W.H. Freeman and Company. 1990.

Kosko, Bart Ph.D. *Fuzzy Thinking: The New Science of Fuzzy Logic.* USA: Hyperion. 1993.

Kosslyn, Stphen M., and Olivier Koenig. *Wet Mind: The New Cognitive Neuroscience.* USA: The Free Press, A Division of Macmillan, Inc. 1992.

Kurzweil, Raymond. *The Age of Intelligent Machines.* Japan: Massachusetts Institute of Technology. 1990.

Levitan, Irwin B. and Leonard K. Kaczmarek. *The Neuron: Cell and Molecular Biology.* USA: Oxford University Press. 1991.

Llinas, Rodolfo R. *The Biology of the Brain: From Neurons to Networks.* USA: Scientific America and W.H. Freeman and Company. 1988.

Luger, George F. and William A. Stubblefield. *Artificial Intelligence: Structures and Strategies for Complex Problem Solving, Second Edition.* USA: The Benjamin/Cummings Publishing Company, Inc. 1993.

Luria, A.R. *The Working Brain: An Introduction to Neuropsychology.* USA: Basic Books. 1973.

Merleau-Ponty, Maurice. *Phenomenology of Perception.* Translated by Colin Smith. Great Britain: Routledge & Kegan Paul Ltd. 1962.

————. *The Structure of Behavior.* France: Beacon Press, 1963.

Ornstein, Robert and Richard F. Thompson. *The Amazing Brain.* USA: Houghton Mifflin Company. 1984.

Pinker, Steven. *How the Mind Works.* USA: W.W. Norton & Company, Inc. 1997.

————. *The Better Angels of Our Nature: Why Violence Has Declined.* USA: Penguin Group, Inc. 2011.

————. *the blank slate: The Modern Denial of Human Nature.* USA: Penguin Group, Inc. 2002.

————. *The Language Instinct: How the Mind Creates Language.* USA: William Morrow and Company, Inc. 1994.

————. *The Stuff of Thought: Language as a Window into Human Nature*. USA: Penguin Group, Inc. 2007.

————. *Words and Rules: The Ingredients of Language*. USA: HarperCollins Publishers, Inc. 1999.

Restak, Richard M.D. *The Brain Has a Mind of Its Own: Insights from a Practicing Neurologist*. USA: Harmony Books, a division of Crown Publishers Inc. 1991.

Sacks, Oliver. *An Anthropologist on Mars: Seven Paradoxical Tales*. USA: Alfred A. Knopf, Inc. 1995.

————. *A Leg to Stand On*. USA: HarperCollins Publishers. 1984.

————. *Seeing Voices: A Journey into the World of the Deaf*. USA: University of California Press. 1990.

————. *The Island of the Colour-blind: From the Major Television Series*. Great Britain: Picador. 1996.

————. *The Man Who Mistook His Wife for a Hat: and Other Clinical Tales*. USA: Summit Books. 1985.

Schwartz, Barry. *Psychology of Learning and Behavior, 3rd Edition*. USA: W. W. Norton & Company, Inc. 1989.

Searle, John R. *The Rediscovery of the Mind*. USA: Massachusetts Institute of Technology. 1992.

Whitehead, Alfred North. *Process and Reality: Corrected Edition*. Eds. David Ray Griffin and Donald W. Sherburne. USA: The Free Press, a Division of Macmillan Publishing Co., Inc. 1978.

Wills, Christopher. *The Runaway Brain: The Evolution of Human Uniqueness*. Great Britain (London): HarperCollins Publishers, Inc. 1993.

Index

Colophon

This book is set in Perpetua typeface along with the Segoe UI typeface family for the title and chapter headings. Perpetua was designed by Eric Gill in 1925 for the Monotype Corporation foundry and is characterized as a transitional serif font similar to the styles of the late 18th and 19th century. The name was derived from the title of its first use, a limited edition of the a new translation by Walter H. Shewring of The Passion of Perpetua and Felicity. The font was also used in the designer's own work *Art Nonsense and Other Essays* written and illustrated by Eric Gill and released in the same year. The Segoe typeface was designed by Steve Matteson for the AGFA Monotype foundry. Its smooth and friendly rounded style makes it a popular and inviting heading font.

- Design by Jill Ryan, Gadfly, Leesburg, Virginia
- Cover Artwork by Paula Ryan, Arcola, Virginia
- Illustrations & Interior Graphics Design by Andrew M. Ryan
- Edited by Kelly Kagamas Tomkies, Bexley, Ohio
- Printed by Lightning Source, Inc. La Vergne, Tennessee

About the Author

   With an insatiable passion for the truth, Andrew M. Ryan naturally gravitated to an education in philosophy, earning his bachelor's degree from Louisiana State University. Beyond his desire to understand the mind, he continues to explore many topics, including cosmology and cognitive science. Ryan is also the author of the novel *The Labbitt Halsey Protocol*. He has a daughter and lives with his wife in Northern Virginia.

CPSIA information can be obtained at www.ICGtesting.com
Printed in the USA
BVOW08s2334020816

456842BV00016B/1/P

9 780980 208849